THE CHRYSOSTOM BIBLE
A Commentary Series for Preaching and Teaching
1 Corinthians: A Commentary

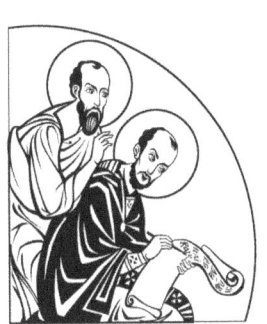

THE CHRYSOSTOM BIBLE
A Commentary Series for Preaching and Teaching

1 Corinthians: A Commentary

Paul Nadim Tarazi

OCABS PRESS
ST PAUL, MINNESOTA 55124
2011

THE CHRYSOSTOM BIBLE
1 CORINTHIANS: A COMMENTARY

Copyright © 2011 by
Paul Nadim Tarazi

ISBN 1-60191-016-9

All rights reserved

PRINTED IN THE UNITED STATES OF AMERICA

Other Books by the Author

I Thessalonians: A Commentary

Galatians: A Commentary

The Old Testament: An Introduction

Volume 1: Historical Traditions, revised edition

Volume 2: Prophetic Traditions

Volume 3: Psalms and Wisdom

The New Testament: An Introduction

Volume 1: Paul and Mark

Volume 2: Luke and Acts

Volume 3: Johannine Writings

Volume 4: Matthew and the Canon

The Chrysostom Bible

Genesis: A Commentary

Philippians: A Commentary

Romans: A Commentary

Colossians & Philemon: A Commentary

Land and Covenant

The Chrysostom Bible
1 Corinthians: A Commentary

Copyright © 2011 by Paul Nadim Tarazi
All rights reserved

ISBN 1-60191-016-9

Published by OCABS Press, St. Paul, Minnesota.
Printed in the United States of America.

Books are available through OCABS Press at special discounts for bulk purchases in the United States by academic institutions, churches, and other organizations. For more information please email OCABS Press at press@ocabs.org.

Abbreviations

Books by the Author

1 Thess	*1 Thessalonians: A Commentary,* Crestwood, NY: St. Vladimir's Seminary Press, 1982
Gal	*Galatians: A Commentary,* Crestwood, NY: St. Vladimir's Seminary Press, 1994
OTI₁	*The Old Testament: An Introduction, Volume 1: Historical Traditions,* revised edition, Crestwood, NY: St. Vladimir's Seminary Press, 2003
OTI₂	*The Old Testament: An Introduction, Volume 2: Prophetic Traditions,* Crestwood, NY: St. Vladimir's Seminary Press, 1994
OTI₃	*The Old Testament: An Introduction, Volume 3: Psalms and Wisdom,* Crestwood, NY: St. Vladimir's Seminary Press, 1996
NTI₁	*The New Testament: An Introduction, Volume 1: Paul and Mark,* Crestwood, NY: St. Vladimir's Seminary Press, 1999
NTI₂	*The New Testament: An Introduction, Volume 2: Luke and Acts,* Crestwood, NY: St. Vladimir's Seminary Press, 2001
NTI₃	*The New Testament: An Introduction, Volume 3: Johannine Writings,* Crestwood, NY: St. Vladimir's Seminary Press, 2004
NTI₄	*The New Testament: An Introduction, Volume 4: Matthew and the Canon,* St. Paul, MN: OCABS Press, 2009
C-Gen	*Genesis: A Commentary.* The Chrysostom Bible. St. Paul, MN: OCABS Press, 2009
C-Phil	*Philippians: A Commentary.* The Chrysostom Bible. St. Paul, MN: OCABS Press, 2009
C-Rom	*Romans: A Commentary.* The Chrysostom Bible. St. Paul, MN: OCABS Press, 2010
C-Col	*Colossians & Philemon: A Commentary.* The Chrysostom Bible. St. Paul, MN: OCABS Press, 2010
LAC	*Land and Covenant,* St. Paul, MN: OCABS Press, 2009

Abbreviations

Books of the Old Testament*

Gen	Genesis	Job	Job	Hab		Habakkuk
Ex	Exodus	Ps	Psalms	Zeph		Zephaniah
Lev	Leviticus	Prov	Proverbs	Hag		Haggai
Num	Numbers	Eccl	Ecclesiastes	Zech		Zechariah
Deut	Deuteronomy	Song	Song of Solomon	Mal		Malachi
Josh	Joshua	Is	Isaiah	Tob		Tobit
Judg	Judges	Jer	Jeremiah	Jdt		Judith
Ruth	Ruth	Lam	Lamentations	Wis		Wisdom
1 Sam	1 Samuel	Ezek	Ezekiel	Sir	Sirach	(Ecclesiasticus)
2 Sam	2 Samuel	Dan	Daniel	Bar		Baruch
1 Kg	1 Kings	Hos	Hosea	1 Esd		1 Esdras
2 Kg	2 Kings	Joel	Joel	2 Esd		2 Esdras
1 Chr	1 Chronicles	Am	Amos	1 Macc		1 Maccabees
2 Chr	2 Chronicles	Ob	Obadiah	2 Macc		2 Maccabees
Ezra	Ezra	Jon	Jonah	3 Macc		3 Maccabees
Neh	Nehemiah	Mic	Micah	4 Macc		4 Maccabees
Esth	Esther	Nah	Nahum			

Books of the New Testament

Mt	Matthew	Eph	Ephesians	Heb	Hebrews
Mk	Mark	Phil	Philippians	Jas	James
Lk	Luke	Col	Colossians	1 Pet	1 Peter
Jn	John	1 Thess	1 Thessalonians	2 Pet	2 Peter
Acts	Acts	2 Thess	2 Thessalonians	1 Jn	1 John
Rom	Romans	1 Tim	1 Timothy	2 Jn	2 John
1 Cor	1 Corinthians	2 Tim	2 Timothy	3 Jn	3 John
2 Cor	2 Corinthians	Titus	Titus	Jude	Jude
Gal	Galatians	Philem	Philemon	Rev	Revelation

*Following the larger canon known as the Septuagint.

Contents

Preface	*15*
Introduction	*19*
Chapter 1	*21*
Vv. 1-3	21
Vv. 4-9	27
Vv. 10-17	31
Vv. 18-31	38
Chapter 2	*49*
Vv. 1-5	49
Vv. 6-16	51
Chapter 3	*71*
Vv. 1-9	71
Vv. 10-17	76
Vv. 18-23	80
Chapter 4	*85*
Vv. 1-5	85
Vv. 6-13	87
Vv. 14-21	94
Chapter 5	*99*
Vv. 1-5	99
Vv. 6-13	101
Chapter 6	*107*
Vv. 1-11	107
Vv. 12-20	116

Chapter 7	**125**
Vv. 1-7	125
Vv. 8-16	131
Vv. 17-24	134
Vv. 25-40	138
Chapter 8	**147**
Vv. 1-13	147
Chapter 9	**155**
Vv. 1-27	155
Chapter 10	**173**
Vv. 1-13	173
Vv. 14-22	180
Vv. 23-33	184
V. 11:1	185
Chapter 11	**191**
Vv. 2-16	191
Vv. 17-34	200
Chapter 12	**217**
Vv. 1-11	217
Vv. 12-31	221
Chapter 13	**231**
Vv. 1-3	231
Vv. 4-7	232
Vv. 8-13	237

Chapter 14	***243***
Vv. 1-25	*243*
Vv. 26-40	*249*
Chapter 15	***259***
Vv. 1-11	*259*
Vv. 12-19	*273*
Vv. 20-28	*277*
Vv. 29-34	*281*
Vv. 35-49	*284*
Vv. 51-58	*292*
Chapter 16	***297***
Vv. 1-4	*297*
Vv. 5-12	*299*
Vv. 13-24	*305*
Further Reading	***315***
Commentaries and Studies	*315*
Articles	*316*

Preface

The present Bible Commentary Series is not so much in honor of John Chrysostom as it is to continue and promote his legacy as an interpreter of the biblical texts for preaching and teaching God's congregation, in order to prod its members to proceed on the way they started when they accepted God's calling. Chrysostom's virtual uniqueness is that he did not subscribe to any hermeneutic or methodology, since this would amount to introducing an extra-textual authority over the biblical texts. For him, scripture is its own interpreter. Listening to the texts time and again allowed him to realize that "call" and "read (aloud)" are not interconnected realities; rather, they are one reality since they both are renditions of the same Hebrew verb *qara'*. Given that words read aloud are words of instruction for one "to do them," the only valid reaction would be to hear, listen, obey, and abide by these words. All these connotations are subsumed in the same Hebrew verb *šama'*. On the other hand, these scriptural "words of life" are presented as readily understandable utterances of a father to his children (Isaiah 1:2-3). The recipients are never asked to engage in an intellectual debate with their divine instructor, or even among themselves, to fathom what he is saying. The Apostle to the Gentiles followed in the footsteps of the Prophets to Israel by handing down to them the Gospel, that is, the Law of God's Spirit through his Christ (Romans 8:2; Galatians 6:2) as fatherly instruction (1 Corinthians 4:15). He in turn wrote readily understandable letters to be read aloud. It is in these same footsteps that Chrysostom followed, having learned from both the Prophets and Paul that the same "words of life" carry also the sentence of death at the hand of the scriptural God, Judge of all

(Deuteronomy 28; Joshua 8:32-35; Psalm 82; Matthew 3:4-12; Romans 2:12-16; 1 Corinthians 10:1-11; Revelation 20:11-15).

While theological debates and hermeneutical theories come and go after having fed their proponents and their fans with passing human glory, the Golden Mouth's expository homilies, through the centuries, fed and still feed myriads of believers in so many traditions and countries. Virtually banned from dogmatic treatises, he survives in the hearts of "those who have ears to hear." His success is due to his commitment to exegesis rather than to futile hermeneutics. The latter behaves as someone who dictates on a living organism what it is supposed to be, whereas exegesis submits to that organism and endeavors to decipher it through trial and error. There is as much a far cry between the text and the theories about it as there is between a living organism and the theories about it. The biblical texts are the reality of God imparted through their being read aloud in the midst of the congregation, disregarding the value of the sermon that follows. The sermon, much less a theological treatise, is at best an invitation to hear and obey the text. Assessing the shape of an invitation card has no value whatsoever when it comes to the dinner itself; the guests are fed by the dinner, not by the invitation or its phrasing (Luke 14:16-24; Matthew 22:1-14).

This commentary series does not intend to promote Chrysostom's ideas as a public relation manager would do, but rather to follow in the footsteps of his approach as true children and heirs are expected to do. He used all the contemporary tools at his disposal to communicate God's written instruction to his hearers, as a doctor would with his patients, without spending unnecessary energy on peripheral debates requiring the use of professional jargon incomprehensible to the commoner. The writers of this series will try to do the same: muster to the best of their ability all necessary contemporary knowledge to communicate to the general readers the biblical message without burdening them with data unnecessary for that purpose. Whenever it will be deemed necessary or even helpful to do so, and in order to curtail burdensome and lengthy technical asides within the commentaries, specialized monographs related either to specific topics or to the scriptural background—literary, sociopolitical, or archeological—will be issued as companions to the series.

Paul Nadim Tarazi
Editor

Introduction

Repeatedly in my commentaries on the Pauline corpus I have shown that the "truth of the gospel" (Gal 2:5, 14), whose sole champion was Paul, did not entail something new to be added to the Old Testament Law, which is the expression of God's will for all ages. Rather, as is evident from Isaiah 40-55, the evangelization of the nations was simply the mission assigned to the "servant of the Lord," namely, to share with them God's law (Is 42:4; 51:4) even though Jacob's progeny did not abide by it (42:19-25; see also 5:24). Paul's "mission statement" at its clearest and in its most concise form is found at the beginning of his letter to the citizens of the Roman empire's capital, the elite of the nations:

> Paul, a servant of Jesus Christ, called to be an apostle, set apart for the gospel of God which he promised beforehand through his prophets in the holy scriptures, the gospel concerning his Son … Jesus Christ our Lord, through whom we have received grace and apostleship to bring about the full and trustworthy submission (to that gospel) … among all the nations, including yourselves… (Rom 1:1-6)

Later in Romans 9-11, Paul will make clear that such submission is required of the nations in spite of the scriptural Israel's disobedience, which in no way could have negated the perennial value of God's word (9:6a). Though circumcised in the flesh, Israel in the Old Testament, time and again, proved to be uncircumcised in the heart against the express summons of the divine law (Deut 10:16; 30:6; see also Jer 4:4; 9:25). Still, Paul's Gentiles were bound to that same directive in order to inherit the promised Kingdom where the scriptural God reigns unobstructed. Consequently, the Pauline letters were conceived to spread this message as scripture, that is, in the form of an authoritative literature consigned in writing.

From this perspective, among all those letters, 1 Corinthians holds the place of honor in that, more than any other epistle, it deals in detail with the multitude of theoretical as well as practical hurdles faced by Paul's Gentiles since, upon meeting him at first, they "were alienated from the commonwealth of Israel, and strangers to the covenants of promise" (Eph 2:12). These covenants were inscribed in the Old Testament writings to which they were not privy. Thus Paul's mission was a two-step endeavor: first to acquaint his flock with scripture and then to explain it to them. This second step was complicated by the perennial hounding of his opponents, especially the followers of James and Cephas. The result was that, in the edification of his Gentile communities, Paul had to battle on two fronts in each and every endeavor. Therefore, my readers are asked to make an extra effort to follow the Apostle's reasoning and argumentation in 1 Corinthians more than they would do when hearing his other letters.

In this commentary series, I have included both Greek and English texts for each verse. The English is the RSV translation, which I have been using in my writings. In my comments, however, I often defer to the Greek with my own translation in order to render the meaning as close as possible to the original text.

Chapter 1

Vv. 1-3 *¹ Παῦλος κλητὸς ἀπόστολος Χριστοῦ Ἰησοῦ διὰ θελήματος θεοῦ καὶ Σωσθένης ὁ ἀδελφὸς ² τῇ ἐκκλησίᾳ τοῦ θεοῦ τῇ οὔσῃ ἐν Κορίνθῳ, ἡγιασμένοις ἐν Χριστῷ Ἰησοῦ, κλητοῖς ἁγίοις, σὺν πᾶσιν τοῖς ἐπικαλουμένοις τὸ ὄνομα τοῦ κυρίου ἡμῶν Ἰησοῦ Χριστοῦ ἐν παντὶ τόπῳ, αὐτῶν καὶ ἡμῶν. ³ χάρις ὑμῖν καὶ εἰρήνη ἀπὸ θεοῦ πατρὸς ἡμῶν καὶ κυρίου Ἰησοῦ Χριστοῦ.*

¹Paul, called by the will of God to be an apostle of Christ Jesus, and our brother Sosthenes, ²To the church of God which is at Corinth, to those sanctified in Christ Jesus, called to be saints together with all those who in every place call on the name of our Lord Jesus Christ, both their Lord and ours: ³Grace to you and peace from God our Father and the Lord Jesus Christ.

As is usual in his letters, Paul begins by identifying himself as an apostle of Christ Jesus. According to the Jerusalem agreement, he is the sole apostle to the Gentiles, just as Peter is the sole apostle to the Jews of the diaspora (Gal 2:7-8). Furthermore, his apostleship is not to be questioned since it originates in God's will (*thelēmatos*) which is a shortened formula (see also 2 Cor 1:1; Eph 1:1; Col 1:1) for the detailed "not from men nor through man, but through Jesus Christ and God the Father" (Gal 1:1). Furthermore, God's will for the apostle can be neither explained nor challenged since it is ultimately for a purpose, as we hear in the letter to the Galatians: "But when he [God] who had set me apart before I was born, and had called me through his grace, was pleased (*evdokēsen*) to reveal his Son to me, *in order that* I might preach him among the Gentiles." (vv.15-16). Indeed, earlier in that same letter Paul used the term "will" in conjunction with the salvation bestowed to all: "Grace to you and peace from God the Father and our Lord Jesus Christ, who gave himself for our sins to deliver us from the present evil age, according to the will of our God and Father." (vv.3-4) In Ephesians we find God's "will" and "pleasure" joined in one action: "He destined us in love to be his sons through Jesus Christ, according to the (good) pleasure (*evdokian*) of his will (*thelēmatos*), to the praise of his glorious grace which he freely bestowed on us in the Beloved." (1:5-6).

Paul alone among the leaders of his churches is the "apostle of the Messiah Jesus." Paul's helper, Sosthenes, is identified as a "brother." The Greek *Sōsthenēs* is a composite of *sōs* (healthy, from the verb *sōzō* whose meaning is "maintain in safety" and thus "save") and *sthenēs* (from *sthenos* whose meaning is "physical strength" and whose opposite is *astheneia* denoting "lack of strength," "weakness," "sickness"). Someone who is lacking *sthenos* is an *asthenēs* (weak, sick). The noun *astheneia*, and more so the adjective *asthenēs*, are used profusely in 1 Corinthians, especially in the debate concerning the attitudes of the "strong" and the "weak" about what food to eat or what to abstain from at table fellowship (8:7-13). Paul's instructions in this regard took a good share of his letter to the Romans (14:1-15:6). The weak brother is clearly the Jew who is bound by dietary rules.[1] Thus it would appear that Sosthenes stands for a Jew who was saved (healed, made whole) and became a "brother" worthy, in spite of his weakness (*astheneia*), to be cited next to Paul himself as putative co-author of the letter. Paul will use the meaning of his name throughout the letter in order to tame the arrogance of the Gentile Corinthians, just as he endeavored to do with the Gentile Romans in Romans (9-11 and 12-15).

---

[1] See my comments on Rom 14:1-15:6 in *C-Rom* 250-8.

Chapter 1

The only other instance of the name Sosthenes is found in Acts in conjunction with Paul's preaching in Corinth:

> When Silas and Timothy arrived from Macedonia, Paul was occupied with preaching, testifying to the Jews that the Christ was Jesus. And when they opposed and reviled him … he left there and went to the house of a man named Titius Justus, a worshiper of God; his house was next door to the synagogue. Crispus, the ruler of the synagogue, believed in the Lord, together with all his household; and many of the Corinthians hearing Paul believed and were baptized … And he stayed a year and six months, teaching the word of God among them. But when Gallio was proconsul of Achaia, the Jews made a united attack upon Paul and brought him before the tribunal … And he [Gallio] drove them from the tribunal. And they all seized Sosthenes, the ruler of the synagogue, and beat him in front of the tribunal. But Gallio paid no attention to this. (Acts 18:5-8, 11-12, 16-17)

The addressee in this letter is the church of God. This double absolute with two definite articles in Greek[2] connotes the uniqueness as well as the fullness of God's—the Lord's—assembly (*qehal yahweh; ekklēsia kyriou*), that is, the totality of God's community, "all the assembly of Israel" (*kol-qehal yisra'el; pasa ekklēsia Israēl*), in the Old Testament. This church of God is essentially one since it is associated with the one God and his one messiah (Gal 3:16). The other common noun used in the Old Testament to refer to God's community is "congregation" (*'edah; synagōgē*), which denoted the Jewish sabbath gatherings extant in Paul's times. The plurality of the synagogues did not hamper the oneness of God's community since the gatherings revolved around the scriptural readings that underscored the reality of that oneness. In other words, it is the sound of the one

---

[2] The Greek *he ekklesia tou Theou* (literally "the church of the God").

shepherd's voice which secures the oneness of the flock despite the number of sheep or where they are scattered. For his mainly Gentile congregations, Paul chose the scriptural appellation of "assembly (church)"[3] (*qehal yahweh; ekklēsia kyriou*). The reason is twofold. On the one hand, the appellation "synagogue" risked that the Pauline churches slip more readily in Peter's camp (Gal 2:7-8) and, by the same token, under the aegis of James and the Jerusalemite leadership (vv.11-14). On the other hand, the term *ekklēsia* was the common name of the Greco-Roman city's body politic and had an appeal to the Gentiles in that it would not sound as though they were uprooted; they would *as Gentiles*— without being forced into circumcision—become members of the scriptural God's household (6:10) and join in "the Israel of God" (v.16; Eph 2:11-13). This was precisely what Paul was continually fighting for. Just as the multiplicity of the synagogues did not void the oneness of God's people, so also the multiplicity of the Pauline churches did not void the oneness of God's community among the Gentiles. It is through the one message of the one gospel that each and every Pauline gathering "assemble as church" (*synerkhomenōn en ekklēsia*; 1 Cor 11:18), the church being none other than "the church of God *which is* (*tē ousē*) at Corinth" (1:2).

From the scriptural perspective there is no flock until the shepherd gathers the sheep. So, also, there is no "church" (*ekklēsia* from the verb *kalō* [call]) until and unless there is someone who "calls" the people to meet as a congregation. And the one who does that in scripture is God, who is referred to as "the caller, the one who calls" (*ho kalōn*; Rom 4:7; 9:12; Gal 5:8;

---

[3] The English "church" originates from the Greek adjective *kyriakos* (lordly) referring to the Lord (*Kyrios*) Jesus.

1 Thess 2:12; 5:24).[4] Everything originates from God, starting with the call of Moses. God is the "caller" through his plenipotentiary representative, the prophet in the Old Testament and the apostle in the New Testament. Location does not matter. In Ezekiel, God's congregation, Israel, was in Babylon, not in Judah. Moreover, this congregation [Israel] was actually dry bones, and it is Ezekiel's word that blew into it a reviving spirit that brought it back to life (Ezek 37:1-14). The same thing occurs with Paul: "For consider your call, brethren; not many of you were wise according to worldly standards, not many were powerful, not many were of noble birth; but God chose what is foolish in the world to shame the wise, God chose what is weak in the world to shame the strong, God chose what is low and despised in the world, *even things that are not, to bring to nothing things that are*, so that no human being might boast in the presence of God." (1 Cor 1:26-29) Thus the church of God *is* wherever the Apostle's teaching resounds. Before Paul arrived in Corinth there was no church in that city; a few weeks later the church (*he ekklēsia*; "the called one") of God was established there.

The church in Corinth was made of members that have been sanctified (made holy; *hēgiasmenois*) in Christ Jesus who was brought among them through the gospel (1 Cor 4:15). However, being "sanctified" is not a done deal. The Hebrew *qadoš* (holy, saint) essentially means separated as in taboo, that is, a person or an area that has been declared off limits. This applies essentially to the deities and their domains, since holiness is, so to speak,

---

[4] See also the instances of the aorist *kalesas, kalesantos* (the one who has called) in Gal 1:6, 15; 2 Tit 1:9. See also 1 Peter (1:15; 2:9; 5:10) and 2 Peter (1:3), which are the products of the Pauline school as is argued for by many scholars. See my *NTI₄* 25-106 and my article "Paul, the One Apostle of the One Gospel" in *The Journal of the Orthodox Center for the Advancement of Biblical Studies* (*JOCABS*) 2 (2009).

basically "divine" and is only secondarily applied to those who are in the immediate service to the deities and their domains, such as angels and priests, and by extension all temple servers. Given that the scriptural God has no statue, he is in no need of either a palace or a temple in which to abide and does not require a king to represent him—he alone is the King of Israel— nor does he require a priestly caste to serve him. It ensues then that it is his entire community that is holy, in the sense of being called to that holiness: "Say to all the congregation of the people of Israel, You shall be holy; for I the Lord your God am holy." (Lev 19:2) That is why, immediately after having addressed the Corinthians as "sanctified," Paul adds "called to be saints" (*klētois hagiois*; 1 Cor 1:2). Later, in 6:5-11, Paul will make clear that holiness is not magical, but has to be lived out:

> I say this to your shame. Can it be that there is no man among you wise enough to decide between members of the brotherhood, but brother goes to law against brother, and that before unbelievers? To have lawsuits at all with one another is defeat for you. Why not rather suffer wrong? Why not rather be defrauded? But you yourselves wrong and defraud, and that even your own brethren. Do you not know that the unrighteous will not inherit the kingdom of God? Do not be deceived; neither the immoral, nor idolaters, nor adulterers, nor sexual perverts, nor thieves, nor the greedy, nor drunkards, nor revilers, nor robbers will inherit the kingdom of God. And such were some of you. But you were washed, you were sanctified, you were justified in the name of the Lord Jesus Christ and in the Spirit of our God.

Along with the Corinthians, Paul greets all the brethren "in every place" (1:2). This, obviously, means "in every place throughout the province Achaia."[5] On the level of the empire,

---

[5] *NTI₄* 74.

the Roman emperor would speak officially *urbi et orbi* (to the city [of Rome] and all the orb), in the same way as heads of states nowadays address their entire nation from the capital city. The believers are qualified as "those who call (*epikaloumenois*) on the name of our Lord Jesus Christ" (1:2; see also Rom 10:12-14). The response to God's "calling" (*kalō*) is to "call on" (*epikalō*) him or his Christ in the double sense of acknowledging and proclaiming him as the Lord and also of entreating him through prayer. Paul ends his initial greeting by wishing his addressees his classic "Grace to you and peace from God our Father and the Lord Jesus Christ" (1 Cor 1:3).[6]

Vv. 4-9 ⁴Εὐχαριστῶ τῷ θεῷ μου πάντοτε περὶ ὑμῶν ἐπὶ τῇ χάριτι τοῦ θεοῦ τῇ δοθείσῃ ὑμῖν ἐν Χριστῷ Ἰησοῦ, ⁵ ὅτι ἐν παντὶ ἐπλουτίσθητε ἐν αὐτῷ, ἐν παντὶ λόγῳ καὶ πάσῃ γνώσει, ⁶ καθὼς τὸ μαρτύριον τοῦ Χριστοῦ ἐβεβαιώθη ἐν ὑμῖν, ⁷ ὥστε ὑμᾶς μὴ ὑστερεῖσθαι ἐν μηδενὶ χαρίσματι ἀπεκδεχομένους τὴν ἀποκάλυψιν τοῦ κυρίου ἡμῶν Ἰησοῦ Χριστοῦ· ⁸ ὃς καὶ βεβαιώσει ὑμᾶς ἕως τέλους ἀνεγκλήτους ἐν τῇ ἡμέρᾳ τοῦ κυρίου ἡμῶν Ἰησοῦ [Χριστοῦ]. ⁹ πιστὸς ὁ θεός, δι' οὗ ἐκλήθητε εἰς κοινωνίαν τοῦ υἱοῦ αὐτοῦ Ἰησοῦ Χριστοῦ τοῦ κυρίου ἡμῶν·

> ⁴*I give thanks to God always for you because of the grace of God which was given you in Christ Jesus,* ⁵*that in every way you were enriched in him with all speech and all knowledge—* ⁶*even as the testimony to Christ was confirmed among you—*⁷*so that you are not lacking in any spiritual gift, as you wait for the revealing of our Lord Jesus Christ;* ⁸*who will sustain you to the end, guiltless in the day of our Lord Jesus Christ.* ⁹*God is faithful, by whom you were called into the fellowship of his Son, Jesus Christ our Lord.*

---

[6] See my comments in *1 Thess* 28-9; *C-Phil* 68-70; *C-Col* 25.

Paul follows his initial greeting with thanksgiving to God.[7] His standard reason for giving thanks is his addressees' positive response to God's grace and their expression of that acceptance in a life filled with trust, love, and hope.[8] But here he seems displeased, as he was with the Galatians. Among the Pauline correspondence to churches, Galatians is the only letter which is striking in both the absence of thanksgiving after the initial greeting and the complete lack of the verb "thank" in the entire letter. Here in 1 Corinthians, Paul's dissatisfaction is expressed obliquely. Instead of thanking God for the Corinthians' behavior, his thanksgiving to God lies in acknowledging (*evkharistō*) God's grace (*khariti*). As for the Corinthians, they are merely the *recipients* of that grace: either they are the complement nouns to verbs whose subject is Jesus Christ (1 Cor 1:8) or, when the subject of the verbs, these verbs are in the passive voice (vv.5, 9). Paul makes it clear right from the beginning that the Corinthians are on the receiving end *in everything*: "… that in every way (*en panti*; in every matter) you were enriched in him with all (*panti*; every kind of) speech and all (*panti*; every kind of) knowledge … so that you are not lacking in any (*mēdeni*) spiritual gift." (vv.5, 7)[9] As in all introductions, the phraseology used both here (enriched, speech, knowledge, spiritual gift) and in v.9 (God is faithful, called, fellowship) prepares for the various topics that will be covered in the letter.

The channel through which God's grace (free gift) was bestowed (v.4) on the Corinthians in all its fullness (v.5) was the

---

[7] See Rom 1:8; 1 Cor 1:4; Eph 1:16; Phil 1:3; Col 1:3; 1 Thess 1:2; 2 Thess 1:3; Philem 1:4.

[8] See Col 1:4-5; 1 Thess 1:3.

[9] *mēdeni* from *mēden* (not one, nothing) is the opposite of *panti* from *pas* (every one, every).

"testimony (*martyrion*; witness) concerning Christ" rendered fully and in all assuredness (*ebebaiōthē*) by Paul "among them" (v.6). Here again, Paul makes sure that his addressees not think they had anything to do with the matter. They are simply at the receiving end. They are not lacking in any spiritual gift (*kahrismati*; the product of the *kharis* [grace]) because of Paul's witnessing to the gospel among them (v.7a). All that the Corinthians are required to do is proceed on the path delineated by the gospel teaching, "awaiting (*apekdekhomenous*) the revealing (*apokalypsin*) of our Lord Jesus Christ" (v.7b), which lies ahead at the end (*heōs telous*; v.8) of that path. Paul makes this clear not only to the Corinthians, but to the other churches he established as well:

> I consider that the sufferings of this present time are not worth comparing with the glory that is to be revealed to us. For the eager expectation (*apokaradokia*) of the creation waits with eager longing (*apekdekhetai*) for the revealing (*apokalypsin*) of the sons of God; for the creation was subjected to futility, not of its own will but by the will of him who subjected it in hope; because the creation itself will be set free from its bondage to decay and obtain the glorious liberty of the children of God. We know that the whole creation has been groaning in travail together until now; and not only the creation, but we ourselves, who have the first fruits of the Spirit, groan inwardly as we wait (*apekdekhomenoi*) for adoption as sons, the redemption of our bodies. For in this hope we were saved. Now hope that is seen is not hope. For who hopes for what he sees? But if we hope for what we do not see, we wait (*apekdekhometha*) for it with patience. (Rom 8:18-25)

> For I know that through your prayers and the help of the Spirit of Jesus Christ this will turn out for my deliverance, as it is my eager expectation (*apokaradokian*) and hope that I shall not be at all ashamed, but that with full courage now as always Christ will be honored in my body, whether by life or by death. (Phil 1:19-20)

> But our commonwealth is in heaven, and from it we await (*apekdekhometha*) a Savior, the Lord Jesus Christ, who will change our lowly body to be like his glorious body, by the power which enables him even to subject all things to himself. (3:20-21)

Since the revelation of Jesus Christ will take place on his "day," that is "judgment day," the Corinthians are not to be careless while awaiting its coming. They need to be found no less "guiltless (*anenklētous*)" (v.8) than the Philippians (Phil 1:10; blameless) and the Colossians (Col 1:22; blameless). Yet again, in order not to give the slightest impression to his hearers that they might earn their ultimate salvation, he makes sure to let them know that the assuredness comes from God and his messiah, and not from themselves:

> ... even as the testimony to Christ was confirmed (*ebebaiōthē*) among you, so that you are not lacking in any spiritual gift, as you wait for the revealing of our Lord Jesus Christ, who also will sustain (*bebaiōsei*; confirm) you to the end, guiltless in the day of our Lord Jesus Christ. (1 Cor 1:6-8)

This corresponds to what Paul wrote to the Philippians: "And I am sure that he who began a good work in you will bring it to completion at the day of Jesus Christ." (Phil 1:6) What is happening with the believers in Corinth through Christ is due to the fact that "God is faithful" to the call he issued to them through Paul, a call which invited them into "the fellowship (*koinōnian*) of his Son, Jesus Christ our Lord" (1 Cor 1:9). This verse is often misunderstood as meaning that one has a "personal" relationship with Christ. It bears repeating here that the understanding of *koinōnia* is bound to table fellowship as will be made amply clear later in the letter (10:14-22). The ultimate test as to whether or not the Corinthians do partake of that fellowship is the extent to which they live a life of love and care

Chapter 1

for the needy neighbor.[10] The Lord Jesus Christ is after all the head of the household. He does not need anything from them; he provides for their needs and requires from them to do his bidding. Fellowship is not so much about an individual's oneness with Christ as it is about oneness with the others around the teaching of the gospel of Christ preached by Paul. This will be corroborated in the verses that follow.

Vv. 10-17 ¹⁰ Παρακαλῶ δὲ ὑμᾶς, ἀδελφοί, διὰ τοῦ ὀνόματος τοῦ κυρίου ἡμῶν Ἰησοῦ Χριστοῦ, ἵνα τὸ αὐτὸ λέγητε πάντες καὶ μὴ ᾖ ἐν ὑμῖν σχίσματα, ἦτε δὲ κατηρτισμένοι ἐν τῷ αὐτῷ νοῒ καὶ ἐν τῇ αὐτῇ γνώμῃ. ¹¹ ἐδηλώθη γάρ μοι περὶ ὑμῶν, ἀδελφοί μου, ὑπὸ τῶν Χλόης ὅτι ἔριδες ἐν ὑμῖν εἰσιν. ¹² λέγω δὲ τοῦτο ὅτι ἕκαστος ὑμῶν λέγει· ἐγὼ μέν εἰμι Παύλου, ἐγὼ δὲ Ἀπολλῶ, ἐγὼ δὲ Κηφᾶ, ἐγὼ δὲ Χριστοῦ. ¹³ μεμέρισται ὁ Χριστός; μὴ Παῦλος ἐσταυρώθη ὑπὲρ ὑμῶν, ἢ εἰς τὸ ὄνομα Παύλου ἐβαπτίσθητε; ¹⁴ εὐχαριστῶ [τῷ θεῷ] ὅτι οὐδένα ὑμῶν ἐβάπτισα εἰ μὴ Κρίσπον καὶ Γάϊον, ¹⁵ ἵνα μή τις εἴπῃ ὅτι εἰς τὸ ἐμὸν ὄνομα ἐβαπτίσθητε. ¹⁶ ἐβάπτισα δὲ καὶ τὸν Στεφανᾶ οἶκον, λοιπὸν οὐκ οἶδα εἴ τινα ἄλλον ἐβάπτισα. ¹⁷ οὐ γὰρ ἀπέστειλέν με Χριστὸς βαπτίζειν ἀλλὰ εὐαγγελίζεσθαι, οὐκ ἐν σοφίᾳ λόγου, ἵνα μὴ κενωθῇ ὁ σταυρὸς τοῦ Χριστοῦ.

¹⁰I appeal to you, brethren, by the name of our Lord Jesus Christ, that all of you agree and that there be no dissensions among you, but that you be united in the same mind and the same judgment. ¹¹For it has been reported to me by Chloe's people that there is quarreling among you, my brethren. ¹²What I mean is that each one of you says, "I belong to Paul," or "I belong to Apollos," or "I belong to Cephas," or "I belong to Christ."¹³Is Christ divided? Was Paul crucified for you? Or were you baptized in the name of Paul? ¹⁴I am thankful that I

---

[10] See further my detailed comments on Phil 1:9-11 in *C-Phil* 77-83 and on Philem 5-7 in *C-Col* 113-6.

baptized none of you except Crispus and Gaius; ¹⁵lest any one should say that you were baptized in my name. ¹⁶(I did baptize also the household of Stephanas. Beyond that, I do not know whether I baptized any one else.) ¹⁷For Christ did not send me to baptize but to preach the gospel, and not with eloquent wisdom, lest the cross of Christ be emptied of its power.

Paul's request is for the Corinthians to "all say the same thing (*to avto*)," that is, to be of one mind[11] and thus not allow schisms (dissensions) among themselves. The request (*parakalō*) of a senior is actually an order,[12] especially if the plenipotentiary messenger is issuing it in the name of the Lord. That his request is indeed that of a senior is confirmed in Paul's use of *katērtismenoi* which unfortunately RSV translates into "united." The same RSV translates its other occurrence in the Corinthian correspondence as "mend your ways" (*katartizesthe*; be corrected in your ways; 2 Cor 13:11), which is closer to the meaning of the original as is substantiated by the instances of the verb in the active voice: "Brethren, if a man is overtaken in any trespass, you who are spiritual should restore (*katartizete*; correct) him in a spirit of gentleness" (Gal 6:1);[13] "... praying earnestly night and day that we may see you face to face and supply (*katartisai*; supplement through correct teaching) what is lacking in your faith?" (1 Thess 3:10) Paul is not asking the Corinthians to "be united in the same mind and the same judgment" as though they were to meet and discuss matters and then find a common ground. Rather, as he subsequently will make clear, Paul is summoning them to abide by his teaching and even be corrected by it if need be, thereby submitting to it all together.

---

[11] See my comments on *to avto* in Phil in *C-Phil* 179.
[12] See *1 Thess* 133-4.
[13] See my comments in *Gal* 310-11 where I show that the addressees are the leaders of the community.

As is the case with all personal names in scripture, the name Chloe is functional in the context of Paul's argument. If Chloe has people whom she can send with a message to Paul which he will not disregard (1 Cor 1:11), then the assumption is that she is important in the community, presumably a patrician whose home is the house church. Her name means "tender nascent grass" and references the young church of Corinth whose members Paul considers "babes in Christ" whom he "fed with milk, not solid food; for you were not ready for it; and even yet you are not ready, for you are still of the flesh" (3:1-3a). The reason he writes in a rhetorical manner is that "while there is jealousy and strife (*eris*) among you, are you not of the flesh, and behaving like ordinary men?" (v.3b). The noun translated in RSV as "strife" is *eris*, the singular of the plural *erides* (translated as "quarreling"), which is precisely the complaint leveled against the Corinthians by the men of Chloe (1:11). That the two statements are closely interrelated is borne out by the fact that these are the only instances of that Greek word in 1 Corinthians.

Paul then proceeds to make clear to the Corinthians that siding with a different leader as though each of those leaders is carrying a different gospel is strictly prohibited by the Jerusalem agreement that stipulated one gospel and one apostleship (Gal 2:7-8).[14] He will comment further on this later in the letter: "Whether then it was I or they, so we preach and so you believed." (1 Cor 15:11) However, Paul is not leveling the value among the four "leaders." He is forcing the hand of the Corinthians by reminding them that they have only "one father in the gospel of Christ" (4:15). The names of the four "leaders" are presented as an *inclusio* (A, B, B', A'), Paul and Christ at both ends, and Apollos and Cephas in the middle. It is only the first

---

[14] See my comments in *Gal* 69-70.

and last names that remain functional in the following verses and throughout the entire epistle as well. Consequently, Apollos and Cephas are "squeezed out," as it were. They are introduced only to be flagrantly dismissed, just as Cephas and the others will be at the beginning of chapters 9 and 15.[15] Another way to look at the *inclusio* is to consider Apollos and Cephas "squeezed in" between Paul and Christ and thus under their control just as Silvanus is between Paul and Timothy in the Thessalonian correspondence (1 Thess 1:1; 2 Thess 1:1).[16] Either way, Apollos and Cephas will be relegated to a secondary position in 1 Corinthians 3.

With the exception of John 1:42 the name Cephas occurs exclusively in Galatians and 1 Corinthians. The letter to the Galatians describes Paul's view as to how Cephas betrayed the Jerusalem agreement. That accounts for the mistrust in Cephas or in his followers expressed in 1 Corinthians and explains Paul's effort to sway the Corinthians away from them. As to Apollos, his name occurs exclusively in 1 Corinthians, with the exception of Titus 3:13, and twice in Acts in conjunction with his activity at Corinth (18:24; 19:1). The name is ominous since it is from the verb *apollymi* (destroy) and is thus linked to the god Apollo, the destroyer (wolf) deity. Those who would follow Apollos away from the saving gospel are bound to *apōleia* (destruction, perdition) as Paul will write a few verses later: "For the word, namely (the word) of the cross, is folly to those who are perishing (*apollymenois*), but to us who are being saved it is the power of God." (1 Cor 1:18) I believe that Apollos is a cryptic reference to Barnabas, Paul's companion who worked with him

---

[15] See my article "Paul, the One Apostle of the One Gospel" in *The Journal of the Orthodox Center for the Advancement of Biblical Studies* (*JOCABS*) 2 (2009).

[16] See my comments in *NTI₄* 95-6. I have shown in *NTI₂* 243 that Silas ended up turning his back on Paul.

and then betrayed him.[17] This scenario would fit 1 Corinthians perfectly. On the one hand, Apollos watered what Paul planted in Corinth (3:6; see also 4:6). On the other hand, later in the letter, Paul refers to Barnabas as his co-worker in that same city (9:6) in conjunction with the mention of Cephas (v.5).

In my commentary on Galatians I have argued in detail for the understanding of "Christ" in the Pauline letters as referring to the one messianic community consisting of both Jews and Gentiles.[18] "Christ" is not so much an individual as he is the "head of the body" as Paul will demonstrate extensively later in 1 Corinthians (5:12-20; 12:12-31). "Is Christ divided (*memeristai*)?" asks Paul in disbelief. If his community is torn apart by dissensions, then the fellowship (*koinōnia*) is broken and Christ—that is, his household—is "divided," in the same way Satan's would be: "Every kingdom divided (*meristheisa*) against itself is laid waste, and no city or house divided (*meristheisa*) against itself will stand; and if Satan casts out Satan, he is divided (*emeristhē*) against himself; how then will his kingdom stand?" (Mt 12:25-26); "How can Satan cast out Satan? If a kingdom is divided (*meristhē*) against itself, that kingdom cannot stand. And if a house is divided (*meristhē*) against itself, that house will not be able to stand. And if Satan has risen up against himself and is divided (*emeristhē*), he cannot stand, but is coming to an end." (Mk 3:23-25) Paul is not about to allow the Corinthians to be split between Christ, the lord of the household, and Paul, his house superintendent (*oikonomos*),[19] let alone between the household's lord and antagonists, the like of Apollos and Cephas. The two main aspects that make the house lord unique in this

---

[17] Gal 2:1-14; Acts 11-15.
[18] See my discussion regarding the term "Christ" being referential to the messianic community in *Gal* 138-43, 187-8.
[19] 1 Cor 4:1-2; 9:17.

case are his crucifixion and the Corinthians' baptism in his name. These are also the two foci of Paul's argument in Galatians behind the oneness of table fellowship (3:1-6, 26-29).

On the practical level, crucifixion is not an issue for Paul since he is assumedly alive and could not have been crucified for the Corinthians' sake. However, he could very well have baptized some of the Corinthians. In spite of the fact that baptism was administered in Christ's name, Paul hurries to say that he baptized only two people, Crispus and Gaius, to make the point that baptism is definitely not in his name. As usual, the names referenced are functional. These two Roman names were very prominent and well-known in those times. Crispus was the name of a famous senator, Lucius Junius Quintus Vibius Crispus, who served under the emperors Nero, Vespasian, and Domitian, and also the name of the 1st century B.C. historian Gaius Sallustius Crispus. Gaius was the name of Julius Caesar and of the emperors Octavian Augustus and Caligula. Thus, Paul is trying to say to the Corinthians that there is no need for him to show off about how many were baptized at his hands, since those he did baptize bore the names of two prominent Romans connected to the city of Rome itself, one of which with no less than an imperial name. Crispus and Gaius function in the same way as Titus (the name of the emperor Titus) does in Galatians (2:1, 3): mighty Rome, the ruler of the world, was brought into obedient submission to the gospel (Rom 1:5; 16:25). Still, there is another twist to the name Crispus. It is the other name of Sosthenes as one can gather from Acts (18:5-17). Like Paul, Crispus is both a Roman citizen and a Jew. Crispus, together with Gaius, who is typically a Gentile, function similarly to Timothy and Titus, as representatives of the Jew and the Gentile who submitted to the gospel, and thus account for its full success from the Pauline perspective. Accordingly, Paul does not need to have baptized more than Crispus and Gaius.

Yet, Paul adds Stephanas' household as recipients of baptism at his hands. The function of this unexpected addition is to invite his hearers to look in another direction, rather than to throw themselves into different camps. The Greek *Stephanas* is another form of *Stephanos* which means crown and thus refers to true witness and eventually its ultimate stage of martyrdom. Indeed later, Paul will present himself as someone vying for the imperishable crown (9:25) while in the service of the gospel (vv.16-17). Since his mission is not to baptize but to evangelize, those who would really want to be "his" (1:12) would have to follow in his footsteps as the members of the household of Stephanas. Notice that by speaking not merely of the person Stephanas, but rather of his household, Paul is obliquely stating that, whenever in Corinth, he would be the guest of that household whose members, by the same token, are effectively "his own." In a nutshell, Paul is saying the following: "If indeed you insist to be considered 'mine' (v.12), then join the 'household' of Stephanas, which is my household." After all, baptism is as secondary to the word of preaching as circumcision is to the word of promise; they are both external signs sealing the actual reality that lies in God's message to us: "We say that faith was reckoned to Abraham as righteousness. How then was it reckoned to him? Was it before or after he had been circumcised? It was not after, but before he was circumcised. He received circumcision as a sign or seal of the righteousness which he had by faith while he was still uncircumcised." (Rom 4:9a-11a)

In preparation for what he will be expanding on, Paul adds after "to evangelize (*evangelisasthai*; to preach the gospel)" "not with cloquent wisdom (*sophia logou*; wisdom of the (human) word), lest the cross of Christ be emptied of its power" (1 Cor 1:17). Indeed, it is this vocabulary—wisdom, word, cross, power—that controls the rest of chapter 1. Moreover, having dismissed the matter of baptism as secondary, Paul reverts to the gospel message that centers round the crucifixion of God's messenger for our sake. It bears repeating again that classical theology, under the influence of Platonic philosophy, was concerned with the divinity of Christ more than anything else and blurred the centrality of crucifixion by equating it with death: "Christ crucified" became equivalent with "Christ having died." All God's messengers are bound to die like any other human being. The main point in Christ's demise is the *kind* of death he underwent: instead of the glorious death of a martyr, he suffered a shameful end. That Paul understood the crucifixion in this way is verified in the vocabulary, replete with shame and boasting, which he used at the conclusion of the first chapter.

Vv. 18-31 ¹⁸ Ὁ λόγος γὰρ ὁ τοῦ σταυροῦ τοῖς μὲν ἀπολλυμένοις μωρία ἐστίν, τοῖς δὲ σῳζομένοις ἡμῖν δύναμις θεοῦ ἐστιν. ¹⁹ γέγραπται γάρ· ἀπολῶ τὴν σοφίαν τῶν σοφῶν καὶ τὴν σύνεσιν τῶν συνετῶν ἀθετήσω. ²⁰ ποῦ σοφός; ποῦ γραμματεύς; ποῦ συζητητὴς τοῦ αἰῶνος τούτου; οὐχὶ ἐμώρανεν ὁ θεὸς τὴν σοφίαν τοῦ κόσμου; ²¹ ἐπειδὴ γὰρ ἐν τῇ σοφίᾳ τοῦ θεοῦ οὐκ ἔγνω ὁ κόσμος διὰ τῆς σοφίας τὸν θεόν, εὐδόκησεν ὁ θεὸς διὰ τῆς μωρίας τοῦ κηρύγματος σῶσαι τοὺς πιστεύοντας· ²² ἐπειδὴ καὶ Ἰουδαῖοι σημεῖα αἰτοῦσιν καὶ Ἕλληνες σοφίαν ζητοῦσιν, ²³ ἡμεῖς δὲ κηρύσσομεν Χριστὸν ἐσταυρωμένον, Ἰουδαίοις μὲν σκάνδαλον, ἔθνεσιν δὲ μωρίαν, ²⁴ αὐτοῖς δὲ τοῖς κλητοῖς, Ἰουδαίοις τε καὶ Ἕλλησιν, Χριστὸν θεοῦ δύναμιν καὶ θεοῦ σοφίαν· ²⁵ ὅτι τὸ μωρὸν τοῦ θεοῦ σοφώτερον τῶν ἀνθρώπων ἐστὶν καὶ τὸ ἀσθενὲς τοῦ θεοῦ ἰσχυρότερον τῶν ἀνθρώπων. ²⁶ Βλέπετε γὰρ τὴν κλῆσιν ὑμῶν, ἀδελφοί, ὅτι οὐ πολλοὶ σοφοὶ κατὰ σάρκα, οὐ πολλοὶ δυνατοί, οὐ πολλοὶ εὐγενεῖς· ²⁷ ἀλλὰ τὰ μωρὰ τοῦ κόσμου ἐξελέξατο ὁ θεός, ἵνα καταισχύνῃ τοὺς σοφούς, καὶ τὰ ἀσθενῆ τοῦ κόσμου ἐξελέξατο ὁ θεός, ἵνα καταισχύνῃ τὰ ἰσχυρά, ²⁸ καὶ τὰ ἀγενῆ τοῦ κόσμου καὶ τὰ ἐξουθενημένα ἐξελέξατο ὁ θεός, τὰ μὴ ὄντα, ἵνα τὰ ὄντα καταργήσῃ, ²⁹ ὅπως μὴ καυχήσηται πᾶσα σὰρξ ἐνώπιον τοῦ θεοῦ. ³⁰ ἐξ αὐτοῦ δὲ ὑμεῖς ἐστε ἐν Χριστῷ Ἰησοῦ, ὃς ἐγενήθη σοφία ἡμῖν ἀπὸ θεοῦ, δικαιοσύνη τε καὶ ἁγιασμὸς καὶ ἀπολύτρωσις, ³¹ ἵνα καθὼς γέγραπται· ὁ καυχώμενος ἐν κυρίῳ καυχάσθω.

¹⁸For the word of the cross is folly to those who are perishing, but to us who are being saved it is the power of God. ¹⁹For it is written, "I will destroy the wisdom of the wise, and the cleverness of the clever I will thwart." ²⁰Where is the wise man? Where is the scribe? Where is the debater of this age? Has not God made foolish the wisdom of the world? ²¹For since, in the wisdom of God, the world did not know God through wisdom, it pleased God through the folly of what we preach to save those who believe. ²²For Jews demand signs and Greeks seek wisdom, ²³but we preach Christ crucified, a stumbling block to Jews and folly to Gentiles, ²⁴but to those who are called, both Jews and Greeks, Christ the power of God and the wisdom of God. ²⁵For the foolishness of God is wiser than men, and the weakness of God is stronger than men. ²⁶For consider your call, brethren; not many of you were wise according to worldly standards, not many were powerful, not many were of noble birth; ²⁷but God chose what is foolish in the world to shame the wise, God chose what is weak in the world to shame the strong, ²⁸God chose what is low and despised in the world, even things that are not, to bring to nothing things that are, ²⁹so that no human being might boast in the presence of God. ³⁰He is the source of your life in Christ Jesus, whom God made our wisdom, our righteousness and sanctification and redemption; ³¹therefore, as it is written, "Let him who boasts, boast of the Lord."

The original Greek that is usually mistranslated as "For the word of the cross" (1 Cor 1:18) is actually "For the word, which is that of the cross" (*Ho logos gar ho tou stavrou*). The subject of the sentence is "the word (*logos*)" which, in Pauline terminology, is another term for "the gospel (*evangelion*)" or "the heralding" (*kērygma*; preaching). This will be made clear a few verses later: "When I came to you, brethren, I did not come proclaiming (*katangellōn* from the same root as *evangelion*) to you the testimony of God in lofty words or wisdom. For I decided to know nothing among you except Jesus Christ and him crucified … and my speech (*logos*; word) and my message (*kērygma*; preaching) were not in plausible words of wisdom" (2:1-2, 4; compare with the terminology of 1:17-18). If the cross is not to be "emptied," it is because it is meant to refer to a "word" that could be robbed of its meaning and this "word" is the gospel (*evangelion*) preached by Paul (Gal 3:1).

In describing the effect of the gospel Paul purposely uses terminology of the Roman arena. In the arena the gladiators are slated to either perdition (*apōleia*) or to salvation (*sōtēria*), both ultimately through the emperor's "power," since the emperor is able and has the right to decide their fate, even against the people's preference. On the other hand, those condemned to death by crucifixion are by definition "perishing" (*apollymenois*). Yet, as he did in Romans 1:1-17, Paul is expressing an anti-imperial stand by saying that the fate of the Corinthians, living within the confines of the Roman empire, is in the power of God who, through his crucified emissary, is able to bestow salvation, a proposition that is obviously sheer "folly" (*mōria*). However, affirms Paul, it is those who refuse that proposition, who will perish. Unlike later theology that uses philosophical intricacies to explain the "folly," Paul simply reasons, "For it is written." This stands to "scriptural" reason since the gospel preached by Paul is none other than what "God promised beforehand through his prophets in the holy scriptures" (Rom 1:2).[20] It is only proper that Paul chose to quote from Isaiah, the prophet par excellence of God's messenger's shameful death: "I will destroy (*apolō*; make perish) the wisdom of the wise, and the cleverness of the clever I will thwart." (1 Cor 1:19; Is 29:14). It is evident that Paul's reasoning is thoroughly scriptural since the scriptural quotation controls the entire passage, and its terminology dictates Paul's own choice of words (1 Cor 1:17-18) when leading up to it (v.19).

In vv.20-21a Paul repeats the argument he developed extensively in Romans 1:18-32 whereby God left the world to its own false wisdom, dooming it to its demise.[21] When God offered humankind the way of salvation, he made sure to do so through the means of the gospel message, which would be considered folly by men (1 Cor 1:21b). Such would close the door even to the possibility that they would have figured it out sooner or later through their wisdom. No human being in his right mind would ever consider to be deemed foolish! In order to put pressure on his hearers, Paul includes himself among the targeted holders of human wisdom. To be sure, the main term "wise (man)" (*sophos*) Paul will apply mostly to the Corinthians (1:26-27; 3:18; 6:5); still he uses it once to speak of himself: "According to the grace of God given to me, like a skilled (*sophos*; wise) master builder I laid a foundation" (3:10). However, he is "wise" inasmuch as he became an apostle preaching "the wisdom of God" (2:6-7), not that of the world (vv.4-5). Such is not a unique instance since he does the same at the beginning of Galatians (1:13-17) and in Philippians (3:4-11). In other words, by giving himself as a

---

[20] See *C-Rom* 31-2.
[21] See *C-Rom* 51-9.

prime example of someone who trusted in God's wisdom in spite of its apparent folly (1 Cor 1:21a), Paul can ask the same of the Corinthians when he tells them that salvation through "the folly of the preaching" is granted to "those who trust (believe)" (v.21b).

This reading is corroborated in Paul's choice of the two terms he uses in apposition to "wise man": scribe (*grammatevs*) and debater (*syzētētēs*) (v.20). Although "scribe" can be understood as a general term referring to a "man of letters," it is a unique instance outside the Gospels where the reference is always and specifically to the Jewish scribes. This would correspond then to his referring to himself as a Pharisee in Philippians 3:5 and as "a member of Judaism, zealous for the fatherly traditions" in Galatians 1:14-15, that is, in the two passages mentioned earlier where he speaks of his turning around. As for "debater," it is similarly unique outside Mark and Luke-Acts where it occurs in reference to debates with Jesus, his disciples, or Stephen regarding the teaching, which debates are often carried by those knowledgeable in the Law.[22]

In dealing with the false wisdom of the world here Paul uses a terminology very close to that used in Romans: "Has not God made foolish (*emōranen*) the wisdom (*sophian*) of the world?" (1 Cor 1:20b); "Claiming to be *wise* (*sophoi*), they *became fools* (*emōranthēsan*)." (Rom 1:20) The closeness in phraseology is part of a parallelism in the approach. In Romans 1:18-2:29 Paul speaks of the ungodliness and wickedness of men in general (1:18), a statement he applies first to the Gentiles (1:19-32) then to the Jews (2:1-29). Here in 1 Corinthians Paul speaks of the false wisdom of the world in general (1:21) and then applies his

---

[22] Mk 1:27; 8:11; 9:10, 14, 16; 12:28; Lk 22:23; 24:15; Acts 6:9.

statement to the Gentiles as well as to the Jews (vv.22-25). In Romans the culmination of folly lay in men's persistence not to abide by God's "just decree" (*dikaiōma*; 1:32) expressed specifically in the Law (2:14-29). Here in 1 Corinthians the fullness of folly lies in the refusal to submit to the gospel message which is carrying God's "folly" as the true and saving wisdom (1:22-25). More important, however, is the fact that the terminology of vv.21-23 is reminiscent of Galatians 1:15-16:

> But when he who had set me apart before I was born, and had called me through his grace, was pleased (*evdokēsen*) to reveal his Son to me, in order that I might preach (*evangelizōmai*) him among the Gentiles, I did not confer with flesh and blood (Gal 1:15-16)

> For since, in the wisdom of God, the world did not know God through wisdom, God was pleased (*evdokēsen*) through the folly of the preaching (*kērygmatos*; proclamation, what is heralded) to save those who believe. For Jews demand signs and Greeks seek wisdom, but we preach (*kēryssomen*; proclaim, herald) Christ crucified, a stumbling block to Jews and folly to Gentiles (1 Cor 1:21-23)

This indicates that Paul was referring specifically to his preaching among the Corinthians and not to an ethereal common preaching. At the most, the plural "we preach" would include Apollos but only to the extent allowed later in 3:6 and 10-11 whereby Apollos' secondary activity is acceptable so long as it corresponds to Paul's foundational work: "I planted, Apollos watered ... According to the grace of God given to me, like a skilled master builder I laid a foundation, and another man is building upon it. Let each man take care how he builds upon it. For no other foundation can any one lay than that which is laid, which is Jesus Christ."

Jews and Gentiles have different reasons to refuse the gospel message (1:22). Here Paul reserves the search for "wisdom" to the Greeks (*Hellēnes*) since the "love for wisdom" (*philosophia*) is an integral part of their quest, whereas he speaks of "signs" as the concern of the Jews. The meaning of "sign" (Hebrew *'ot*; Greek *sēmeion*) is technical in scripture. It refers to an event, whether miraculous or not, which is assigned as such by God; whenever that event takes place, then one will know that God has spoken truthfully. That is why the Jewish leaders in the Gospels keep asking Jesus to show them a sign that he is sent by God. For both Gentiles and Jews it is impossible to consider that a crucified person can be an expression of wisdom, much less of strength, or a sign from God (v.23). Yet, writes Paul, it is through such medium that God has called Hellenes as well as Jews, and those who accept the call will have to accept that kind of messiah as the medium of God's power and wisdom (v.24). This combination is challenging to the power of Rome and to the wisdom of Greece, the two foci of the Roman empire's greatness. In order to drive home his point, Paul administers the ultimate blow to the arrogance of any and all of his hearers: "For the foolishness (the foolish expression) of God is wiser than men, and the weakness (the weak expression) of God is stronger than men." (v.25)

Then, to forego any retort, Paul uses an argument *ad hominem*, that is, an argument appealing to the Corinthians' personal experience concerning the gospel in the same way as he did with the Galatians: "Let me ask you only this: Did you receive the Spirit by works of the law, or by hearing with faith?" (Gal 3:2).[23] Most of Paul's addressees, the object of God's benevolent choice, were not wise according to the flesh, that is, in terms of human

---

[23] See my comments in *Gal* 94-101.

wisdom, nor were they socially powerful, yet he adds the mention of nobility by birth (*evgeneis*; 1 Cor 1:26). This is a clear strike at the Roman nobility—those who were free citizens by birth, through their being members of a given extended family or clan (Greek *genos*; Latin *gens*)—which was held in the highest esteem in the empire. By introducing nobility along with wisdom and power, the two elements pertinent to the discussion, Paul is intentionally belittling the Corinthians, citizens of Corinth, the capital of the Roman province Achaia that covered the area of ancient Greece, by reminding them that they, the Greeks, who centuries earlier looked down on all others, including the Romans, whom they considered barbarians, now lie under the Roman boot, vying for the status of Roman citizenry as the ultimate goal in life.

The mention of nobility is definitely not done in passing since it (1) takes the lion's share in Paul's counterstatement, (2) introduces new terminology, and (3) prepares for the conclusion:

> ... but God chose what is foolish in the world to shame the wise, God chose what is weak in the world to shame the strong, God chose what is low (*agenē*) and despised in the world, even things that are not, to bring to nothing things that are, so that no human being (*sarx*; flesh) might boast in the presence of God. (1 Cor 1:27-28)

Notice the expansion of the third element into "low and despised ... even things that are not," compared to the simple "foolish" and "weak." "Low" (*agenē*) should have sufficed since it is the opposite of "noble" (*evgeneis*) just as "foolish" is the opposite of "wise" and "weak" that of "strong." By adding "despised" Paul is stressing that he is talking of "the lowest of the lowest." Indeed, someone of low social standing, like a slave or even a freedman, could still be respectable. The house superintendent (*oikonomos*), as Paul no less considers himself (4:1-2; 9:17), is after all a slave trusted by the master to manage the matters of his household and, as such, has authority even over the master's children. Paul pushes the matter to the extreme by referring to the lowliest as "things that are not," that is, "those who are (amount to) nothing" as we would put it nowadays. The functional and intentional purpose of this addition is confirmed by the fact that (1) the result of God's counteraction mentions its opposite, "things that are," "those who are something," rather than "noble" or "held in esteem," and (2) God's intervention is expressed through a new verb, the more forceful "bring to nothing" (*katargēsē*; void, destroy), rather than "shame" (*kataiskhynē*) which was used in conjunction with both "the wise" and "the strong."

All that astute orchestration of differing terminology and phraseology functions as a literary buildup for the concluding result: "so that all (every) flesh (*sarx*; human being) not boast in the presence of God" (1:29). "Boasting," obviously the opposite of "being shamed (put to shame)," would be a fitting conclusion to v.27. Yet, "every flesh" harks back to "things that are not" (v.28). Indeed, in scripture "flesh" refers to what is essentially human, not divine (which would be "spirit"), and as such is bound to decay (reflected in the verb *katargēsē*) and "return to the ground, for out of it you were taken; you are dust, and to dust you shall return" (Gen 3:19). Later Paul will revisit this matter when he sternly reminds the "fleshly" Corinthians (3:1-3): "Food is meant for the stomach and the stomach for food—and God will destroy (*katargēsei*) both one and the other." (6:13a).

It is God who chose that the unworthy Corinthians be granted the grace of being "in Christ Jesus," that is, members of the one messianic community, "the church of God" (1:1). True wisdom, which is from God, flows from the lips of Christ Jesus, the head and teacher of that household, who speaks through his apostle Paul (4:15). Yet, more important than the wisdom of the gospel is what it bestows on those who put their trust in it (1:21): righteousness which ensures sanctification and, by the same token, ultimate redemption from the state of exile and death brought about by our Law-less behavior (v.30). This is what Paul teaches in a comprehensive manner in Romans 5-8.[24] Finally, in order to make sure that what he wrote in 1 Corinthians 1:29 not be mistaken as his personal opinion, Paul seals it with the full authority of scripture itself: "therefore (*hina*; so that), as it is written, 'Let him who boasts, boast of the Lord.'" (v.31) Indeed scripture was looming in the background in vv.18-19: Paul started by extensively using the terminology of the scriptural text and ended by quoting it. One should remember that the quotations, although usually short, function as an invitation for the hearers to recollect the entire passage.[25] Listen to the full original statement in Jeremiah:

> Thus says the Lord: "Let not the wise man (*sophos*) glory (*kavkhasthō*) in his wisdom (*sophia*), let not the mighty man (*iskhyros*) glory (*kavkhasthō*) in his might (*iskhyi*), let not the rich man glory (*kavkhasthō*) in his riches; but let him who glories (*kavkhōmenos*) glory (*kavkhasthō*) in this, that he understands and knows me, that I am the Lord who practice steadfast love, justice,

---

[24] See my comments in *C-Rom* 105-147.
[25] See especially the case of Gal 4:27 where Paul quotes only a verse from Isaiah, inviting the hearer of scripture (v.21) to go back to the Book of Isaiah in order to fully understand the relation between Sarah and the heavenly Jerusalem whose children the Galatians are in the same manner as Isaac is Sarah's son. See my detailed comments in *Gal* 242-51.

and *righteousness* in the earth; for in these things I delight, says the Lord." (Jer 9:22-23)[26]

The Jeremianic text is definitely the source for Paul's vocabulary in 1 Corinthians 1:24-30. Still, the influence is astonishing. When analyzing Paul's text closely, one notices that, although he begins with *dynamis* (power; vv.18 and 24) which he keeps in v.26 (*dynatoi*; powerful), he introduces the parallel root *iskhyr—* (strong) in vv.25 and 27, which is precisely Jeremiah's terminology. The third element of "nobility" in 1 Corinthians, introduced besides wisdom and power (strength), is prompted by the third element of "richness" in Jeremiah. In the Roman empire, power (strength) was an attribute of the Roman nobility, which power was rooted in that nobility's richness in earthly possessions.

---

[26] Throughout the LXX text the original for "glory" is the verb *khavkhōmai* which is used in 1 Corinthians and translated as "boast."

Chapter 2

Vv. 1-5 *¹Κἀγὼ ἐλθὼν πρὸς ὑμᾶς, ἀδελφοί, ἦλθον οὐ καθ' ὑπεροχὴν λόγου ἢ σοφίας καταγγέλλων ὑμῖν τὸ μυστήριον τοῦ θεοῦ. ² οὐ γὰρ ἔκρινά τι εἰδέναι ἐν ὑμῖν εἰ μὴ Ἰησοῦν Χριστὸν καὶ τοῦτον ἐσταυρωμένον. ³ κἀγὼ ἐν ἀσθενείᾳ καὶ ἐν φόβῳ καὶ ἐν τρόμῳ πολλῷ ἐγενόμην πρὸς ὑμᾶς, ⁴ καὶ ὁ λόγος μου καὶ τὸ κήρυγμά μου οὐκ ἐν πειθοῖ[ς] σοφίας [λόγοις] ἀλλ' ἐν ἀποδείξει πνεύματος καὶ δυνάμεως, ⁵ ἵνα ἡ πίστις ὑμῶν μὴ ᾖ ἐν σοφίᾳ ἀνθρώπων ἀλλ' ἐν δυνάμει θεοῦ.*

> *¹When I came to you, brethren, I did not come proclaiming to you the testimony of God in lofty words or wisdom. ²For I decided to know nothing among you except Jesus Christ and him crucified. ³And I was with you in weakness and in much fear and trembling; ⁴and my speech and my message were not in plausible words of wisdom, but in demonstration of the Spirit and of power, ⁵that your faith might not rest in the wisdom of men but in the power of God.*

Paul proceeds to speak of his proclamation among the Corinthians using paradoxical terminology. He refers to the gospel as "the mystery of God"[1] and yet he did not impart it in loftiness of word or wisdom. In chapter 1, Paul denigrated philosophy that flourished in ancient Greece around Athens, an area that became the Roman province Achaia whose capital was Corinth. This same area boasted of arguably the most famous religious center of ancient Greece. Just a short distance north of Athens was the locale of the well-known Eleusinian mysteries dating from as early as 1700 B.C. and continuing to the era of

---

[1] RSV opted for the reading "the testimony of God" (*to martyrion tou Theou*) found in some manuscripts. However, I consider "the mystery of God" as the original which copyists have probably changed into "the testimony of God" to correspond to "the testimony of Christ" in 1 Cor 1:6.

the Roman Empire. These mysteries reenacted the goddess Demeter's search for her daughter Kore or Pesephone who was abducted by the god Hades. The goal was to give hope for life after death, a view not common among ancient Greeks. Thus, by introducing the terminology of "mystery," Paul was molding the gospel's message in a cast that was appealing to the commoner rather than to the philosopher, after having reminded his hearers that they were of the former kind (1 Cor 1:20, 26). In so doing, he was blocking a way for them to cop out and throw themselves into the world of mystery religions. A few verses later he will assert that his proclamation of the "word" (1:18) entails "wisdom" (2:6) despite any appearance to the contrary (1:19-31). By the same token, throughout the epistle, he is opening the way for the culmination of his teaching in chapter 15 where he will discuss the resurrection from the dead and life eternal should one pass the test of divine judgment.[2]

Still, in continuation with chapter 1, the concern here remains anti-human (anti-ancient Greek) wisdom. The mystery of Paul's God is communicated not through loftiness of "wise words" that belittles the common people. Scripturally, mystery is a counsel, that is, God's plan, which is shared with the people through specifically assigned emissaries, the prophet in the Old Testament[3] and the apostle in the New Testament. The total discrepancy, if not opposition, between Greek philosophy and the "mystery of God" that Paul is proclaiming is at its clearest in Paul's statement, "For I decided (judged necessary) to know nothing among you except Jesus Christ and him crucified" (2:2), which is precisely "folly" in the eyes of the erudite Greeks (1:21)

---

[2] Notice the use of the noun "mystery" in 15.51 (Lo! I tell you a mystery. We shall not all sleep, but we shall all be changed).
[3] See in particular Is 6:5-13; Jer 1:4-10; Ezek 2:1-5; 3:1-11; Am 7:7-15.

and "weakness" in those of the powerful Romans who use crucifixion as the ultimate expression of shaming an opponent by exposing his utter frailty and ineptitude. The emissary who presents this message does so "in much fear and trembling." However, if his proclamation of the gospel word is not delivered with convincing (*peithois*) words of wisdom, this only enhances the fact that its validity lay in the power of God's spirit.[4] The result, intended all along by Paul himself, is for the Corinthians to put their trust in God's power, not in human wisdom. The subtle shift from "wisdom" to "power" is evidenced in that Paul introduces his "weakness" (2:3) and then God's "power" (v.5) in contradistinction to human wisdom. The reason is clear. Although he will talk about wisdom (vv.6-7), his real target is Roman power as is apparent from the double reference to "the rulers of this age" (vv.6 and 8). By the same token, the terminology of power allows Paul to slowly slip in reference to God's spirit (vv.10-15) which he introduced in v.5 in conjunction with power.

Vv. 6-16 ⁶ Σοφίαν δὲ λαλοῦμεν ἐν τοῖς τελείοις, σοφίαν δὲ οὐ τοῦ αἰῶνος τούτου οὐδὲ τῶν ἀρχόντων τοῦ αἰῶνος τούτου τῶν καταργουμένων· ⁷ ἀλλὰ λαλοῦμεν θεοῦ σοφίαν ἐν μυστηρίῳ τὴν ἀποκεκρυμμένην, ἣν προώρισεν ὁ θεὸς πρὸ τῶν αἰώνων εἰς δόξαν ἡμῶν, ⁸ ἣν οὐδεὶς τῶν ἀρχόντων τοῦ αἰῶνος τούτου ἔγνωκεν· εἰ γὰρ ἔγνωσαν, οὐκ ἂν τὸν κύριον τῆς δόξης ἐσταύρωσαν. ⁹ ἀλλὰ καθὼς γέγραπται· ἃ ὀφθαλμὸς οὐκ εἶδεν καὶ οὖς οὐκ ἤκουσεν καὶ ἐπὶ καρδίαν ἀνθρώπου οὐκ ἀνέβη, ἃ ἡτοίμασεν ὁ θεὸς τοῖς ἀγαπῶσιν αὐτόν. ¹⁰ ἡμῖν δὲ ἀπεκάλυψεν ὁ θεὸς διὰ τοῦ πνεύματος· τὸ γὰρ πνεῦμα πάντα ἐραυνᾷ, καὶ τὰ βάθη τοῦ θεοῦ. ¹¹τίς γὰρ οἶδεν ἀνθρώπων τὰ τοῦ ἀνθρώπου εἰ μὴ τὸ πνεῦμα τοῦ ἀνθρώπου

---

[4] In scripture power is intimately connected with spirit, as is evident throughout the New Testament. The Hebrew *ruaḥ* means wind and thus a mighty movement of air which, though unseen, produces a visible effect.

τὸ ἐν αὐτῷ; οὕτως καὶ τὰ τοῦ θεοῦ οὐδεὶς ἔγνωκεν εἰ μὴ τὸ πνεῦμα τοῦ θεοῦ. ¹²ἡμεῖς δὲ οὐ τὸ πνεῦμα τοῦ κόσμου ἐλάβομεν ἀλλὰ τὸ πνεῦμα τὸ ἐκ τοῦ θεοῦ, ἵνα εἰδῶμεν τὰ ὑπὸ τοῦ θεοῦ χαρισθέντα ἡμῖν· ¹³ἃ καὶ λαλοῦμεν οὐκ ἐν διδακτοῖς ἀνθρωπίνης σοφίας λόγοις ἀλλ' ἐν διδακτοῖς πνεύματος, πνευματικοῖς πνευματικὰ συγκρίνοντες. ¹⁴ψυχικὸς δὲ ἄνθρωπος οὐ δέχεται τὰ τοῦ πνεύματος τοῦ θεοῦ· μωρία γὰρ αὐτῷ ἐστιν καὶ οὐ δύναται γνῶναι, ὅτι πνευματικῶς ἀνακρίνεται. ¹⁵ὁ δὲ πνευματικὸς ἀνακρίνει [τὰ] πάντα, αὐτὸς δὲ ὑπ' οὐδενὸς ἀνακρίνεται. ¹⁶τίς γὰρ ἔγνω νοῦν κυρίου, ὃς συμβιβάσει αὐτόν; ἡμεῖς δὲ νοῦν Χριστοῦ ἔχομεν.

⁶Yet among the mature we do impart wisdom, although it is not a wisdom of this age or of the rulers of this age, who are doomed to pass away. ⁷But we impart a secret and hidden wisdom of God, which God decreed before the ages for our glorification. ⁸None of the rulers of this age understood this; for if they had, they would not have crucified the Lord of glory. ⁹But, as it is written, "What no eye has seen, nor ear heard, nor the heart of man conceived, what God has prepared for those who love him," ¹⁰God has revealed to us through the Spirit. For the Spirit searches everything, even the depths of God. ¹¹For what person knows a man's thoughts except the spirit of the man which is in him? So also no one comprehends the thoughts of God except the Spirit of God. ¹²Now we have received not the spirit of the world, but the Spirit which is from God, that we might understand the gifts bestowed on us by God. ¹³And we impart this in words not taught by human wisdom but taught by the Spirit, interpreting spiritual truths to those who possess the Spirit. ¹⁴The unspiritual man does not receive the gifts of the Spirit of God, for they are folly to him, and he is not able to understand them because they are spiritually discerned. ¹⁵The spiritual man judges all things, but is himself to be judged by no one. ¹⁶"For who has known the mind of the Lord so as to instruct him?" But we have the mind of Christ.

If the apostle does not impart human wisdom, he nevertheless, says Paul, "speaks" (*laloumen*) wisdom to the "fulfilled" (*teleiois*; mature). The verb *lalō* (speak) is usually associated with speaking out and thus teaching, especially in the Pauline corpus.[5] By referring to the mature, Paul is preparing for the harsh criticism he is about to level against the Corinthians whom he will dub as "babes" (3:1-4). For the time being, he continues to dismantle Greco-Roman arrogance and, indirectly, that of his hearers who are befuddled by it. The wisdom of the gospel message that Paul imparts is not of this age, that is, of the Roman world (2:6; see 1:20) and, more specifically, of the rulers who are bound to be brought to nothingness (*katargoumenōn*). The agent of this destruction is God. This is evident from the parallel statement, "God chose what is low and despised in the world, even things that are not, to bring to nothing (*katargēsē*) things that are" (1:28). Paul imparts the wisdom of God according to his mystery; moreover, this mystery is communicated through the gospel preaching according to the apostolic words, as reflected in the verb "(we) speak" (*laloumen*) which is repeated on purpose. The reference to the gospel is corroborated by the use of "hidden" (*apokekrymmenēn*) and "decreed beforehand" (*proōrisen*) in conjunction with the wisdom of God. "Hidden" also occurs in Colossians in a context that references Paul's commission to preach the gospel and uses terminology (mystery, wisdom, mature) that is similar to that of 1 Corinthians:

> And you, who once were estranged and hostile in mind, doing evil deeds, he has now reconciled in his body of flesh by his death, in order to present you holy and blameless and irreproachable before him, provided that you continue in the faith, stable and steadfast,

---

[5] See e.g. Rom 15:18; 2 Cor 2:17; 4:13-14; 7:14; 12:19; Eph 6:19-20; Phil 1:14; Col 4:3-4; 1 Thess 2:2, 4, 16.

not shifting from the hope of the gospel which you heard, which has been preached to every creature under heaven, and of which I, Paul, became a minister. Now I rejoice in my sufferings for your sake, and in my flesh I complete what is lacking in Christ's afflictions for the sake of his body, that is, the church, of which I became a minister according to the divine office which was given to me for you, to make the word of God fully known, the mystery hidden (*apokekrymmenon*) for ages and generations but now made manifest to his saints. To them God chose to make known how great among the Gentiles are the riches of the glory of this mystery, which is Christ in you, the hope of glory. Him we proclaim, warning every man and teaching every man in all wisdom, that we may present every man mature (*teleion*) in Christ. (Col 1:21-28)[6]

The "decreed beforehand" (*proōrisen*; from the verb *proorizō*) refers to the fact that God's plan was set even before the rulers of this world were at hand; thus it could not have been an effect of their "wise" planning. The other instances of the verb *proorizō* in the New Testament sound as though they are expanded comments on 1 Corinthians 2:7-8. Romans 8:28-30 and Ephesians 1:5-12 detail what Paul writes in 1 Corinthians 2:7 concerning God's plan to glorify those whom he called through Paul's preaching (But we impart a secret and hidden wisdom of God, which God decreed before the ages for our glorification):

We know that in everything God works for good with those who love him, who are called according to his purpose (*prothesin*). For

---

[6] See also the parallel passage in Ephesians 3:7-9 (Of this gospel I was made a minister according to the gift of God's grace which was given me by the working of his power. To me, though I am the very least of all the saints, this grace was given, to preach to the Gentiles the unsearchable riches of Christ, and to make all men see what is the plan of the mystery hidden for ages in God who created all things).

those whom he foreknew (*proegnō*) he also predestined (*proōrisen*) to be conformed to the image of his Son, in order that he might be the first-born among many brethren. And those whom he predestined (*proōrisen*) he also called; and those whom he called he also justified; and those whom he justified he also *glorified*. (Rom 8:28-30)

He destined (*proorisas*) us in love to be his sons through Jesus Christ, according to the purpose of his will, to the praise of the *glory* of his grace which he freely bestowed on us in the Beloved ... For he has made known to us in all *wisdom* and insight the *mystery* of his will, according to his purpose which he set forth (*proetheto*; from the same root as *prothesin*) in Christ as a plan for the fullness of time, to unite all things in him, things in heaven and things on earth. In him, according to the purpose (*prothesin*) of him who accomplishes all things according to the counsel of his will, we who first hoped in Christ have been destined (*prooristhentes*; from the verb *proorizō*) and appointed to live for the praise of his *glory*. (Eph 1:5-6, 9-12)

Acts 4:26-28 speaks to the kind of death Christ was subjugated to by the rulers of this world, which is referred to in 1 Corinthians 2:8:

The kings of the earth set themselves in array, and *the rulers* were gathered together, against the Lord and against his Anointed—for truly in this city there were gathered together against thy holy servant Jesus, whom thou didst anoint, both Herod and Pontius Pilate, with the Gentiles and the peoples of Israel, to do whatever thy hand and thy plan had predestined (*proōrisen*) to take place. (Acts 4:26-28)

In 1 Corinthians 2:8 Paul ridicules the rulers of this world. In spite of their wisdom that was alleged to impart knowledge, those who were supposedly God's representatives on earth (Rom 13:1-7) did not know the plan of God. And how could they—

given that God's plan revolved around the Roman crucifixion which is a sign of shame and not glory? Yet, the Lord Jesus acceded to God's glory through his total obedience in submitting to a shameful death (Phil 2:5-11). That plan of God, unknown to the rulers of this world, was imparted by Paul through his preaching "the gospel of God which he promised beforehand (*proepēngeilato*)[7] through his prophets in the holy scriptures" (Rom 1:1-2) The scriptural quotations in 1 Corinthians 2:9 and 16 which bracket the passage that covers Paul's apostolic mission and teaching in Corinth (vv.10-15) are ingeniously chosen. The main scriptural reference Paul uses in dealing with Christ's shameful death on the cross is the fourth passage on the Lord's Servant in Isaiah (52:1-53:12).[8] That passage lies at the center of the second part of Isaiah (chs.40-66) and constitutes the backbone of the Pauline gospel.[9] In Romans, especially in chapters 9-11, Paul uses his scriptural quotations not only in sequence, but also in a way that covers the entire scripture.[10] This is precisely what he is doing here in 1 Corinthians.

The first part of the quotation in 1 Corinthians 2:9 is from Isaiah 64:4; the quotation in 1 Corinthians 2:16 is from Isaiah 40:13. Thus Paul is inviting his hearers to review in their minds Isaiah 40-66 in order to be convinced of his argument. Actually, his teaching is not so much an argumentation as it is a reminder of God's plan (*prothesis*; purpose) inscribed in the "holy scriptures" (Rom 1:2). Why did he start with the end of Isaiah

---

[7] Notice again the preposition *pro* (pre—, beforehand) which we have encountered in the verbs I pointed out in Acts, Romans, and Ephesians as well as 1 Corinthians.
[8] See my comments on Phil 2:6-11 in *C-Phil* 110-33 and on Col 1:15-20 in *C-Col* 43-44, 52.
[9] As early as Gal 4:21-31, where Is 54 is the central scriptural reference for the establishment that the Gentile believers, though uncircumcised, were nevertheless Sarah's children in the same manner as Isaac.
[10] See *C-Rom* 174-5, 177-9, 185-9, 198-200.

(40-66) and end with its beginning? He did this to dismantle the edifice of Greco-Roman arrogance reflected in their so-called wisdom and their false power (1 Cor 1:18-2:8). In so doing he was forced to conclude his introductory part of the letter by pointing out the end of God's plan: the glorification of those who trust in him (1 Cor 2:7) rather than trust in the false glory promised by the Roman rulers of this world or in the false glory of Rome's Jewish counterpart, the earthly Jerusalem.[11] Once this is established through a reference to the *end* of God's plan from the *end* of Isaiah 40-66, Paul returns to his main concern: the Corinthians are to persevere in their trust in his teaching by referring to its source, God's spirit (1 Cor 2:10-15). Thus he ends up by inviting them to go back to the beginning of Isaiah 40-66 and review God's plan from its start. Just before Isaiah 40:13 one hears the following verses pitting God's glory against that of man, which is precisely Paul's point here regarding God's superior power over that of the Roman and Jewish authorities:

A voice cries: "In the wilderness prepare the way of the Lord, make straight in the desert a highway for our God. Every valley shall be lifted up, and every mountain and hill be made low; the uneven ground shall become level, and the rough places a plain. And the glory of the Lord shall be revealed, and all flesh shall see it together, for the mouth of the Lord has spoken." A voice says, "Cry!" And I said, "What shall I cry?" All flesh is grass, and all its beauty (all glory of man [LXX]) is like the flower of the field. The grass withers, the flower fades, when the spirit (*ruaḥ*) of the Lord blows upon it; surely the people is grass. The grass withers,

---

[11] Notice that the challenge to the Corinthians' trust in Paul's gospel came from his Jewish opponents as well as from the Hellenes (1 Cor 1:22-24). See also on this matter Acts 4:26-28 quoted earlier.

the flower fades; but the word of our God will stand for ever. (Is 40:3-8)

This is Paul's usual strategy: bringing his addressees back to the "earth" of their daily lives and challenging them to proceed on the path (1 Cor 15:58) since God's last word still lies ahead (4:1-5; 15:46). The path starts with their calling through the preaching of the Apostle (Rom 1:5; Phil 1:5; Col 1:5-6a; 1 Thess 1:4-5), which has its origin in God's revelation of the content of the gospel to Paul (1 Cor 2:10):

> For I would have you know, brethren, that the gospel which was preached by me is not man's gospel. For I did not receive it from man, nor was I taught it, but it came through a revelation of Jesus Christ ... But when he who had set me apart before I was born, and had called me through his grace, was pleased to reveal his Son to me, in order that I might preach him among the Gentiles. (Gal 1:11-12, 15-16)

A caveat is in order here. The "us" of 1 Corinthians 2:10 and the "we" in v.12 are often taken as being inclusive of the addressees. This is usually done to make what is said of "the spiritual man" in v.14 a general statement potentially applicable to all believers, or at least applicable to some elect among them. Such an understanding distorts the meaning of the text and is simply guru-ism. Self-assigned "spiritual" persons view the apostles, or more precisely the Old Testament prophets, as being the first in a continuing series of spiritual leaders. This is completely unscriptural. In each scriptural book there is only one representative of God who stands alone against all others.[12] The prime example of this is Moses who alone went up the mountain

---

[12] A classic example is Ezekiel who is alone on God's side not only against the rebellious people (2:3-8; 3:4-9) but also against the equally rebellious "elders" (9:4-6; 14:1-3; 20:1-3) and even prophets (13:1-16) and prophetesses (vv.17-23). See also Paul in 1 Cor, 2 Cor, Gal.

and who alone received the divine revelation which he in turn communicated to the people. Looking closely at 1 Corinthians 2:10-16, one will notice that one of the "we" verbs is "speak" (*laloumen*) which is the same verb used earlier (vv.6 and 7) that applies exclusively to the apostolic preaching. On the other hand, the Corinthian addressees cannot possibly be "spiritual" and "mature"—at least in the same sense as Paul is[13]—since, a few verses later, Paul will refer to them as "fleshly" and immature "babes" (3:1-3); rather they are judged by Paul's verdict.

In preparation for dubbing the Corinthians as "fleshly" and not "spiritual," Paul begins by writing that God reveals (to the Apostle) through the spirit, which is quintessentially divine in scripture. Another caveat is in order here against the teaching, championed mainly by early Alexandrian theologians: that the tripartite composition of the human being consists of spirit, soul, and body. In scripture the human being is not even bipartite; he is one totality viewed from the two perspectives, the soul and the flesh. One should not rush to the conclusion that spirit and soul (or breath) are equivalent.

In Hebrew spirit (*ruaḥ*), soul (*nepheš*; breathing), and *nešamah* (breath; breeze) are interrelated in that they are connected with moving air and, accordingly, the first and the third appear as complement of the verb *naphah* (breathe). We have a similar phenomenon in Greek. *pnevma* (spirit) and *pnoē* (breeze, breath, breathing, and thus "soul" [breathing being]) are from the same root as the verb *pneō* (breathe). This interconnection accounts for the interplay between the different nouns. In Genesis, *nepheš*

---

[13] To make this matter more pointed I often say to my students "You may well be *better* than Paul but will never be *like* him, simply because he is one of a kind just as Ezekiel and Moses are."

ḥayyah refers to animals (1:20, 21, 30) as well as humans (2:7). By the same token, the spirit as breath can be used in lieu of soul as breath:

When thou hidest thy face, they are dismayed; when thou takest away their breath (*ruaḥ*), they die and return to their dust. When thou sendest forth thy spirit (*ruaḥ*), they are created; and thou renewest the face of the ground. (Ps 104:29-30)

> Who knows whether the spirit (*ruaḥ*) of man goes upward and the spirit (*ruaḥ*) of the beast goes down to the earth? (Eccl 3:21)

> He who observes the wind (*ruaḥ*) will not sow; and he who regards the clouds will not reap. As you do not know how the spirit (*ruaḥ*) comes to the bones in the womb of a woman with child, so you do not know the work of God who makes everything. (11:4-5)

> ... and the dust returns to the earth as it was, and the spirit (*ruaḥ*) returns to God who gave it. (12:7)

The Hebrew *nepheš* translated as *psykhē* in Greek and "soul" in English is simply the "breath" or breathing that, like the pulsating flow of blood (Hebrew *damim*), reflect that a human being is alive. Breathing and pulse are the two most immediate "signs" or indicators of life. Due to its connotation of destructive power, the Hebrew *ruaḥ* (wind or rushing air; Greek *pnevma*), when associated with the divine, expresses an essential judging function of the deity. Another feature of the wind is its speed, which reflects the possibility for the deity to suddenly make itself present. This explains why divine epiphanies are often expressed in conjunction with the whirlwind. Unlike breathing which is a recurrent and thus "passing" phenomenon that does not have an effect beyond itself, the wind produces an effect beyond itself. The most classic example of differentiation between the two is actually found in 1 Corinthians itself: "Thus it is written, 'The first man Adam became a living being (*psykhēn zōsan*; living soul)'; the last Adam[14] became a life-giving spirit (*pnevma zōopoioun*). It is the physical (*psykhikon*; soul-ly) which is first and then the spiritual (*pnevmatikon*). The first man was from the earth, a man of dust; the second man is from heaven." (15:45-47) Translations usually distort the original Greek and are misleading. Notice how the two terms "being" and "physical" are disjointed, whereas in the original Greek they have the same root *psykhē*. What is of further importance is the correspondence between soul and dust, which is found in Genesis 1:7, the text behind 1 Corinthians 15:45 and 47: "then the Lord God formed man of *dust* from the ground, and *breathed* into his nostrils the *breath* of life; and man became a living being (*nepheš ḥayyah*, *psykhēn zōsan* [living soul])." If spirit is opposed to soul as it is to flesh, then the spirit is not, as it were, a higher instance of the soul as it is usually assumed by many. Both soul and flesh pertain to the human realm. Spirit is strictly and exclusively of the divine domain.

Then in which sense does Paul speak of the spirit of man (2:11)? When referring to the human being, spirit is used to mean soul or breath, and usually in a setting where it functions in contradistinction, even in opposition, to God's spirit. A classic example is found in Ezekiel: "Son of man, prophesy against the prophets of Israel, prophesy and say to those who prophesy out of their own minds (*libbam*; hearts [centers of human thoughts]): 'Hear the word of the Lord!' Thus says the Lord God, Woe to the foolish prophets who follow *their own spirit* (*ruaḥ*), and have seen nothing!" (13:2-3) The same intention is on Paul's mind in 1 Corinthians 2:10-11. He uses the "spirit of man" not to bring

---

[14] Who is Christ (v.22).

out the similarity between man and God, but rather to bring to the fore the opposition between the "human spirit" and the "spirit of God." As far as the human "spirit" can dig, it always does so within the depths of the human mindset. Consequently, a human being is soul-ly as well as fleshly to the extent that he lives according to his own will; the same human being is spiritual to the extent that he lives according to the teaching God revealed through his spirit (1 Cor 3:1-3). However, God's thoughts and intentions, communicated through his spirit, are essentially contrary to human thoughts (1:20-2:9). There is no universal spirit of which every human has a spark, so to speak. Put otherwise, and in scriptural terminology, the human "soul" or "breath," even if it appears as powerful as the "spirit" (*ruaḥ*; mighty wind), remains human and thus is bound to dust just as are the mighty empires. This is corroborated in 1 Corinthians 2:12: "Now we have received not the spirit of the world, but the spirit which is from God." On the one hand, Paul speaks of the spirit of man as being the spirit of the world and, on the other hand, the spirit *of God* (*tou Theou* [v.11]) is clearly explicated as being the spirit *which is from God* (*to ek tou Theou* [v.12]). This is precisely what Paul received and what makes him an apostle; he knows that everything he has and has become is ultimately a gift from God (v.12).[15] In turn, what he received, he is to "speak," impart through the gospel which, as he earlier explained (vv.1-7) and now repeats, is not made out of words learned according to human wisdom, but of words taught through God's spirit (v.13; see also v.10).

---

[15] Compare 1 Cor 2:12 (Now we have received [*elabomen*] not the spirit of the world, but the Spirit which is from God, that we might understand the gifts [*ta kharisthenta*] bestowed on us by God) and Rom 1:5 (through whom [Jesus Christ, our Lord] we have received [*elabomen*] grace [*kharin*] and apostleship to bring about the obedience of faith for the sake of his name among all the nations).

When taken as a philosophic-theological compendium of self-standing statements that have value on their own, 1 Corinthians 2:13-16 becomes a classic example of how the meaning of scriptural texts can be twisted and even outright misconstrued. Doing so obscures the meaning of the text which is ultimately controlled by the flow and thus intention of the narrative. The only sense a text has is contextual. Thus advanced dictionaries give many examples of the entry word by using phrases to explain the different connotations and meanings of that word. Phrases, in turn, are parts of sentences, which are parts of paragraphs, which are parts of chapters or sections, which are parts of books.[16] Very widely accepted is the premise that the term "spiritual" in v.13 (*pnevmatikois*)[17] and v.15 (*pnevmatikos*) include or refer to actual persons other than Paul himself. However, such is excluded by what Paul writes immediately thereafter: "But I, brethren, could not address you as spiritual men, but as men of the flesh, as babes in Christ." (3:1) Still, even this will not convince those who read scripture as theological statements since they would retort that 2:13 and 15 could still apply to other non-Corinthian believers. This is precisely where the real mishandling lies, namely, in forgetting that 1 Corinthians was written to the Corinthians and that, in order to understand the letter's message, one is to hear it as the original addressees were intended to hear it since Paul's corrective writing is assumed to be aimed at those creating problems in Corinth. That is why, even though all seven letters of Revelation 2-3 are intended for the hearers of each of the seven churches (2:7, 11,

---

[16] Case in point are articles or books entitled, e.g., "Salvation in the Book of Isaiah," "Harlotry in Hosea and Ezekiel," "The Function of the Mountain in the Gospel of Matthew," or "The Holy Spirit in Luke-Acts."
[17] The RSV translation "those who possess the Spirit" is, at worst, erroneous and, at best, misleading, especially in view of the fact that the same RSV has "spiritual men" for the same Greek word in 3:1.

17, 29; 3:6, 13, 22), the message to be gathered from each letter cannot be understood unless one puts oneself within the special problems raised by the specific situation of the addressed church. Otherwise, why would the author have conceived seven problematic letters different in content? Furthermore, when "non-Corinthian" hearers assume that they are spiritual and not fleshly, then not only will they end up as self-righteous as the Pharisee in the parable of the Pharisee and the tax-collector (Lk 18:14), but also, and more importantly, Paul's corrective teaching ceases to be addressed to them and, by the same token, they cease to be hearers of the letter. And since they are not concerned with the letter, they cannot possibly apply any part of it to themselves; the letter is not functional for them. To put it scripturally, potential hearers of the Pauline corpus who consider themselves among the "righteous" fall under scripture's verdict underscored pointedly by the Apostle: "What then? Are we Jews any better off? No, not at all; for I have already charged that all men, both Jews and Greeks, are under the power of sin." (Rom 3:9) In the same vein, Paul addresses *all* the Corinthians as men of the flesh and babes (1 Cor 3:1). He alone is "the spiritual man" (2:15), which he confirms by no less than a scriptural quotation (v.16).

Paul is saying in v.13 that the "wisdom of God" he is "speaking" to the Corinthians (v.7) is imparted in words that correspond to that wisdom, which is folly in the eyes of men (1:21). As he already indicated in 2:1 and 4, the vocabulary he uses does not consist of words learned through human wisdom, but through God's spirit, and thus is spiritual. The most common translation of the ending of v.13 (*pnevmatikois pnevmatika synkrinontes*), "interpreting spiritual truths to those who possess the Spirit (who are spiritual)," is incorrect. It reflects the erroneous assumption that there are "spiritual men" in

Corinth. Furthermore, such a translation gives unusual meaning to the verb *synkrinontes* (from *synkrinō*) which is used only twice more in the New Testament, in 2 Corinthians 10:12; there it is translated as "compare, judge by comparison" which is its customary meaning: "Not that we venture to class or compare (*synkrinai*) ourselves with some of those who commend themselves. But when they measure themselves by one another, and compare (*synkrinontes*) themselves with one another, they are without understanding." So, it is preferable to follow RSV's "other" translation suggested in the footnote, "interpreting spiritual truths in spiritual language," or more preferably "interpreting spiritual matters in spiritual language" since "truth" is associated with the philosophical jargon that Paul is precisely attacking.[18] This fits perfectly the context of 1 Corinthians 2:13 where, in the first part of the verse, *didaktois* (learned; taught) is an adjective qualifying the *logois* (words) of human wisdom. In opposition to these (*alla*; but), Paul tells us in the second part of the verse that he uses words taught (*didaktois*) by the spirit and thus are *pnevmatikois* (spiritual), which is appositional to the preceding *didaktois*. So in v.13b Paul is making sure through critical assessment (*synkrinontes*) that his "spiritual words" correspond to, *compare with*, the spiritual matters he is imparting.

What is usually missed in the translations of as well as the comments on v.14 is *psykhikos* (soul-ly; with a soul) which qualifies a man who does not receive or accept the matters of the spirit of God. The use of that adjective is clearly intentional since a few verses later Paul speaks of persons who are not spiritual as "fleshly" (of the flesh; *sarkinois* [3:1] and *sarkikoi* [v.3]). By

---

[18] This again shows how exegesis—since every translation is interpretive—has been influenced by classical philosophical theology.

translating *psykhikos* as "unspiritual" in 2:14 and "physical," as it does in 15:44 [twice] and 46,[19] RSV obscures the intended connection between what the Apostle is writing in chapter 2, on the one hand, and chapter 15, on the other hand. These four instances account for all the occurrences of this adjective in the Pauline corpus. Given that 1 Corinthians 1:18-2:16 is oppositional to the prevailing Greek wisdom (*sophia*) and thus philosophy (love for wisdom), the aim behind the unexpected use of *psykhikos* in referring to the "non-spiritual" man is unmistakably anti-Platonic. Plato embraced the fallacy that the soul was not only an eternal element but also the essence of our being, an assumption still plaguing our mindset.[20] Such a stand completely undermines one of the central tenets of scripture— God's universal judgment of every "fleshly" human being who lives on earth. The soul (Hebrew *nepheš*; Greek *psykhē*; breathing) ends with the demise of the flesh (Hebrew *baśar*; Greek *sarx*), and consequently *psykhikos* (pertaining to the soul) is fully equivalent to *sarkikos* (pertaining to the flesh). Neither attains eternal life except after God's judgment; moreover, eternal life is not a done deal as in Platonism, since condemnation or perdition can well be the lot of a given "flesh and soul" human person (1:18a; 6:9-10; see also Gal 5:20-21; Rev. 21:12-13). By interjecting *psykhikos* here, Paul is looking ahead to detailing this matter at the end of the letter, with the literary device of *inclusio* that brackets a book, a chapter, or a

---

[19] "It is sown a *physical* body, it is raised a spiritual body. If there is a *physical* body, there is also a spiritual body ... But it is not the spiritual which is first but the *physical*, and then the spiritual."

[20] Theology has not succeeded to eliminate Plato's hold since it still speaks of an immortal, though not eternal, soul. The difference is merely academic since our ultimate interest is life *after* death. Thus, for better or worse, Platonic philosophy still controls our theological thinking, which leads us more often than not into *eisegeting* [reading unwarranted meaning into] scripture.

section thereof with the same thought, which in this case is the behavior or mode of life of the Corinthians.[21] The only other occurrences of *psykhikos* in the New Testament are James 3:15 and Jude 19. Since the letter of James was arguably written in response to Galatians[22] and Jude is the "brother of James" (Jude 1), their witness is all the more pertinent:

> Who is wise and understanding among you? By his good life let him show his works in the meekness of wisdom. But if you have bitter jealousy (*zēlon*) and selfish ambition (*eritheian*) in your hearts, do not boast and be false to the truth. This wisdom is not such as comes down from above, but is earthly, unspiritual (*psykhikē*), devilish. For where jealousy (*zēlos*) and selfish ambition (*eritheian*) exist, there will be disorder and every vile practice. But the wisdom from above is first pure, then peaceable, gentle, open to reason, full of mercy and good fruits, without uncertainty or insincerity. And the harvest of righteousness is sown in peace by those who make peace. (Jas 3:13-18)

> But you must remember, beloved, the predictions of the apostles of our Lord Jesus Christ; they said to you, "In the last time there will be scoffers, following their own ungodly passions."[23] It is these who set up divisions, worldly people (*psykhikoi*), devoid of the Spirit. But you, beloved, build yourselves up on your most holy faith; pray in the Holy Spirit; keep yourselves in the love of God; wait for the mercy of our Lord Jesus Christ unto eternal life. (Jude 17-21)

---

[21] In my discussion of 1 Corinthians 15 I shall argue that that chapter is not dealing with the resurrection from the dead per se or its possibility, but rather with such resurrection as prelude for God's final judgment.

[22] See *NTI₄* 103.

[23] This statement is found in 2 Pet (3:3) which is usually viewed as a product of the Pauline school (*NTI₄* 103-4).

The first passage is replete with both the thought and the terminology of 1 Corinthians: wisdom, jealousy and selfish ambition (compare with 1 Cor 3:3 where we have *zēlos kai eris*[24] [jealousy and strife]). In the second passage "soul" is clearly in opposition to spirit. And in both cases, the stress is on behavior.

If a soul-ly man does not receive or accept the matters of God's spirit (*ta tou pnevmatos tou Theou*), it is because they are folly for him (2:14a). He is not able to know (*gnōnai*) those matters because his means of knowledge is only compatible with human wisdom. Nevertheless, he will be assessed (*anakrinetai*) according to the rules of the spiritual court (*pnevmatikōs*) (v.14b) where "no one comprehends (*egnōken*; has known) the matters of God (*ta tou Theou*) except the Spirit of God (*to pnevma tou Theou*)" (v.11). Paul concludes that, as the (only) spiritual person in the church of God in Corinth, he assesses all and everyone, yet he is not subjugated to the assessment of anyone (v.15). No one else knows the Lord's mind, therefore no one, except his messiah, is able to counsel Paul, an apostle of Christ Jesus (v.16; see 1:1), in his assessment of all. That this is Paul's understanding is corroborated in the following passage where the verb *anakrinō* (assess fully, judge as in a court of law) is used no less than three times in five verses:

> This is how one should regard us, as servants of Christ and stewards of the mysteries of God. Moreover it is required of stewards that they be found trustworthy. But with me it is a very small thing that I should be judged (*anakrithō*) by you or by any human court. I do not even judge (*anakrinō*) myself. I am not aware of anything against myself, but I am not thereby acquitted. It is the Lord who judges (*ho anakrinōn*) me. Therefore do not pronounce judgment (*krinete*) before the time, before the Lord

---

[24] From the same root as *eritheia*.

comes, who will bring to light the things now hidden in darkness and will disclose the purposes of the heart. Then every man will receive his commendation from God. (1 Cor 4:1-5)

Chapter 3

Vv. 1-9 ¹Κἀγώ, ἀδελφοί, οὐκ ἠδυνήθην λαλῆσαι ὑμῖν ὡς πνευματικοῖς ἀλλ' ὡς σαρκίνοις, ὡς νηπίοις ἐν Χριστῷ. ² γάλα ὑμᾶς ἐπότισα, οὐ βρῶμα· οὔπω γὰρ ἐδύνασθε. ἀλλ' οὐδὲ ἔτι νῦν δύνασθε, ³ ἔτι γὰρ σαρκικοί ἐστε. ὅπου γὰρ ἐν ὑμῖν ζῆλος καὶ ἔρις, οὐχὶ σαρκικοί ἐστε καὶ κατὰ ἄνθρωπον περιπατεῖτε; ⁴ ὅταν γὰρ λέγῃ τις· ἐγὼ μέν εἰμι Παύλου, ἕτερος δέ· ἐγὼ Ἀπολλῶ, οὐκ ἄνθρωποί ἐστε; ⁵ Τί οὖν ἐστιν Ἀπολλῶς; τί δέ ἐστιν Παῦλος; διάκονοι δι' ὧν ἐπιστεύσατε, καὶ ἑκάστῳ ὡς ὁ κύριος ἔδωκεν. ⁶ ἐγὼ ἐφύτευσα, Ἀπολλῶς ἐπότισεν, ἀλλὰ ὁ θεὸς ηὔξανεν· ⁷ ὥστε οὔτε ὁ φυτεύων ἐστίν τι οὔτε ὁ ποτίζων ἀλλ' ὁ αὐξάνων θεός. ⁸ ὁ φυτεύων δὲ καὶ ὁ ποτίζων ἕν εἰσιν, ἕκαστος δὲ τὸν ἴδιον μισθὸν λήμψεται κατὰ τὸν ἴδιον κόπον· ⁹ θεοῦ γάρ ἐσμεν συνεργοί, θεοῦ γεώργιον, θεοῦ οἰκοδομή ἐστε.

¹But I, brethren, could not address you as spiritual men, but as men of the flesh, as babes in Christ. ²I fed you with milk, not solid food; for you were not ready for it; and even yet you are not ready, ³for you are still of the flesh. For while there is jealousy and strife among you, are you not of the flesh, and behaving like ordinary men? ⁴For when one says, "I belong to Paul," and another, "I belong to Apollos," are you not merely men? ⁵What then is Apollos? What is Paul? Servants through whom you believed, as the Lord assigned to each. ⁶I planted, Apollos watered, but God gave the growth. ⁷So neither he who plants nor he who waters is anything, but only God who gives the growth. ⁸He who plants and he who waters are equal, and each shall receive his wages according to his labor. ⁹For we are God's fellow workers; you are God's field, God's building.

Paul introduced the verb *dynatai* (is able) in 2:14 in view of its intensive use in 3:1-2 (three times in 2 verses).[1] The intention is to stress the total incompatibility between Paul, who is "spiritual," and the Corinthians, who are "fleshly:"[2] Paul is not able (v.1) and the Corinthians still are not able (v.2) to overcome this. He drives home the point of the impossible compatibility between the spiritual and fleshly by accusing them of being babes who *cannot* (are not able to) *possibly* eat adult food (v.2). Their being fleshly is not a matter of inability to comprehend fully the "mystery of God" as the later Alexandrian theology surmised; rather it is a matter of behavior as is clear from v.3. Actually it is the same behavior of strife and quarreling Paul alluded to in 1:11.[3] The behavioral reference of "fleshly" is corroborated in Paul's use of the verb "walk" (*peripateite*), which RSV translated here as "behave" and elsewhere as "conduct oneself"[4] or "live (lead a life)."[5] The verb *peripatō* is the Greek rendering of the Hebrew *halak* (walk) which is used in the Old Testament to speak of one's walking on the "way" (Hebrew *derek*; Greek *hodos*), that is, according to the commandments of the Law. Hence, "walking according to man" (*kata anthrōpon*; like

---

[1] The wordplay is totally lost in RSV which translates the first instance as "is not able" (2:14), but then switches to "could not" (3:1) and then to "were not ready" and "are not ready" (v.2).

[2] See the similar use of "not being able" of Christ himself: "And Jesus said to them, 'A prophet is not without honor, except in his own country, and among his own kin, and in his own house.' And he could do no (*ou edynato poiēsai*; was not able to do any) mighty work there, except that he laid his hands upon a few sick people and healed them. And he marveled because of their unbelief." (Mk 6:4-6a)

[3] See earlier my comments on this verse where I point out that the noun *eris* (translated as "strife") found in 3:3 is the singular of the same noun *erides* (translated as the singular "quarreling") found in 1:11. The close connection is also evident in that these are the only two instances of that noun in 1 Corinthians.

[4] Rom 13:13; Col 4: 5.

[5] 1 Cor 7:17; 2 Cor 2:3; Eph 4:1, 17; Phil 3:17, 18; Col 1:10; 2:6; 1 Thess 2:12; 4:12 (v.11 in the original Greek); 2 Thess 3:6, 11.

ordinary men [RSV]) is the opposite of "walking by the spirit" (Gal 5:16). This confirms my earlier comments on the opposition between the spirit of man and the spirit of God. Before *eris* (strife; 1 Cor 3:3), which occurred earlier in the plural *erides* (quarreling) in 1:11, Paul mentions *zēlos* (zeal) in the sense of jealousy, misplaced zeal. This noun is introduced in view of Paul's later discussion in chapter 14 where he invites the Corinthians to seek zealously (*zēloute*; earnestly desire, v.1) to communicate God's teaching to the others, rather than use it for one's own glory, and to seek to build up the church as one body instead of dismantling it through strife and divisions.

The intended link between *eris* (3:3) and *erides* (1:11) is evident in how Paul reverts in 3:4 to the terminology of 1:12:

> For it has been reported to me by Chloe's people that there is quarreling (*erides*) among you, my brethren. What I mean is that each one of you says, "I belong to Paul," or "I belong to Apollos," or "I belong to Cephas," or "I belong to Christ." (1:11-12)

> For while there is jealousy and strife (*eris*) among you, are you not of the flesh, and behaving like ordinary men? For when one says, "I belong to Paul," and another, "I belong to Apollos," are you not merely men? (3:3-4)

Paul and Apollos, though God's emissaries to Corinth, are still merely *diakonoi* (table servants) through whom the Corinthians trusted in God's message (v.5a). Paul's choice of *diakonos* to refer to himself and Apollos is definitely pointed. As I explained in my comments on 1:4-17, the main thrust of the letter is the unity of the Corinthian community. As was the case in Galatians 2:11-14, the ultimate test of that unity takes place at table fellowship, which is a recurring topic in 1 Corinthians (8:1-13; 10:14-33; 11:17-34). At the end of the letter, Paul even refers to the entire apostolic effort in Corinth as subsumed under the term *diakonia* (table service): "Now, brethren, you know that the household of Stephanas were the first converts in Achaia, and they have devoted themselves to the service (*diakonia*) of the saints." (16:15) Finally, at the beginning of chapter 12 which is dedicated to the oneness of the community as the one body of Christ, who is the head (of the household) as any Roman lord would be, Paul subsumes all the different household chores as *diakoniai* (table services): "Now there are varieties of gifts, but the same Spirit; and there are varieties of service (*diaireseis diakoniōn*), but the same Lord; and there are varieties of working, but it is the same God who inspires them all in every one. To each is given the manifestation of the Spirit for the common good." (vv.4-7) Within that perspective, it is understandable that Paul and Apollos would be merely chief *diakonoi*.

However, Paul hurries to differentiate between Apollos and himself regarding primacy in that matter, which has been assigned by God himself: "... as the Lord assigned to each. I planted, Apollos watered, but God gave the growth. So neither he who plants nor he who waters is anything, but only God who gives the growth." (3:5b-7) Although God is all in all, so to speak, nevertheless planting not only precedes but also is the reason behind the watering. In other words, God's work in Corinth started with Paul, not Apollos. This teaching is reflected in the story Luke narrates in Acts:

> After this he [Paul] left Athens and went to Corinth. And he found a Jew named Aquila, a native of Pontus, lately come from Italy with his wife Priscilla, because Claudius had commanded all the Jews to leave Rome ... Now a Jew named Apollos, a native of Alexandria, came to Ephesus. He was an eloquent man, well

versed in the scriptures. He had been instructed in the way of the Lord; and being fervent in spirit, he spoke and taught accurately the things concerning Jesus, though he knew only the baptism of John. He began to speak boldly in the synagogue; but when Priscilla and Aquila heard him, they took him and expounded to him the way of God more accurately. And when he wished to cross to Achaia, the brethren encouraged him, and wrote to the disciples to receive him. When he arrived, he greatly helped those who through grace had believed, for he powerfully confuted the Jews in public, showing by the scriptures that the Christ was Jesus. While Apollos was at Corinth, Paul passed through the upper country and came to Ephesus. (18:1-2, 24-28; 19:1)

The primacy of Paul despite the oneness of his work with that of Apollos is further reflected in Paul's conclusion: "He who plants and he who waters are at one (*hen eisin*; working in harmony),[6] still (*de*; on the other hand)[7] each shall receive his wages *according to his labor*." (1 Cor 3:8) As I indicated in my discussion of 1:1, Paul singles himself as the sole apostle to Corinth. Then Paul finishes with a statement that underscores

---

[6] RSV's "are equal" does not render the meaning of the original Greek.

[7] Here again RSV's "and" does not reflect the original's intention. RSV's translation of v.8 seems to suggest that the difference in wages has to do with the personal effort of each worker. But the Greek *kopon* in the Pauline corpus is linked to the apostolic activity and thus reflects the kind of work rather than the level of effort put into it. In Corinth Paul is the chief apostle as he will stress later in the letter, although he mentions Barnabas along with himself: "Am I not free? Am I not an apostle? Have I not seen Jesus our Lord? Are not you my workmanship in the Lord? If to others I am not an apostle, at least I am to you; for you are the seal of my apostleship in the Lord ... Or is it only Barnabas and I who have no right to refrain from working for a living?" (1 Cor 9:1-2, 6) See also 2 Cor 3:1-4 (Are we beginning to commend ourselves again? Or do we need, as some do, letters of recommendation to you, or from you? You yourselves are our letter of recommendation, written on your hearts, to be known and read by all men; and you show that you are a letter from Christ delivered by us, written not with ink but with the Spirit of the living God, not on tablets of stone but on tablets of human hearts. Such is the confidence that we have through Christ toward God).

the centrality of God in the entire matter: "For we are *God's* fellow workers; you are *God's* field, *God's* building." (3:9)[8] Since ultimately the work is God's—twice he is referred to as giving the growth (vv.6 and 7)—Paul and Apollos engage in that work simply as *fellow* workers, and thus dispensable; in his "good pleasure" God chose whom he chose (1:21; see also Gal 1:15). The reality God is interested in is *his* field, *his* building, and for that purpose he chooses *his* co-workers. In switching from field to building, Paul is preparing to seal his point, namely, that not only Apollos but also any other "apostolic" authority is subordinate to his in Corinth.

Vv. 10-17 ¹⁰ Κατὰ τὴν χάριν τοῦ θεοῦ τὴν δοθεῖσάν μοι ὡς σοφὸς ἀρχιτέκτων θεμέλιον ἔθηκα, ἄλλος δὲ ἐποικοδομεῖ. ἕκαστος δὲ βλεπέτω πῶς ἐποικοδομεῖ. ¹¹ θεμέλιον γὰρ ἄλλον οὐδεὶς δύναται θεῖναι παρὰ τὸν κείμενον, ὅς ἐστιν Ἰησοῦς Χριστός. ¹² εἰ δέ τις ἐποικοδομεῖ ἐπὶ τὸν θεμέλιον χρυσόν, ἄργυρον, λίθους τιμίους, ξύλα, χόρτον, καλάμην, ¹³ ἑκάστου τὸ ἔργον φανερὸν γενήσεται, ἡ γὰρ ἡμέρα δηλώσει, ὅτι ἐν πυρὶ ἀποκαλύπτεται· καὶ ἑκάστου τὸ ἔργον ὁποῖόν ἐστιν τὸ πῦρ [αὐτὸ] δοκιμάσει. ¹⁴ εἴ τινος τὸ ἔργον μενεῖ ὃ ἐποικοδόμησεν, μισθὸν λήμψεται· ¹⁵ εἴ τινος τὸ ἔργον κατακαήσεται, ζημιωθήσεται, αὐτὸς δὲ σωθήσεται, οὕτως δὲ ὡς διὰ πυρός. ¹⁶ Οὐκ οἴδατε ὅτι ναὸς θεοῦ ἐστε καὶ τὸ πνεῦμα τοῦ θεοῦ οἰκεῖ ἐν ὑμῖν; ¹⁷ εἴ τις τὸν ναὸν τοῦ θεοῦ φθείρει, φθερεῖ τοῦτον ὁ θεός· ὁ γὰρ ναὸς τοῦ θεοῦ ἅγιός ἐστιν, οἵτινές ἐστε ὑμεῖς.

¹⁰According to the grace of God given to me, like a skilled master builder I laid a foundation, and another man is building upon it. Let each man take care how he builds upon it. ¹¹For no other foundation can any one lay than that which is laid, which is Jesus Christ. ¹²Now if any one builds on the foundation with

---

[8] The Greek is much more impressive since all three phrases start with "God" (*Theou gar esmen synergoi; Theou geōrgion, Theou oikodomē este*).

gold, silver, precious stones, wood, hay, straw— ¹³*each man's work will become manifest; for the Day will disclose it, because it will be revealed with fire, and the fire will test what sort of work each one has done.* ¹⁴*If the work which any man has built on the foundation survives, he will receive a reward.* ¹⁵*If any man's work is burned up, he will suffer loss, though he himself will be saved, but only as through fire.* ¹⁶*Do you not know that you are God's temple and that God's Spirit dwells in you?* ¹⁷*If any one destroys God's temple, God will destroy him. For God's temple is holy, and that temple you are.*

A preferred image that Paul uses is that of the building, which he prefaces with reference to the grace of apostleship granted him (compare 1 Cor 3:10 with 1:1:4). Moreover, by referring to himself as a *wise architect* (*sophos arkhitektōn*)⁹ he brings in the element of wisdom which is central to his presentation. Still his main point is to underscore that any building has only one foundation, and in Corinth the foundation has already been laid by him. Consequently, anyone else involved in the erection of the building can only "build upon" (*epoikodomei*)¹⁰ that foundation and, more importantly, that person is to take care as to how he builds since whatever he is doing has to fit with the foundation, which is Jesus Christ *as viewed and preached by Paul* (3:10-11). Sometimes people are amazed at this last statement since the widespread assumption is that there is and cannot be but one Christ. But this is not at all Paul's stand when he writes to the Corinthians, "For if some one comes and preaches another Jesus than the one we preached, or if you receive a different spirit from the one you received, or if you accept a different gospel

---

⁹ By translating "skilled master builder" RSV overlooks the link to wisdom.
¹⁰ Construed from the preposition *epi* (over, upon) and the verb *oikodomei* (builds).

from the one you accepted, you submit to it readily enough" (2 Cor 11:4).

The input of those who "build upon" the foundation will be assessed on the "day" (of the Lord) when all work will be brought to light and judged through fire as to its value (1 Cor 3:12-13). The imagery of testing the value of a building through fire is a classic metaphor in the Old Testament. The reason is evident. A society's "world" in those times was the city. Entire kingdoms were known as city-states since they revolved around their capital city. The two main biblical instructional stories found in Ezekiel 16 and 23 are presented in conjunction with the three "sisters": Samaria, Jerusalem and Sodom. Jerusalem takes center stage in Isaiah and Jeremiah as well as in Ezekiel. The end of a city is usually by destruction following a siege. The classic four expressions of divine punishment against a people are the result of a siege: death by famine, sickness, or the sword, on the one hand, and exile of the survivors, on the other hand.[11] The destruction of the city itself is through burning since fire "consumes" everything and does not leave any viable remains. Fire, though, does not usually consume metal and stone. Hence Paul's choice of three building materials that would resist consumption (gold, silver, precious stones), and three that would be easily consumed (wood, hay, straw). Since "building upon" has a positive connotation, the motive behind such an action is assumed to be well intentioned, that is, in accordance with the foundation. The main thrust of the immediate context is one of comparison between Paul and Apollos and, more specifically, Paul's primacy over Apollos. So it stands to reason to view those who "build upon" (*epoikodomei*) as being in a position of

---

[11] See e.g. Lev 26:23-26, 33, 41; Deut 28:20-37; 47-68; 1 Kg 8:35-40, 46; Ezek 5:12; 6:11; 7:15, 21; 11:8-12; 12:11, 16; 14:12-23; Am 4:6-12; Rev 6:1-8.

leadership comparable to the prophets whose function is to "build up" (*oikodomei*; *oikodomē*) the congregation (1 Cor 14:3-5, 12). Still, only if their work sustains the test of fire (3:13) and proves worthy will they receive their wages for having upheld God's building (v.14), the same way the caretakers of God's field will receive theirs (v.8). Their work will be tested through fire and if proven unfit will be consumed (v.15a); however, Paul leaves the decision to save them to God in his mercy (v.15b), since at the end no one but he will judge all his "chief stewards" (*oikonomous*; 4:1-5).

Yet—and this is precisely what Paul is driving at—remains the case of a leader's activity intentionally aimed against the foundation laid by Paul. Such is not excusable nor is it forgivable since it is an attack on God's "holy ones" (1:2), among whom the spirit of God dwells (3:16b)[12] and thus are, metaphorically speaking, God's holy temple not made by human hand (v.17b). In Romans 8:9, 11 the same phrase, "the spirit of God dwells among you," is used thrice in a context where the metaphor is the household and the believers are said to be children of God in conjunction with the same spirit (vv.15-16). Later in 1 Corinthians 12, the metaphor used is that of the human body to describe the community of believers; here the metaphor of

---

[12] Very often the original *en hymin* (among you [plural]) is understood and even translated as "in you (plural)" in the sense of "in each of you" as though God's spirit dwells in each of the believers individually. This understanding has plagued theology and spirituality throughout the centuries due to mysticism, which is nothing else but a religious Platonism that was championed by the school of Plotinus. But, if this were true, then the scriptural God would end up with *many* temples in one place, which would be against the prohibition of such in scripture. God has only *one* church congregation in Corinth and even in the entire province Achaia: "… To the church of God which is at Corinth, to those sanctified in Christ Jesus, called to be saints together with all those who in every place call on the name of our Lord Jesus Christ, both their Lord and ours." (1 Cor 1:2) See my comments earlier on this verse and also those on *en hymin* in 6:19.

temple fits perfectly with that of building (3:10-15). However, when speaking of the sure punishment unto oblivion Paul uses the verb *phtheirei* (destroys from inside as a termite or a vermin does; makes perish through rottenness) which is applicable to agriculture[13] as well as to buildings or cities constructed by humans. In doing so, Paul sums up his entire argument, which began in 3:1, by using a verb in his final verdict that would apply to both metaphors, field and building, which, he states, the Corinthians are at the same time (v.9).

Vv. 18-23 ¹⁸ Μηδεὶς ἑαυτὸν ἐξαπατάτω· εἴ τις δοκεῖ σοφὸς εἶναι ἐν ὑμῖν ἐν τῷ αἰῶνι τούτῳ, μωρὸς γενέσθω, ἵνα γένηται σοφός. ¹⁹ ἡ γὰρ σοφία τοῦ κόσμου τούτου μωρία παρὰ τῷ θεῷ ἐστιν. γέγραπται γάρ· ὁ δρασσόμενος τοὺς σοφοὺς ἐν τῇ πανουργίᾳ αὐτῶν· ²⁰ καὶ πάλιν· κύριος γινώσκει τοὺς διαλογισμοὺς τῶν σοφῶν ὅτι εἰσὶν μάταιοι. ²¹ ὥστε μηδεὶς καυχάσθω ἐν ἀνθρώποις· πάντα γὰρ ὑμῶν ἐστιν, ²² εἴτε Παῦλος εἴτε Ἀπολλῶς εἴτε Κηφᾶς, εἴτε κόσμος εἴτε ζωὴ εἴτε θάνατος, εἴτε ἐνεστῶτα εἴτε μέλλοντα· πάντα ὑμῶν, ²³ ὑμεῖς δὲ Χριστοῦ, Χριστὸς δὲ θεοῦ.

> ¹⁸*Let no one deceive himself. If any one among you thinks that he is wise in this age, let him become a fool that he may become wise.* ¹⁹*For the wisdom of this world is folly with God. For it is written, "He catches the wise in their craftiness,"* ²⁰*and again, "The Lord knows that the thoughts of the wise are futile."* ²¹*So let no one boast of men. For all things are yours,* ²²*whether Paul*

---

[13] See later 1 Cor 15:42 where Paul uses the noun *phthora* from the same root as *phtheirei*: "What is sown is perishable (*en phthora*; unto perishability), what is raised is imperishable (*en aphtharsia* [from the same root as *phthora*]; unto imperishability)." See also Galatians where *phthora* occurs in conjunction with the spirit as well as God's final judgment, which fully corresponds with 1 Cor 3:13-17: "Do not be deceived; God is not mocked, for whatever a man sows, that he will also reap. For he who sows to his own flesh will from the flesh reap corruption (*phthoran*); but he who sows to the Spirit will from the Spirit reap eternal life." (Gal 6:7-8)

or Apollos or Cephas or the world or life or death or the present or the future, all are yours; ²³*and you are Christ's; and Christ is God's.*

In the last verses of chapter 3 Paul concludes the discussion he started in 1:10. The vocabulary reflects that 3:22-23 forms an *inclusio* with 1:12. He begins by briefly repeating in 3:18-19a what he said earlier in 1:18-25, prefacing it with the caveat not to deceive oneself. In my commentary on Romans I pointed out that in his scriptural quotations, Paul was referencing the entirety of the Old Testament: Law, Prophets, and Wisdom Literature.[14] It was his way of showing his hearers that he was not coming up with something novel, which was precisely what his opponents were accusing him of, but actually "reciting" the scriptural story in its entirety. He does the same in 1 Corinthians. Earlier in the letter Paul quoted from Isaiah in 1:19, then from Jeremiah in 1:31, then again from Isaiah in 2:9 and 16. At the end of his discussion he quotes from Job (1 Cor 3:19b) and Psalms (1 Cor 3:20), two writings from the third part of the Old Testament.

However, a closer look at the three quotations in 1 Corinthians 2:9 and 3:19b, 20 will show that Paul writes in a way that invites the addressees not only to hear the quotations in their larger context in order to follow his argument, but also to review the entire Old Testament scripture, interconnecting its parts, in order to be persuaded of what he is saying. It is "what is written" that is the ultimate authority and not Paul's "personal opinion." Only by having the mind of the "scriptural" Christ, God's plenipotentiary emissary *as presented in scripture, and preached as such by Paul*, is Paul "a servant of Jesus Christ, called to be an

---

[14] See *C-Rom* 174-5, 177-9, 185-9, 198-200.

apostle, set apart for the gospel of God which he promised beforehand through his prophets in the holy scriptures, the gospel concerning his Son" (Rom 1:1-3).

The quotation in 1 Corinthians 2:9 starts with Isaiah, but its last part is taken from Sirach. Since Paul referred to God's plan he is preaching as God's wisdom (1 Cor 2:7), he finishes the Isaianic quotation in v.9 by referring to the unexpectedness on the part of the rulers of this world with a line from Sirach that speaks of wisdom:

> There is One who is wise, greatly to be feared, sitting upon his throne. The Lord himself created wisdom; he saw her and apportioned her, he poured her out upon all his works. She dwells with all flesh according to his gift, and he supplied her to those who love him. (Sirach 1:6-8)

In 1 Corinthians 3:19b-20 the two quotations are from Job and Psalms and yet incorporate terminology from Sirach. This stress on wisdom is reflected in the choice as well as the rephrasing of these quotations. The first is taken from LXX Job 5:13 that reads "He takes (*katalambanōn*) the wise in their own craftiness (*phronēsei*)" compared to Paul's "He catches (*drassomenos*) the wise in their craftiness (*panourgia*)." Craftiness is taken from the preceding verse in Job, "He frustrates the devices of the crafty (*panourgōn*), so that their hands achieve no success" (v.12), which bespeaks of the crafty person's utter failure in the pursuit of his goal. Paul takes this opportunity to change Job's *katalambanōn* (catches) in v.13 into *drassomenos* (catches) which occurs, outside 1 Corinthians 3:19b, in the entire LXX only twice more in Sirach and both times in contexts that speak precisely of man's failure to attain his goal, the second of which belittles his false understanding and thus wisdom: "An evil wife is an ox yoke which chafes; taking hold of her is like grasping (*drassomenos*; someone grasping) a scorpion" (26:7); "A man of no understanding has vain and false hopes, and dreams give wings to fools. As one who catches (*drassomenos*) at a shadow and pursues the wind, so is he who gives heed to dreams." (34:1-2)

As for the second quotation, Paul changes *anthrōpōn* (men) in the original (the Lord knows that the thoughts of men are futile [Ps 94/LXX 93:11]) into *sophōn* (wise ones): "The Lord knows that the thoughts of the wise are futile." (1 Cor 3:20) Obviously this change reflects criticism leveled against false human wisdom (vv.18-19a). Still, here again, there is more than meets the ear. When the Psalm is read up to the verses quoted, one finds not only mention of "wise" but also the terminology used in the concluding v.21a as well as in vv.18-19a: "O Lord, how long shall the wicked, how long shall the wicked exult (*kavkhēsontai*; 1 Cor 3:21)? ... Understand, O dullest of the people! Fools (*mōroi*; 1 Cor 3:18, 19), when will you be wise?" (Ps 94/LXX Ps 93:3, 8) Paul's use of terminology in his text taken from the upcoming quotation is a literary device I discussed earlier in conjunction with boasting in 1 Corinthians 1:26-31.

It would be indeed silly, if not foolish, to boast in regard to men since God himself ordained everything including the leaders themselves to be at the service of the Corinthians. Put otherwise, from the perspective of God's plan, Peter, Paul, and Apollos are merely *diakonoi* (ministers, table servants) of the Corinthians (3:5) who, by the same token, should refrain from acting *lordly*. This is the reality so long as the Corinthians remember that the true lord of the apostles is Christ who ordained the "free" Paul to be the Corinthians' "slave" (9:19). In turn, Christ himself is *the* Lord inasmuch as he pertains to God as his obedient slave (Phil 2:6-11). All leaders are merely functional in God's plan; he alone gives the growth to the seed that was planted in his field in

Corinth (1 Cor 3:6-7, 9) and his sheer will is at the origin of everything that is taking place in that field (1:1).

Chapter 4

Vv. 1-5 ¹οὕτως ἡμᾶς λογιζέσθω ἄνθρωπος ὡς ὑπηρέτας Χριστοῦ καὶ οἰκονόμους μυστηρίων θεοῦ. ² ὧδε λοιπὸν ζητεῖται ἐν τοῖς οἰκονόμοις, ἵνα πιστός τις εὑρεθῇ. ³ἐμοὶ δὲ εἰς ἐλάχιστόν ἐστιν, ἵνα ὑφ' ὑμῶν ἀνακριθῶ ἢ ὑπὸ ἀνθρωπίνης ἡμέρας· ἀλλ' οὐδὲ ἐμαυτὸν ἀνακρίνω. ⁴ οὐδὲν γὰρ ἐμαυτῷ σύνοιδα, ἀλλ' ἐν τούτῳ δεδικαίωμαι, ὁ δὲ ἀνακρίνων με κύριός ἐστιν. ⁵ὥστε μὴ πρὸ καιροῦ τι κρίνετε ἕως ἂν ἔλθῃ ὁ κύριος, ὃς καὶ φωτίσει τὰ κρυπτὰ τοῦ σκότους καὶ φανερώσει τὰς βουλὰς τῶν καρδιῶν· καὶ τότε ὁ ἔπαινος γενήσεται ἑκάστῳ ἀπὸ τοῦ θεοῦ.

> ¹*This is how one should regard us, as servants of Christ and stewards of the mysteries of God.* ²*Moreover it is required of stewards that they be found trustworthy.* ³*But with me it is a very small thing that I should be judged by you or by any human court. I do not even judge myself.* ⁴*I am not aware of anything against myself, but I am not thereby acquitted. It is the Lord who judges me.* ⁵*Therefore do not pronounce judgment before the time, before the Lord comes, who will bring to light the things now hidden in darkness and will disclose the purposes of the heart. Then every man will receive his commendation from God.*

Paul immediately confirms the status of the apostles, whoever they might be. The Corinthians are to consider the apostles not as their masters but as subalterns (*hyperetas*) of Christ and chief stewards (*oikonomous*) of the mysteries of God. Paul has been stressing this all along. What is required of stewards is that each be found faithful to the task when his master decides to assess him and his work. Consequently, Paul refuses to be called to judgment by the Corinthians. To speak of judgment, Paul uses the verb *anakrinō*, which reflects a full and final verdict. He used this same verb earlier to speak of the spiritual man, namely himself, judging the fleshly Corinthians (2:14-15). So it stands to reason for him to summarily dismiss even the slightest possibility that he would be judged by his addressees. Still, he pushes the matter to the extreme by saying that he does not stand judged by any human court, be it even a summit of the "pillars" (Gal 2:1-10). Speaking of such court he ingeniously and intentionally uses the phrase "human day" (*anthrōpinēs hēmeras*). The term "day" clearly mimics the Lord's Day and thus accuses as inadmissible arrogance any human court that considers itself entitled to emit a "divine" verdict.[1] Yet, Paul goes further still by saying that even his own judgment of himself is of no value, in spite of the fact that he is the spiritual one par excellence. The reason is not that he feels guilty of anything; to the contrary, he does not. Still, what he thinks of himself does not allow him to declare his own acquittal. In a court of law one is entitled to plead innocent, but this is one's own perception. The only valid verdict comes out of the mouth of the judge. In scripture, only God is the judge.

The conclusion is incontrovertible. The Corinthians, deemed by Paul as fleshly, are not to emit any judgment regarding any matter before the allotted time (*kairou*), that is, before the Lord himself comes, "who will bring to light the things now hidden (*ta krypta*) in darkness and will disclose the purposes of the heart" (1 Cor 4:5). However, as Paul indicates elsewhere, "on that day God will judge the secrets (*ta krypta*) of men *according to my gospel*" (Rom 2:16). That is why he is assured of what he is writing to the Corinthians here. The commendation that will come "then" (*tote*) to every man is from God and from him

---

[1] RSV correctly translates the original *anthrōpinēs hēmeras* (human day)—meaningwise—as "human court."

alone (1 Cor 4:5b). Until then, "may every mouth be stopped and the whole world be held accountable to God" (Rom 3:19).

Vv. 6-13 ⁶ Ταῦτα δέ, ἀδελφοί, μετεσχημάτισα εἰς ἐμαυτὸν καὶ Ἀπολλῶν δι' ὑμᾶς, ἵνα ἐν ἡμῖν μάθητε τὸ μὴ ὑπὲρ ἃ γέγραπται, ἵνα μὴ εἷς ὑπὲρ τοῦ ἑνὸς φυσιοῦσθε κατὰ τοῦ ἑτέρου. ⁷ τίς γάρ σε διακρίνει; τί δὲ ἔχεις ὃ οὐκ ἔλαβες; εἰ δὲ καὶ ἔλαβες, τί καυχᾶσαι ὡς μὴ λαβών; ⁸ ἤδη κεκορεσμένοι ἐστέ, ἤδη ἐπλουτήσατε, χωρὶς ἡμῶν ἐβασιλεύσατε· καὶ ὄφελόν γε ἐβασιλεύσατε, ἵνα καὶ ἡμεῖς ὑμῖν συμβασιλεύσωμεν. ⁹ δοκῶ γάρ, ὁ θεὸς ἡμᾶς τοὺς ἀποστόλους ἐσχάτους ἀπέδειξεν ὡς ἐπιθανατίους, ὅτι θέατρον ἐγενήθημεν τῷ κόσμῳ καὶ ἀγγέλοις καὶ ἀνθρώποις. ¹⁰ἡμεῖς μωροὶ διὰ Χριστόν, ὑμεῖς δὲ φρόνιμοι ἐν Χριστῷ· ἡμεῖς ἀσθενεῖς, ὑμεῖς δὲ ἰσχυροί· ὑμεῖς ἔνδοξοι, ἡμεῖς δὲ ἄτιμοι. ¹¹ ἄχρι τῆς ἄρτι ὥρας καὶ πεινῶμεν καὶ διψῶμεν καὶ γυμνιτεύομεν καὶ κολαφιζόμεθα καὶ ἀστατοῦμεν ¹² καὶ κοπιῶμεν ἐργαζόμενοι ταῖς ἰδίαις χερσίν· λοιδορούμενοι εὐλογοῦμεν, διωκόμενοι ἀνεχόμεθα, ¹³ δυσφημούμενοι παρακαλοῦμεν· ὡς περικαθάρματα τοῦ κόσμου ἐγενήθημεν, πάντων περίψημα ἕως ἄρτι.

> ⁶I have applied all this to myself and Apollos for your benefit, brethren, that you may learn by us not to go beyond what is written, that none of you may be puffed up in favor of one against another. ⁷For who sees anything different in you? What have you that you did not receive? If then you received it, why do you boast as if it were not a gift? ⁸Already you are filled! Already you have become rich! Without us you have become kings! And would that you did reign, so that we might share the rule with you! ⁹For I think that God has exhibited us apostles as last of all, like men sentenced to death; because we have become a spectacle to the world, to angels and to men. ¹⁰We are fools for Christ's sake, but you are wise in Christ. We are weak, but you are strong. You are held in honor, but we in disrepute. ¹¹To the present hour we hunger and thirst, we are ill-clad and buffeted and homeless, ¹²and we labor, working with our own hands.

When reviled, we bless; when persecuted, we endure; ^{13}*when slandered, we try to conciliate; we have become, and are now, as the refuse of the world, the offscouring of all things.*

Here we have yet another example of how translations miss the value and intention of the original text. RSV renders the Greek *meteskhēmatisa* as "applied" which is unexpected, to say the least, since its actual meaning is "transformed" and thus "changed" (Phil 3:21) or "disguised" (2 Cor 11:13, 14, 15), as is verified in all occurrences of that verb in the New Testament. In order to understand Paul's intention one is to start with the conclusion "(*so*) *that* (*hina*) none of you may be puffed up in favor of one against another" (1 Cor 4:6b). To be "puffed up" (*physioumai*) is clearly Paul's main point since it will appear twice in the conclusion of his argumentation (vv.19, 20). This, in turn, prepares for the following 5:1-6:11 where he adduces two examples which do not allow the Corinthians to be puffed up and of which they should indeed be ashamed.

The topic of *meteskhēmatisa* used in conjunction with Paul and Apollos began with 3:4. Throughout the passage 3:4-4:5 Paul is describing himself and Apollos as examples against arrogance in that, though apostles with full authority, this does not grant them license to be puffed up before God, since they have been "transformed" *in the letter* (4:1-5) into beings, like all others, still under the verdict of the coming divine judgment.[2] Moreover, Paul presents their transformation as a lesson to be "learned" by

---

[2] When one considers the oneness of the Corinthian correspondence, one realizes that the strangeness of *meteskhēmatisa* will be solved at 2 Corinthians 11:13-15 where Paul is accusing his opponents of "transforming themselves" (*metaskhēmatizomenoi*) in the opposite direction and thus turning from "Christ's apostles" (v.14) into Satan's "table ministers" (*diakonoi*; v.15) instead of God's as Paul and Apollos are described (1 Cor 3:5).

the Corinthians who, should they heed the lesson, would not "be puffed up in favor of one against another" by saying "I belong to Paul" or "I belong to Apollos."

Still the real lesson is "not to go beyond what is (was just) written." How should one take this unique instance in the Pauline corpus where "is written" (*gegraptai*) is not referring to a scriptural quotation but to what the Apostle has just laid down in writing?[3] The only plausible explanation is that Paul was "scripturalizing" his letter, that is to say, making it a reading to be heard at church gatherings in the same way as the Old Testament scriptures were heard. This phenomenon is noticeable throughout the Pauline corpus beginning with the earliest letter addressed to the Galatians. After having referred to the Law as "ordained by angels through (*en kheiri*; by the hand of) an intermediary" (Gal 3:19), Paul finishes his letter by sealing it with these words: "See with what (large) letters I am writing (*egrapsa*; just wrote) to you *with my own hand* (*tē emē kheiri*)." (6:11). By closing the same letter a few verses later with the words "Henceforth let no man trouble me" (v.17a), Paul was sending a clear message: "Do not get back to me regarding what I just wrote; what is written is written." Paul follows the same approach here in 1 Corinthians. After a series of Old Testament quotations introduced with "as is written" (*gegraptai*; 1:19, 31; 2:9; 3:19) he suddenly introduces his own words with the same intent. He will later seal his intent at the end of the letter by

---

[3] Notice how the neuter plural relative pronoun *ha* (what, all these things which) before "is written" (*gegraptai*) corresponds to the neuter plural demonstrative pronoun *tavta* (all this, all these things) at the beginning of the verse, which pronoun is the direct complement of the verb "applied" (*meteskhēmatisa*; transformed).

saying "I, Paul, write this greeting with my own hand (*tē emē kheiri*)" (16:21).[4]

Paul then revisits his status and that of Apollos in more detail in order to show the wide discrepancy between them and the puffed up Corinthians. The first rhetorical question (For who sees anything different [*diakrinei*] in you? [4:7]), though, seems out of sync with the questions that follow (What have you that you did not receive? If then you received it, why do you boast as if it were not a gift?), which clearly function as an introduction to the following vv.8-10 that compare the Corinthians with the apostles. Just as he did earlier with the verb *physioumai* (be puffed up), Paul introduces the verb *diakrinei* in preparation for its later use in 6:1-12 where he will rhetorically ask, "Can it be that there is no man among you wise enough to decide (*diakrinai*) between members of the brotherhood?" (v. 5)

The meaning of *diakrinai* in this case is "judge between," "discern," "assess a matter or a person against a standard." Thus the meaning in 4:7 is "For who can discern anything special in you when you are even not capable of exercising discernment?" or "You do not have the minimum level of wisdom to exercise discernment in basic matters, and you are expecting others to find you special and different from the rest?"

Paul's criticism of the Corinthians, which will culminate in chapter 15, is their assumption that somehow "spiritually" they are already enjoying God's coming kingdom. Yet, how could they even begin to think such when Paul is still toiling on the roads and in the cities of the Roman empire? Paul reminds them that whatever they have, or think they have, they received as a

---

[4] See in more detail on this matter of scripturalizing the Pauline corpus my comments on Col 4:16 and 18 and Philemon 19 in *C-Col* 103-6, 124-5.

gift and, consequently, they have no right to boast as though they acquired it through their own efforts (4:7). Indeed, they are like *nouveaux riches* acting as though they became rich (*eploutēsate*; v.8)[5] through their own efforts, and satiating themselves (*kekoresmenoi*; v.8) without thinking of others, when in fact they were made rich (*eploutisthēte*; 1:4)[6] by God. And this richness was granted them through the grace given to Paul (1:4; 3:10), which would make him the prime partaker of that richness. So how is it possible, asks Paul, that the Corinthians could already be enjoying the kingdom without him? In order to emphasize this point, he ridicules their assumption by telling them he wishes they were reigning since this would mean that he also would be reigning with them (4:8). But this is a sheer impossibility since his status, which he describes in detail to shame them, belies their false claim.

To speak of God's decision regarding his apostles, Paul intentionally opts for the verb *apedeixen* (exhibited) (v.9) which is from the same root as the noun *apodeixei* that he used earlier to refer to his preaching of the gospel as God's intervention in power through the spirit: "And I was with you in weakness and in much fear and trembling; and my speech and my message were not in plausible words of wisdom, but in demonstration (*apodeixei*) of the Spirit and of power, that your faith might not rest in the wisdom of men but in the power of God." (2:3-5)[7] At the same time, by using "last of all," Paul is looking ahead to

---

[5] The intransitive verb *ploutō* means "become (oneself) rich" and thus is in the active voice.

[6] The transitive verb *ploutizō* means "enrich; make (someone else) rich" and thus is in the passive voice.

[7] The intentionality of the choice is evident in that these are the only instances, besides 2 Thess 2:4, in the Pauline corpus of the root *apodeik—*. Worthy of note is that in 2 Thess the verb describes the arrogant action of the "man of apostasy" in showing himself as God, which is the opposite of the apostles' fate.

chapter 15 where the only other occurrences of "last" (*eskhatous*) are used in this letter (vv.8, 26, 45, 52), the first applying to himself as "the last" of the apostles. The metaphor Paul often uses to speak of the apostles is that of gladiators in the arena (*theatron*)[8] exposed to the view of the entire world, so to speak. The Greek *epithanatious* (sentenced to death) is the rendering of the original Latin *morituri* (those about to die) that is part of the salutation with which gladiators in the arena addressed the emperor: *Ave Caesar, morituri te salutant* (Hail Caesar, those who are about to die salute you). The emperor reserved the right at the end of a fight to have the loser's life ended or spared. The metaphor is befitting for an apostle whose life is in the hand of God instead of the emperor.

The terminology used to shame the Corinthians when compared to Paul (4:9-13) fits the context perfectly. The first two pairs hark back to 1:18-31 that revolve around wisdom and power compared to folly and weakness, however, instead of *sophoi* (wise; 1:19, 20, 26, 27) he uses *phronimoi* (wise, sensible; 4:10). This looks ahead to chapter 10 where Paul will appeal to the Corinthians to be *phronimois* (sensible) in exercising their judgment concerning table fellowship (v.15), which has the lion's share in this letter. He also revisits this same topic of the "fool" versus the "wise" in 2 Corinthians 11: "For you gladly bear with fools (*aphronōn*), being wise (*phronimoi*) yourselves!" (v.19) The third pair *endoxoi* (held in honor, worthy of glory) and *atimoi* (in disrepute, lacking honor) is very interesting because it plays on *doxa* (glory) and *timē* (honor) that are linked to life eternal (Rom 2:7, 10) in God's kingdom (*basileia*) which

---

[8] In the Greco-Roman world, the *theatron* (theater) was an enclosed arena to protect the viewers from harm, whereas the *amphitheatron* (amphitheater) was a semi-circle theater for plays and musical performances.

Paul hinted at two verses earlier (1 Cor 4:8) in his use of the verbs *basilevō* (become king, reign) and *symbasilevō* (co-reign, share the rule).

The expressions of Paul's foolishness, weakness, and lack of honor are actual and thus real, not psychological or perceived (v.11). The list culminates, after the last "and," with "we labor (*kopiōmen*), working with our own hands" (v.12a), which confirms that the previous physical want and suffering are linked to Paul's apostolic activity and not due to random events. Indeed, the verb "labor" (*kopiō*) used here refers, in the Pauline corpus, specifically to a taxing effort in conjunction with preaching the gospel.[9] The same applies to the phrase "working with our own hands."[10] Notice that there are six verbs in vv.11-12a, which are the double of the contradictory pairs (vv.10). Three pairs of verbs that follow describe the apostle's beneficent response to aggressive behavior on the part of the world (vv.12b-13a). The last statement (v.13b) wraps up the previous details and alludes to gladiators who, for the entertainment of the crowd, are thrown in the arena to fight not only one another, but also wild beasts. And when they die, their carcasses are disposed of like refuse and others are brought in to continue the show. Furthermore, v.13b forms with v.9 an *inclusio*[11] enwrapping three series of statements that are constructed according to a well-devised pattern. The first and last series are made out each of three opposing double statements: the first series opposes Paul's behavior with that of the Corinthians,[12]

---

[9] 1 Cor 15:10; 16:16; Gal 4:11; Phil 2:16; Col 1:29; 1 Tim 4:10.
[10] 1 Cor 9:14-15; 1 Thess 2:9; 2 Thess 3:8; see also Acts 20:34.
[11] Both speak of the "world" watching the apostles being belittled and thrown aside into oblivion.
[12] "We are fools for Christ's sake, but you are wise in Christ. We are weak, but you are strong. You are held in honor, but we in disrepute" (v.10).

while the third series pins down Paul's attitude against that of the world at large.[13] The middle series consists of six statements describing the physical costs of apostolic labor.[14] Such is hardly random but rather intended, three being the number reflecting fullness.

Vv. 14-21 ¹⁴ Οὐκ ἐντρέπων ὑμᾶς γράφω ταῦτα ἀλλ' ὡς τέκνα μου ἀγαπητὰ νουθετῶ[ν]. ¹⁵ ἐὰν γὰρ μυρίους παιδαγωγοὺς ἔχητε ἐν Χριστῷ ἀλλ' οὐ πολλοὺς πατέρας· ἐν γὰρ Χριστῷ Ἰησοῦ διὰ τοῦ εὐαγγελίου ἐγὼ ὑμᾶς ἐγέννησα. ¹⁶ Παρακαλῶ οὖν ὑμᾶς, μιμηταί μου γίνεσθε. ¹⁷ Διὰ τοῦτο ἔπεμψα ὑμῖν Τιμόθεον, ὅς ἐστίν μου τέκνον ἀγαπητὸν καὶ πιστὸν ἐν κυρίῳ, ὃς ὑμᾶς ἀναμνήσει τὰς ὁδούς μου τὰς ἐν Χριστῷ [Ἰησοῦ], καθὼς πανταχοῦ ἐν πάσῃ ἐκκλησίᾳ διδάσκω. ¹⁸ Ὡς μὴ ἐρχομένου δέ μου πρὸς ὑμᾶς ἐφυσιώθησάν τινες· ¹⁹ ἐλεύσομαι δὲ ταχέως πρὸς ὑμᾶς ἐὰν ὁ κύριος θελήσῃ, καὶ γνώσομαι οὐ τὸν λόγον τῶν πεφυσιωμένων ἀλλὰ τὴν δύναμιν· ²⁰ οὐ γὰρ ἐν λόγῳ ἡ βασιλεία τοῦ θεοῦ ἀλλ' ἐν δυνάμει. ²¹ τί θέλετε; ἐν ῥάβδῳ ἔλθω πρὸς ὑμᾶς ἢ ἐν ἀγάπῃ πνεύματί τε πραΰτητος;

¹⁴I do not write this to make you ashamed, but to admonish you as my beloved children. ¹⁵For though you have countless guides in Christ, you do not have many fathers. For I became your father in Christ Jesus through the gospel. ¹⁶I urge you, then, be imitators of me. ¹⁷Therefore I sent to you Timothy, my beloved and faithful child in the Lord, to remind you of my ways in Christ, as I teach them everywhere in every church. ¹⁸Some are arrogant, as though I were not coming to you. ¹⁹But I will come to you soon, if the Lord wills, and I will find out not the talk of these arrogant people but their power. ²⁰For the kingdom of God

---

[13] "When reviled, we bless; when persecuted, we endure; when slandered, we try to conciliate (vv.12b-13a).

[14] "To the present hour we hunger and thirst, we are ill-clad and buffeted and homeless, and we labor, working with our own hands" (vv.11-12a).

does not consist in talk but in power. ²¹ What do you wish? Shall I come to you with a rod, or with love in a spirit of gentleness?

After his harsh indictment against the Corinthians' misconceptions about themselves, Paul hurries to say that his intention is not simply to shame them; rather he is using shame as a tool to draw their attention to acceptance of his instruction. A true father would do this. God does this in the Prophets, especially in Ezekiel. Shaming is a very effective tool because, shy of excising someone from the community, as Paul will momentarily do (5:1-8), it is the closest one gets to capital punishment: death of a person or destruction of a city. How often do shamed people wish they were dead? So Paul is trying to admonish rather than punish his addressees. The countless other leaders, such as Apollos and Cephas, are unlike the one paterfamilias. Moreover, on purpose, Paul refers to such leaders as "guides" (*paidagōgous*; pedagogues). The pedagogue in Greco-Roman society was a slave assigned to supervise and guide (*agō*) the household's children (*paides*), more specifically to take them to school and back. The execution of his task was not always easy, so he was allowed to use a rod to threaten and even beat the children when necessary. In choosing the term "guide" to speak of the other leaders, Paul not only was diminishing their authority, but also was preparing for the last verse of the chapter where he writes "Shall I come to you with a rod?"

Later in the letter Paul states: "If to others I am not an apostle, at least I am to you; for you are the seal of my apostleship in the Lord." (9:2) Paul was the first to introduce Christ to the Corinthians (3:11) through the gospel he preached. Thus he "became their father in Christ Jesus," and a person can have only one father (4:15). Consequently he urges them to imitate him and not the pedagogues (v.16), and his urging is that of a parent and thus an order.[15] This imitation does not take place through seeing Paul since he is away; otherwise why would he write a letter? Nor does imitating Paul consist in following in his footsteps, doing as he does, since a child cannot be a father and much less act like one. Rather, the father is a teacher and the child is a disciple following the father's *teaching* and not his behavior. Given that a father cannot be duplicated, Paul sends as his representative his eldest child, his "firstborn" Timothy. The value of Timothy does not lie so much in his being "beloved" (v.17), since the Corinthians are also "beloved" (v.14). Rather, Timothy's real value lies in his being "faithful" (*pistos*) to Paul "in the Lord" (v.17) just as Paul is faithful (*pistos*; trustworthy) to God (v.2). The Corinthians can hardly be considered "faithful." Were they so, there would have been in no need for the harsh letter. Paul is faithful as the apostle who teaches the gospel (v.15); Timothy is faithful insofar as he accomplishes his mission "to remind you of *my ways* in Christ, as *I teach* them everywhere in every church" (v.17). To put it simply, Timothy is not sent to Corinth with a "video" of Paul. He is sent to remind the Corinthians, his brethren, that the gospel teaching invites its hearers to "walk the way" leading to God's kingdom.[16] Timothy is sent by Paul the way Paul was sent by God. If Timothy is coming to them instead of Paul, the arrogant Corinthians are not to conclude that Paul is not coming at all and take it as an opportunity or excuse to persevere with impunity in their arrogant attitude (v.18). The same God who chose Paul by his will (*thelēmatos*; 1:1) may very well will (*thelēsē*) that Paul himself come to Corinth and, should that happen soon, he will show them what (God's) power is all about (vv.19-20). In order to

---

[15] See *1 Thess* 133-4.
[16] See Gal 5:16-21; Eph 5:1-5; Col 1:9-14; 1 Thess 1:11-12; 2 Thess 1:3-7.

make them feel the pressure, Paul uses the same terminology of 2:1-5 where he belittled the value of the (human) word:

> When I came to you, brethren, I did not come proclaiming to you the testimony of God in lofty words (*logou*) or wisdom. For I decided to know nothing among you except Jesus Christ and him crucified. And I was with you in weakness and in much fear and trembling; and my speech (*logos*) and my message were not in plausible words (*logois*) of wisdom, but in demonstration of the Spirit and of *power*, that your faith might not rest in the wisdom of men but in the *power* of God. (2:1-5)

> But I will come to you soon, if the Lord wills, and I will find out not the talk (*logon*) of these arrogant people but their *power*. For the kingdom of God does not consist in talk (*logō*) but in *power*. (4:19-20)

Considering that such is the "will" of God, Paul ends his rhetoric by asking the Corinthians about *their* "will": "What do you wish (*ti thelete*; what will you, which way do you want it)?" (v.21a) God's will is that Paul be an apostle (1:1) and thus a father (4:15). Yet, if they still want to perceive him as equal to the other leaders, then he is a "pedagogue" and, if so, then he would come with a rod. However, if he is delaying his coming and sending Timothy in his stead, it is to give extra time for the Corinthians to reconsider and take seriously this opportunity to change their behavior. Should they do so, he would come as a loving father with a spirit of gentleness. What is interesting in his choice of words here (with love in a spirit of gentleness) is that they are a carbon copy of what he teaches in Galatians regarding love and the "spiritual" elders' manner of dealing with a junior who was erring: "But the fruit of the Spirit is love, joy, peace, patience, kindness, goodness, faithfulness, gentleness, self-control … Brethren, if a man is overtaken in any trespass, you who are spiritual should restore him in a spirit of gentleness" (5:22-23; 6:1) The conclusion is that Paul is proving to them that indeed he alone is "the spiritual man" and has "the mind of Christ" when it comes to Corinth (2:15-16).

Chapter 5

Vv. 1-5   ¹Ὅλως ἀκούεται ἐν ὑμῖν πορνεία, καὶ τοιαύτη πορνεία ἥτις οὐδὲ ἐν τοῖς ἔθνεσιν, ὥστε γυναῖκά τινα τοῦ πατρὸς ἔχειν. ² καὶ ὑμεῖς πεφυσιωμένοι ἐστὲ καὶ οὐχὶ μᾶλλον ἐπενθήσατε, ἵνα ἀρθῇ ἐκ μέσου ὑμῶν ὁ τὸ ἔργον τοῦτο πράξας; ³ ἐγὼ μὲν γάρ, ἀπὼν τῷ σώματι παρὼν δὲ τῷ πνεύματι, ἤδη κέκρικα ὡς παρὼν τὸν οὕτως τοῦτο κατεργασάμενον· ⁴ ἐν τῷ ὀνόματι τοῦ κυρίου [ἡμῶν] Ἰησοῦ συναχθέντων ὑμῶν καὶ τοῦ ἐμοῦ πνεύματος σὺν τῇ δυνάμει τοῦ κυρίου ἡμῶν Ἰησοῦ, ⁵ παραδοῦναι τὸν τοιοῦτον τῷ σατανᾷ εἰς ὄλεθρον τῆς σαρκός, ἵνα τὸ πνεῦμα σωθῇ ἐν τῇ ἡμέρᾳ τοῦ κυρίου.

> ¹It is actually reported that there is immorality among you, and of a kind that is not found even among pagans; for a man is living with his father's wife. ²And you are arrogant! Ought you not rather to mourn? Let him who has done this be removed from among you. ³For though absent in body I am present in spirit, and as if present, I have already pronounced judgment ⁴in the name of the Lord Jesus on the man who has done such a thing. When you are assembled, and my spirit is present, with the power of our Lord Jesus, ⁵you are to deliver this man to Satan for the destruction of the flesh, that his spirit may be saved in the day of the Lord Jesus.

Paul proceeds in his attack against the conceit of the Corinthians by singling out an example to totally deflate their arrogance. However, before engaging this passage, I should like to clarify for my readers the meaning of "immorality" (*porneia*; fornication, harlotry) in scripture. Whenever we have a list of sins, *porneia* virtually always heads that list (1 Cor 5:10, 11; 6:9; Eph 5:3, 5). The same *porneia* is singled out as the sin par excellence (1 Cor 6:15-19; Rev 17-19). The reason is that harlotry is the classic metaphoric expression of turning away from God to follow other kings and their deities (see, e.g., Ezek 16; 23; Hos 2). It is the expression of idolatry, which is clear from the cases where the one parallels the other (1 Cor 10:7-8; Rev 2:14, 20) or, more impressively, where the one is explained as being the other: "Put to death therefore what is earthly in you: fornication, impurity, passion, evil desire, and covetousness, which is idolatry." (Col 3:5) The punishment for idolatry in the Old Testament is either death or excision from God's people, which amounts to the same thing, especially in the wilderness context where the Law was promulgated. This is precisely what Paul is about to do with the fornicator: "Let him who has done this be removed from among you." (1 Cor 5:2b) In pointing out that the sin committed is not known even among pagans (*tois ethnesin*; the nations), Paul is mimicking Jeremiah:

> Thus says the Lord: "What wrong did your fathers find in me that they went far from me, and went after worthlessness, and became worthless? ... For cross to the coasts of Cyprus and see, or send to Kedar and examine with care; see if there has been such a thing. Has a nation changed its gods, even though they are no gods? But my people have changed their glory for that which does not profit." (2:5, 10-11)

Since he alone is "the spiritual man," Paul does not have any qualms about acting in the name of God's spirit: "For though absent in body I am present in spirit, and as if present, I have already pronounced judgment in the name of the Lord Jesus on the man who has done such a thing." (1 Cor 5:3-4a) Immediately following is Paul's request that the assembled community execute his decision *without voting on it*: "When you are assembled, and my spirit is present, with the power of our Lord Jesus, you are to deliver this man to Satan." (vv.4b-5a) As in the Old Testament, the community does not deliberate, let alone decide, but it merely executes the dictates of the Law. However, since Paul is acting along the lines of God's behavior, thus punishment is unto instruction rather than destruction. If the sinner is not disciplined, he may assume that his behavior is acceptable in God's eyes, and ultimately he will succumb to eternal perdition on the Lord's Day. Paul's decision is not to ruin the fornicator, but to give him the opportunity to repent. Should Paul's decision to judge the fornicator's "flesh," that is, the fleshly actions, be heeded, then the fornicator will change his ways and act according to God's spirit, that is, he will become "spiritual" (see 3:1-2), which in turn will secure his salvation (1:18).[1]

Vv. 6-13 ⁶ Οὐ καλὸν τὸ καύχημα ὑμῶν. οὐκ οἴδατε ὅτι μικρὰ ζύμη ὅλον τὸ φύραμα ζυμοῖ; ⁷ἐκκαθάρατε τὴν παλαιὰν ζύμην, ἵνα ἦτε νέον φύραμα, καθώς ἐστε ἄζυμοι· καὶ γὰρ τὸ πάσχα ἡμῶν ἐτύθη Χριστός. ⁸ ὥστε ἑορτάζωμεν μὴ ἐν ζύμῃ παλαιᾷ μηδὲ ἐν ζύμῃ κακίας καὶ πονηρίας ἀλλ' ἐν ἀζύμοις εἰλικρινείας καὶ ἀληθείας. ⁹ Ἔγραψα ὑμῖν ἐν τῇ ἐπιστολῇ μὴ συναναμίγνυσθαι πόρνοις, ¹⁰ οὐ πάντως τοῖς πόρνοις τοῦ κόσμου τούτου ἢ τοῖς πλεονέκταις καὶ ἅρπαξιν ἢ εἰδωλολάτραις, ἐπεὶ ὠφείλετε ἄρα ἐκ τοῦ κόσμου ἐξελθεῖν. ¹¹ νῦν δὲ ἔγραψα ὑμῖν μὴ συναναμίγνυσθαι ἐάν τις ἀδελφὸς ὀνομαζόμενος ᾖ πόρνος ἢ πλεονέκτης ἢ εἰδωλολάτρης ἢ λοίδορος ἢ μέθυσος ἢ ἅρπαξ, τῷ τοιούτῳ μηδὲ συνεσθίειν. ¹² τί γάρ μοι τοὺς ἔξω κρίνειν; οὐχὶ τοὺς ἔσω ὑμεῖς κρίνετε; ¹³ τοὺς δὲ ἔξω ὁ θεὸς κρινεῖ. ἐξάρατε τὸν πονηρὸν ἐξ ὑμῶν αὐτῶν.

⁶*Your boasting is not good. Do you not know that a little leaven leavens the whole lump?* ⁷*Cleanse out the old leaven that you may be a new lump, as you really are unleavened. For Christ,*

---

[1] One should not understand 1 Cor 5:5 as speaking of two parts in the human being, his flesh that is *per se* bound to destruction and his spirit that is *per se* destined to immortality.

our paschal lamb, has been sacrificed. ⁸Let us, therefore, celebrate the festival, not with the old leaven, the leaven of malice and evil, but with the unleavened bread of sincerity and truth. ⁹I wrote to you in my letter not to associate with immoral men; ¹⁰not at all meaning the immoral of this world, or the greedy and robbers, or idolaters, since then you would need to go out of the world. ¹¹But rather I wrote to you not to associate with any one who bears the name of brother if he is guilty of immorality or greed, or is an idolater, reviler, drunkard, or robber—not even to eat with such a one. ¹²For what have I to do with judging outsiders? Is it not those inside the church whom you are to judge? ¹³God judges those outside. "Drive out the wicked person from among you."

Paul uses the common metaphor of leaven, which he appealed to in Galatians 5:9, to convince the Corinthians to be rid of the immoral man (1 Cor 5:7b-8a). After the mention of leaven, Paul moves on to the Passover and to Christ as the paschal lamb. The reason is that, in scripture, the feasts of Passover and unleavened bread are connected, the first following immediately after the second.² This move from the common metaphor of leaven to the feast of Passover and the sacrificed lamb is not haphazard when one considers the vocabulary of chapter 5. A few verses earlier the assembly of the Corinthians "in the name of the Lord Jesus," during which they were to expel the immoral man, was described with the verb *synakhthentōn* (having been brought together; from the verb *synagomai* [be brought together]). This is from the same root as the noun *synagōgē* (assembly; synagogue; Hebrew *'edah*) which, together with *ekklēsia* (congregation; church; Hebrew *qahal*), is the common scriptural name to speak of Israel when officially gathered around God. The next occurrence of the verb

---

² Ex 23:15; 34:18; Lev 23:5-6; Deut 16:1-8.

synerkhomai (come together) corresponding to *synagomai*[3] is in chapter 11, where it is used in conjunction with the Eucharistic gathering (vv.18, 20, 33).[4] There Paul explains Christ's sacrifice as the basis for the coming together; thus when this is not the case, that same gathering is one "unto condemnation" (v.33) rather than salvation. So, in both cases (chapters 5 and 11), Paul is reminding the Corinthians that the church in Corinth is the church *of God* (1:1)—not theirs—and that the church gathering is the *Lord's* supper (11:20)—not theirs (v.21). Any behavior that threatens this reality is condemnable with destruction by God himself (3:17). Consequently, here in chapter 5, Paul is informing the Corinthians that, should they not excise the immoral man, they would risk being leavened by the "old" lump and not be "renewed" by the leaven of Christ into a "new" lump, which is precisely what happened at their baptism through the gospel (6:11; see also Rom 6). Not excising the immoral man is tantamount to betraying their call (*klēsin*; 1:26) by God (v.27) into becoming his church (called one; *ekklēsia*, 1:1-2).

A good number of scholars take the combination of "For Christ, our paschal lamb, has been sacrificed" (5:7b) and "Let us, therefore, celebrate the festival" (v.8a) as a sign that Paul was writing just before the feast of Pascha-Easter. I am convinced that this is not actually the case. The Greek differentiates between two kinds of imperatives or cohortatives (let me or let us do something); one is in the aorist tense, and the other in the present tense. The present tense, imperative or cohortative, aims at a recurrent action: do this or let us do this time and again. The aorist tense, imperative or cohortative, is directed toward a

---

[3] Notice how both use the preposition *syn* meaning together: *syn-agomai* (be led together) and *syn-erkhomai* (come together).
[4] The only other instance is found in the phrase *synelthē hē ekklēsia* (the church is assembled) in 14:23, *synelthē* being the aorist tense from *synerkhomai*.

once and for all action. For example: if you want me to write to inform you that I arrived at my destination you would use the aorist tense imperative, whereas if you want me to write to you on a regular basis you would use the present tense imperative. Here, in 5:8a, we have "let us celebrate" in the present tense (*heortazōmen*) and not in the aorist tense (*heortasōmen*). So Paul was saying "let us every time celebrate" and not "let us celebrate soon." Purposely I said "every time" and not "every year" because the reference is, as in chapter 11, to the Eucharistic gathering where every time the commemoration of Christ as sacrificed lamb takes place (11:23-26). "For Christ, our paschal lamb, has been sacrificed" (5:7b) recounts a once and for all action.[5] There is no reference to a yearly Christian Pascha-Easter in the New Testament, unless one considers 5:7b as such, which would be begging the question. The present tense cohortative, "let us celebrate," refers to a recurring event in the life of the household church. Furthermore, according to chapter 11, Christ's once and for all sacrifice is remembered, not reenacted, during the Eucharistic meal. The addition of "the festival" after celebrate (1 Cor 5:8a) in RSV is misleading and might be understood to mean a Pascha-like gathering where a new lamb was sacrificed each time. That would be contrary to Paul's teaching. The unique use of the verb *heortazō* in the Pauline corpus must then be explained through the reference to Christ as *paskha* (Passover lamb) and not necessarily intended as a reference to the Passover *heortē* (feast, festival, celebration) itself.[6]

---

[5] RSV's translation of the aorist *etythē* (*was* sacrificed) into "*has been* sacrificed" is misleading because it connotes a recent past event rather than an event that took place at any point in the past without reference to an intended specific time, which is the actual meaning of the Greek *aoristos* (without any defined limits).

[6] The RSV translation "Let us, therefore, celebrate the festival" (1 Cor 5:8a) gives undue value to the common root *heort*— in *heortē* (feast, festival) and *heortazō* (celebrate festively, as one would a feast, and thus simply "celebrate").

As for the Christian feast of Pascha-Easter, one should be wary of reading later developments back into the Pauline literature.[7]

Another usual misreading is made in conjunction with "the letter" (*tē epistolē*) in 5:9-11 which is translated sometimes as "my letter" (RSV; NEB) or "my previous letter" (Phillips)[8] or "an epistle" (KJV), and in all cases assumes a letter written earlier than the passage 5:6-13. This, however, may not be the case. When looking at 2 Thessalonians 3:14 one finds the following: "If any one refuses to obey what we say (*tō logō hēmōn*; through our [gospel] word) in this letter (*tēs epistolēs*; the letter), note that man, and have nothing to do with him (*synanamignysthai*), that he may be ashamed (*entrapē*)." (RSV) The same original "*the* letter" is rendered as "*this* letter" by RSV in 2 Thessalonians, while it is translated as "my letter" in 1 Corinthians. So RSV has no qualms in understanding "the letter" in 2 Thessalonians as referring to that letter itself and not to an earlier one.[9] Moreover, the topic in both epistles (1 Cor and 2 Thess) is the same: shaming a disobedient person, with the intent of inducing repentance. The similarity between the two letters is further evidenced in the use of the verb *synanamignysthai* (associate with, have to do with) that occurs only in 1 Corinthians 5:9, 11 and 2 Thessalonians 3:14 in the entire New Testament. Adducing *egrapsa* (I wrote; 1 Cor 5:9) in support of the earlier letter theory founders since the same verb is translated differently in v.11: "I have written" (KJV); "I tell you" (Phillips); "I write" (NEB); RSV has in the footnote "I write." The aorist *egrapsa* refers to

---

[7] It is beyond the scope of this commentary to discuss the rise of the Christian Pascha-Easter.
[8] Phillips further adds the phrase "in this letter" in v.11, which does not exist in the original.
[9] See also Col 4:16 (*hē epistlolē*) and 1 Thess 5:27 (*tēn epistolēn*) where RSV renders the original "the letter" as "this letter."

what Paul has just finished writing as is clear from the following instance in the same letter (9:15) which is rendered by the same RSV as "I write."[10] Therefore, there is no reason to understand 1 Corinthians 5:9 otherwise. After the digression in vv.6-8 explaining his apparent harsh decision in vv.1-5, Paul refers to that decision—not to mingle with immoral men—by saying that it does not extend to all sinners in the world, since this would amount to virtually excising oneself from society (vv.9-10). Rather, "what I am writing now (in the sense of here)" is that for the Corinthians not to associate *at the Eucharistic table fellowship* (*synesthiein*) with an immoral man known as "brother" (v.11); rather, such "brother" is to be excised from those gatherings (vv.1-5; also v.13b). However, such an apostolic order does not necessarily extend outside that setting; otherwise where would one find the opportunity to exhort that brother to repentance? This is corroborated by the verb "judge" used three times in vv.12-13a, which action Paul applied to the immoral man (v.3). Just as the domain of a Roman paterfamilias is limited to his own household, so also the authority of the apostle, as father, is over "the insiders" (v.12b) of God's congregation. Paul's authority does not extend to "the outsiders" (v.12a), who are the exclusive domain of God (v.13a) since God alone is the ruler of the world. And in order to put an end to any potential discussion concerning his harsh decision, Paul concludes by appealing, as usual, to scripture itself: "Drive out the wicked person from among you." (v.13b; see Deut 17:7; 19:19; 22:21, 24; 24:7).

---

[10] See further not only the Pauline corpus (Rom 15:15; Gal 6:11; Philem 19, 21) but also the other epistles (1 Jn 2:14, 21, 26; 5:13; 3 Jn 9).

Chapter 6

Vv. 1-11 ¹ *Τολμᾷ τις ὑμῶν πρᾶγμα ἔχων πρὸς τὸν ἕτερον κρίνεσθαι ἐπὶ τῶν ἀδίκων καὶ οὐχὶ ἐπὶ τῶν ἁγίων;* ² *ἢ οὐκ οἴδατε ὅτι οἱ ἅγιοι τὸν κόσμον κρινοῦσιν; καὶ εἰ ἐν ὑμῖν κρίνεται ὁ κόσμος, ἀνάξιοί ἐστε κριτηρίων ἐλαχίστων;* ³ *οὐκ οἴδατε ὅτι ἀγγέλους κρινοῦμεν, μήτι γε βιωτικά;* ⁴ *βιωτικὰ μὲν οὖν κριτήρια ἐὰν ἔχητε, τοὺς ἐξουθενημένους ἐν τῇ ἐκκλησίᾳ, τούτους καθίζετε;* ⁵ *πρὸς ἐντροπὴν ὑμῖν λέγω. οὕτως οὐκ ἔνι ἐν ὑμῖν οὐδεὶς σοφός, ὃς δυνήσεται διακρῖναι ἀνὰ μέσον τοῦ ἀδελφοῦ αὐτοῦ;* ⁶ *ἀλλὰ ἀδελφὸς μετὰ ἀδελφοῦ κρίνεται καὶ τοῦτο ἐπὶ ἀπίστων;* ⁷ *Ἤδη μὲν [οὖν] ὅλως ἥττημα ὑμῖν ἐστιν ὅτι κρίματα ἔχετε μεθ' ἑαυτῶν. διὰ τί οὐχὶ μᾶλλον ἀδικεῖσθε; διὰ τί οὐχὶ μᾶλλον ἀποστερεῖσθε;* ⁸ *ἀλλὰ ὑμεῖς ἀδικεῖτε καὶ ἀποστερεῖτε, καὶ τοῦτο ἀδελφούς.* ⁹ *Ἢ οὐκ οἴδατε ὅτι ἄδικοι θεοῦ βασιλείαν οὐ κληρονομήσουσιν; μὴ πλανᾶσθε· οὔτε πόρνοι οὔτε εἰδωλολάτραι οὔτε μοιχοὶ οὔτε μαλακοὶ οὔτε ἀρσενοκοῖται* ¹⁰ *οὔτε κλέπται οὔτε πλεονέκται, οὐ μέθυσοι, οὐ λοίδοροι, οὐχ ἅρπαγες βασιλείαν θεοῦ κληρονομήσουσιν.* ¹¹ *καὶ ταῦτά τινες ἦτε· ἀλλὰ ἀπελούσασθε, ἀλλὰ ἡγιάσθητε, ἀλλὰ ἐδικαιώθητε ἐν τῷ ὀνόματι τοῦ κυρίου Ἰησοῦ Χριστοῦ καὶ ἐν τῷ πνεύματι τοῦ θεοῦ ἡμῶν.*

¹When one of you has a grievance against a brother, does he dare go to law before the unrighteous instead of the saints? ²Do you not know that the saints will judge the world? And if the world is to be judged by you, are you incompetent to try trivial cases? ³Do you not know that we are to judge angels? How much more, matters pertaining to this life! ⁴If then you have such cases, why do you lay them before those who are least esteemed by the church? ⁵I say this to your shame. Can it be that there is no man among you wise enough to decide between members of the brotherhood, ⁶but brother goes to law against brother, and that before unbelievers? ⁷To have lawsuits at all with one another is defeat for you. Why not rather suffer wrong? Why not rather be defrauded? ⁸But you yourselves wrong and defraud, and that even your own brethren. ⁹Do you not know that the unrighteous will not inherit the kingdom of God? Do not be deceived; neither the immoral, nor idolaters, nor adulterers, nor sexual perverts, ¹⁰nor thieves, nor the greedy, nor drunkards, nor revilers, nor robbers will inherit the kingdom of God. ¹¹And such were some of you. But you were washed, you were sanctified, you were justified in the name of the Lord Jesus Christ and in the Spirit of our God.

The main line of thought in chapter 5 was judgment, and this same topic is discussed in verses 1-11 in chapter 6, which is filled with terms from the root *kri—* (judge; vv.1, 2 [three times], 3, 4, 5, 6, 7) and *dik—* (justice; vv.1, 7, 8, 9, 11). This passage is linked to the preceding chapter in that it forces the hand of the Corinthians to accept Paul's verdict over the immoral man without giving even the slightest consideration that his decision might be overturned by the Roman legal system. If Paul does not judge outsiders (5:12), it follows that neither he nor the Corinthian believers are to submit to outsiders' justice. To drive his point home he belittles Roman justice as being handled by the "unrighteous" (unjust, *adikōn*; 6:1) when viewed from the perspective of God's righteousness. The internal matters of the household church, according to Paul's directive in 5:1-15, are to be handled among the "saints," the members of the congregation. It would be indeed ludicrous if the saints who are to behold the judgment of the Roman "world"[1] would end up being judged by it (v.2a). If they are to

---

[1] RSV, KJV and Phillips all misread the original by translating it as "if the world is to be judged by you (if you are to judge the world)." NEB is the closest to the original when it renders it into "if the world is to come before you for judgment."

judge the world, they should be able to judge trivial cases (little legal matters; v.2b). Paul pushes the matter even further by reminding his hearers that he and they will judge the angels and, even more so, earthly matters (matters pertaining to this life; v.3).

The way the saints are to judge the world would explain the rather unexpected switch from the second person plural in v.2 to the first person plural in v.3, especially in view of the fact that the second person plural is used throughout the rest of the passage. One is not to understand that the "saints" will actually take part in the process of judging the world. That is the prerogative of God alone as Paul underscores in 5:13. Rather the believers, assuming they inherit the kingdom (6:9-11), will be seated around God in the same way as the author of Revelation depicts the status of the martyrs (20:4).[2] Put otherwise, while seated in God's company, the "saints" will be witnessing God's judgment of the world. If they will be in this position in the Kingdom, writes Paul, how could they allow themselves to be judged by a human court (1 Cor 6:1; see earlier 4:3). Paul ups the ante further by speaking of the judgment of the angels. Since the "saints" will not actually judge the world, neither will they judge the angels, God's ministers. The solution to understanding this statement must lie elsewhere, and this is where it becomes very important to take the "we" into serious consideration. Until now in this letter the "we" referred to either the apostles or the Corinthians together with Paul *as God's apostle to them*. Consequently, the "we" includes the apostolic office and thus authority. In Romans, Paul writes that the angels will have no power whatsoever regarding God's decision toward Paul and the Roman believers: "For I am sure that neither death, nor life, nor

---

[2] See my comments in *NTI*₃ 115-8.

angels, nor *principalities*, nor things present, nor things to come, nor *powers*, nor height, nor depth, nor anything else in all creation, will be able to separate us from the love of God in Christ Jesus our Lord." (8:38-39) In Ephesians, he even goes a step further by asserting that the apostolic office is actually on a higher level than that of the heavenly powers:

> Of this gospel I was made a minister according to the gift of God's grace which was given me by the working of his power. To me, though I am the very least of all the saints, this grace was given, to preach to the Gentiles the unsearchable riches of Christ, and to make all men see what is the plan of the mystery hidden for ages in God who created all things; that through the church the manifold wisdom of God might now be made known to the *principalities* and *powers* in the *heavenly places*. (3:7-10)

In this passage the gospel is equated with God's wisdom hidden from the heavenly powers and principalities, which corresponds to what Paul wrote earlier in 1 Corinthians concerning God's wisdom which was hidden from the rulers of this world (2:6-8), yet revealed through the gospel preached by Paul (1:21-25). In Ephesians, Paul addressed this on two levels. On the one hand, instead of the rulers of *this world* he spoke of the *heavenly* principalities and powers. On the other hand, he wrote that the heavenly principalities and powers did not know of that wisdom until the gospel was preached by Paul and accepted by Gentiles. Put otherwise, Paul and the believing Gentiles will "precede" and are superior to the angels from the perspective of the gospel. In comparison with those worthy believers who will be seated around God on judgment day, the angels are mere ministers performing their duty and are not seated. And this is precisely what Paul is hinting at in 1 Corinthians 6:2-3 when he says that the Roman world is judged "among you" (*en hymin*; 6:2),[3] that is to say, when you are gathered as the church (5:4).

1 Corinthians 6:4 elaborates on the imagery of being seated, which is the position of the judge, in contradistinction with those who are standing awaiting the verdict. The most telling passages that reflect the fact that being seated is the status of an elder, especially in his function as a judge, are found in Ezekiel:

> Then came certain of the elders of Israel to me; and sat before me. And the word of the Lord came to me: "Son of man, these men have taken their idols into their hearts, and set the stumbling block of their iniquity before their faces; should I let myself be inquired of (*'iddaroš 'iddareš*) at all by them?" (14:1-3)

> In the seventh year, in the fifth month, on the tenth day of the month, certain of the elders of Israel came to inquire of (*deroš*) the Lord, and sat before me. And the word of the Lord came to me: "Son of man, speak to the elders of Israel, and say to them, Thus says the Lord God, Is it to inquire of (*deroš*) me that you come? As I live, says the Lord God, I will not be inquired of (*'iddareš*) by you. Will you judge them, son of man, will you judge them?" (20:1-4)

The Hebrew verb *daraš* translated as "inquire of" actually means "study, examine the case of someone." Notice how in the second passage we clearly hear that the elders came to examine the Lord and *thus* sat before Ezekiel, that is to say, sat *in order to* examine the Lord's case, that is, to judge him rather than to inquire of him as their elder in the matter. Only such an understanding can explain God's harsh retort, which otherwise would seem out of place: "As I live, says the Lord God, I will not be inquired of (*'iddareš*; examined, brought to task) by you. Will you judge

---

[3] And not "by you" as RSV has it.

them, son of man, will you judge them?" Not only is God not going to let himself be judged by them, but in fact he is going to judge them. The elders have arrogantly reversed the roles, and in no way will God tolerate that.

In 1 Corinthians 6:4 we find the combination of "legal cases" (*kritēria*; cases to be judged) and "make sit, set" (*kathizete*).[4] However, the perennial debate concerning this verse is whether it is to be taken as a (rhetorical) question accusing the Corinthians of mismanagement ([why] do you lay them before those who are least esteemed by the church? [RSV]), or as an indicative describing the wanton behavior of the Corinthians (JB), or as an imperative requesting to do as Paul is commanding (set as judge those who are least esteemed in the church [KJV]).[5] The first two possibilities boil down to the same harsh critique, and the weakness in such interpretations is that they contradict what Paul is accusing the Corinthians of in v.1. Therefore, the last option (KJV) seems to fit the context best. Indeed, the clue to this most plausible choice, in context and line of thought, is to be found in the original Greek of v.4b. A literal translation of v.4b would be "*the* (*tous*) least esteemed (*exouthenēmenous*) in the church, *these* (*toutous*; those, such) you set (to judge)" or "*the* (*tous*) least esteemed, *these* (*toutous*; those, such) set (to judge) in the church." What is usually eliminated in the translations is the emphatic demonstrative pronoun "these" after the definite article "the." In so doing, one is weakening, if not virtually discarding, the case for the last option. Moreover, taking seriously the obviously intended—since it is unnecessary—demonstrative

---

[4] RSV completely loses the original. A close translation of the original v.4 would be: "Therefore, whenever you have legal cases of matters pertaining to this life, *set* those who are least esteemed *to judge* in the church."

[5] My readers are reminded that the original manuscripts do not contain punctuation marks.

pronoun opens the possibility of taking "in the church" together with "set (to judge)" rather than with "the least esteemed" thus making v.4b sound "the least esteemed, set these (to judge) in (the context of) the church (gathering)." The "least esteemed" usually reflects a derogatory connotation, but earlier in the letter Paul specifically wrote:

> For consider your call, brethren; not many of you were wise according to worldly standards, not many were powerful, not many were of noble birth; but God chose what is foolish in the world to *shame* (*kataiskhynē*) the wise, God chose what is weak in the world to *shame* the strong, God chose what is low and despised (*exouthenēmena*) in the world, even things that are not, to bring to nothing things that are, so that no human being might *boast* in the presence of God. (1:26-29)

The two instances of the passive participle of the verb *exouthenō* (disdain, despise) are closely related as is evident in that they occur only twice in the letter until 16:11 where it is in the active voice when Paul is asking that "no one despise (*exouthenēsē*) him [Timothy]." Furthermore, in both instances (1:28 and 6:4) they are used in conjunction with the notion of shame in spite of the fact that the root in either case is not the same.[6] This shows that by using *exouthenēmenous* in 6:4 Paul is clearly drawing the attention to what he wrote in 1:26-28. The intention is further underscored through the unnecessary demonstrative *toutous* in 6:4, which makes sense only if one takes it as meaning "precisely (such as) these." In the church gathering where correction of the brethren should occur, as Paul requested in 5:1-5, it would be more advisable to proceed with the trial even if those available to

---

[6] "But God chose what is foolish in the world to shame (*kataiskhynē*) the wise, God chose what is weak in the world to shame (*kataiskhynē*) the strong" (1:27); "I say this to your shame (*entropēn*)." (6:5a)

preside are "the least esteemed" members since they were chosen *as such* in order to belittle the wisdom of the Roman world (1:27-28) including its legal system.

Paul then goes further by asking rhetorically if there is not a wise person among them to conduct such trials (6:5). The fact that they have trials would be an indication that they suffered "defeat" (*hēttēma*; v.7a) and, more importantly, that God, in spite of his power (1:24), must have been defeated in his plan to shame the Roman world through his "saints" (6:1b and 2a). The Corinthians should be ashamed that they have to go to unbelievers (*apistōn*) to settle matters between brethren, that is, believers (v.6), which is a repetition of v.1. This repetition is done to underscore the magnitude of the blasphemy and to prepare for the extreme request of vv.7a-8: the believers are better off suffering injustice (*adikeisthe*; suffer wrongdoing), even to the extent of being bereaved of their own needs (*apostereisthe*), rather than seek their own just cause if, by so doing, they potentially wrong their own brethren in the name of justice (*adikeite*) and rob them or bereave them of their needs (*apostereite*). What precisely is Paul's thinking here, especially in view of v.9 where he reminds his hearers that the unrighteous (*adikoi*; those who wrong others) will not inherit God's kingdom? To answer this question it is necessary to review what Paul said previously in the letter concerning God's gift to the Corinthians. From the beginning he writes that God's grace is expressed in richness through Christ (1:4). Moreover, unused to such wealth, the Corinthians misinterpreted it as being rightfully their own (4:7-8). One of the facets of divine grace is the righteousness that was bestowed through Christ (1:30). That this verse was on Paul's mind here is evident in that righteousness and sanctification (1:30) are picked up in his conclusion in 6:11:

"... you were sanctified, you were justified (made righteous)."[7] In 1:30 righteousness and sanctification are appositional to wisdom. In 6:5 Paul appeals to wisdom to shame the Corinthians who are not supposed to be boasting about it in the first place (1:29, 31). Since the entire new status of the Corinthians is sheer grace and since this new status includes righteousness as well as richness, the believers are already filled with whatever a human court can and might grant them. Consequently, should a Corinthian pursue a legal case in a Roman court against a poorer brother, who may have a family to sustain, and eventually win that case, then that Corinthian would have "robbed" the poorer brother and proved unworthy of God's righteousness granted to him. Thus he will end up among the unrighteous (*adikoi*) who shall not inherit the kingdom (6:9a). The importance of that aspect of robbing a brother is evident in the list of the "unrighteous," which begins with the "immoral" (*pornoi*), reminiscent of the man judged by Paul in 5:1-5, and ends with the "robbers" (*arpages*; snatchers, 6:10), unique in the Pauline corpus. Someone who is "enriched in every way in Christ" ought not to stoop so low as to "snatch away" the livelihood of a brother.

Then Paul finishes by saying that "such were some of you, but you were washed, you were sanctified, you were justified" (v.11), which is reminiscent of "He is the source of your life in Christ Jesus, whom God made our wisdom, our righteousness and sanctification and redemption" (1:30). The verb "wash oneself, be washed" (*apolouomai*) occurs only here and in Acts 22:16 where it is clearly linked with baptism (Rise and be baptized, and wash away your sins, calling on his name). Redemption, on the

---

[7] The closeness is actually tighter as I shall show in my discussion of that verse further below.

other hand, is often related to the forgiveness of sins (Rom 3:24-25; Eph 1:7; Col 1:14; Heb 9:15). Here in 1 Corinthians, it is mentioned at the end of a passage that began with the extensive mention of baptism (1:13-17). Accordingly, 6:11 is a fitting conclusion to the discussion that started with the subordination of baptism to the word of preaching which calls the believers to a new way of life rather than to a cleansing of their earthly bodies, a teaching he discusses in detail in Romans 6. In that chapter, he introduces the imagery of the body (vv.6, 12) and its members (twice in v.13 and twice in v.19) which he then applies to the body of Christ in 12:3-8 where he recalls the newness of life (v.2) mentioned earlier in conjunction with baptism (6:4). Here also in 1 Corinthians, the lengthy unitary discussion that started with 1:10 culminates with the passage on the body of Christ (6:12-20). That this latter passage pertains to the preceding is evident in that (1) it relates to the topic of *porneia* (harlotry, fornication) that began in 5:1 and carried through to 6:9-10 (Do not be deceived; neither the immoral [*pornoi*], ... nor robbers will inherit the kingdom of God), and (2) a new topic of discussion begins in 7:1: "Now concerning the matters about which you wrote (*Peri de hōn egrapsate*)."

Vv. 12-20 ¹² Πάντα μοι ἔξεστιν ἀλλ' οὐ πάντα συμφέρει· πάντα μοι ἔξεστιν ἀλλ' οὐκ ἐγὼ ἐξουσιασθήσομαι ὑπό τινος. ¹³ τὰ βρώματα τῇ κοιλίᾳ καὶ ἡ κοιλία τοῖς βρώμασιν, ὁ δὲ θεὸς καὶ ταύτην καὶ ταῦτα καταργήσει. τὸ δὲ σῶμα οὐ τῇ πορνείᾳ ἀλλὰ τῷ κυρίῳ, καὶ ὁ κύριος τῷ σώματι· ¹⁴ ὁ δὲ θεὸς καὶ τὸν κύριον ἤγειρεν καὶ ἡμᾶς ἐξεγερεῖ διὰ τῆς δυνάμεως αὐτοῦ. ¹⁵ οὐκ οἴδατε ὅτι τὰ σώματα ὑμῶν μέλη Χριστοῦ ἐστιν; ἄρας οὖν τὰ μέλη τοῦ Χριστοῦ ποιήσω πόρνης μέλη; μὴ γένοιτο. ¹⁶ [ἢ] οὐκ οἴδατε ὅτι ὁ κολλώμενος τῇ πόρνῃ ἓν σῶμά ἐστιν; ἔσονται γάρ, φησίν, οἱ δύο εἰς σάρκα μίαν. ¹⁷ ὁ δὲ κολλώμενος τῷ κυρίῳ ἓν πνεῦμά ἐστιν. ¹⁸Φεύγετε τὴν πορνείαν. πᾶν ἁμάρτημα ὃ ἐὰν ποιήσῃ ἄνθρωπος ἐκτὸς τοῦ σώματός ἐστιν· ὁ δὲ πορνεύων εἰς τὸ ἴδιον σῶμα ἁμαρτάνει. ¹⁹ ἢ οὐκ οἴδατε ὅτι τὸ σῶμα ὑμῶν ναὸς τοῦ ἐν ὑμῖν ἁγίου πνεύματός ἐστιν οὗ ἔχετε ἀπὸ θεοῦ, καὶ οὐκ ἐστὲ ἑαυτῶν; ²⁰ ἠγοράσθητε γὰρ τιμῆς· δοξάσατε δὴ τὸν θεὸν ἐν τῷ σώματι ὑμῶν.

> ¹²"All things are lawful for me," but not all things are helpful. "All things are lawful for me," but I will not be enslaved by anything. ¹³"Food is meant for the stomach and the stomach for food"—and God will destroy both one and the other. The body is not meant for immorality, but for the Lord, and the Lord for the body. ¹⁴And God raised the Lord and will also raise us up by his power. ¹⁵Do you not know that your bodies are members of Christ? Shall I therefore take the members of Christ and make them members of a prostitute? Never! ¹⁶Do you not know that he who joins himself to a prostitute becomes one body with her? For, as it is written, "The two shall become one flesh." ¹⁷But he who is united to the Lord becomes one spirit with him. ¹⁸Shun immorality. Every other sin which a man commits is outside the body; but the immoral man sins against his own body. ¹⁹Do you not know that your body is a temple of the Holy Spirit within you, which you have from God? You are not your own; ²⁰you were bought with a price. So glorify God in your body.

This last section concludes the discussion regarding harlotry and makes clear that the decision to oust the immoral man was not only meant to give him an opportunity to repent and be saved, but also and more importantly, as was pointed out in 5:6-8, it was necessary to preserve the church of God. To explain this, Paul appeals to the metaphor of that community as being the body of Christ. He begins by saying that the new status of empowerment granted to the believers by God should not be misconstrued. They are not entitled to use it for their own gain.

Rather, it was granted for the common good of the community, as he will explain in detail in chapters 12-14.

Verse 6:12 is another example of crafty literary construct on two levels, both intended to impress on the hearers the need to heed the message. The first level is that of rhetorical debate. The text is structured as a conversation between the hearers and Paul, who would be correcting false conclusions they may have drawn from his teaching. This methodology pervades chapters 8-10 as well. RSV actually divides 6:12-13a into three statements by the Corinthians put in quotation marks, each followed by Paul's retort. The second level is the play on the understanding of "authority" (*exousia*) that is linked to empowerment. This second level is completely missed, or at least misrepresented, by the RSV translation of *exestin* into "lawful" and *exousiasthēsomai* into "enslaved." A literal translation of v.12 would be: "'All things are (stand out) within the reach of my hand (power),' but not all things are for the common good. 'All things are (stand out) within the reach of my hand (power),' but I will not be under the authority (power) of anything." The verb *exestin* is made out of the verb *estin* (it is) with the preposition *ex* (out of): it means literally "it stands out, it is within my reach" and thus "it is possible" and, by extension, "it is permissible, within my authority." The noun derived from that verb is *exousia* and carries the notion of capability and power as well as possibility and right and, by extension, includes its ultimate expression of the absolute authority, that of the Roman paterfamilias and the emperor; see, e.g., Romans 13:1-3 where *exousia* clearly refers to the Roman authorities:

> Let every person be subject to the governing authorities (*exousiais*). For there is no authority (*exousia*) except from God, and those that exist have been instituted by God. Therefore he who resists

the authorities (*tē exousia*: the authority) resists what God has appointed, and those who resist will incur judgment. For rulers (*arkhontes*) are not a terror to good conduct, but to bad. Would you have no fear of him *who is in authority* (*tēn exousian*; the authority)? Then do what is good, and you will receive his approval.

In turn, out of the noun *exousia* is produced the verb *exousiazō* which means "to have or exercise (absolute) authority over" as a master would have over his slaves. The passive voice verb *exousiazomai* means "be under the authority of" the way a slave is under the absolute authority of his master. So what Paul is saying to the Corinthians is the following: should you indulge in everything that is in your power and at hand's reach, then you will end up enslaved to your own power (1 Cor 6:12b), and you will never be able to discern if you have the willpower to refrain from some things. Put otherwise, one will never know if you are in control of what you do, or if you are under the control of what is permissible and possible to you. The only way for you to show that you are in charge is to refrain from doing something that is not for the common good, much as a true Roman paterfamilias would refrain from doing anything that would prove to be harmful for his household (v.12a).

That the meaning of the verb *sympherei* is "(works) for the common good"[8] is corroborated in a similar statement in 10:23 where it is used in parallel with the verb "builds (up)" (*oikodomei*) and repeats the entire statement of 6:12: "'All things are (stand out) within the reach of my hand (power),' but not all things are for the common good (*sympherei*). 'All things are

---

[8] The RSV translation as "helpful" allows the hearer or reader the possibility of understanding it as "helpful for oneself," which would be in total opposition to Paul's intent.

(stand out) within the reach of my hand (power),' but not all things build up (*oikodomei*)." The verb *oikodomei* and its correlated noun *oikodomē* (building, building up) occur profusely in chapter 14, which is the concluding chapter of the lengthy section (chapters 12-14) that deals with the topic of the common good of the community *as a body* which overrules the interest of the individual *as a member of that body*. Toward the beginning of that section, and thus as a preamble to it, Paul writes: "Now there are varieties of gifts, but the same Spirit ... *To each* (*hekastō*) is given the manifestation of the Spirit *for the common good* (*pros to sympheron*)[9]." (12:4, 7) So 6:12 is a fitting introduction to a passage dealing with the community as the body of Christ (vv.13b-20).

But what about v.13a[10] that seems unnecessary in this context dealing with harlotry? The only plausible explanation is that it is a literary device used to hold together the unity of the letter. The addition of v.13a prepares for the later passage that starts with "All things are (stand out) within the reach of my hand (power),' but not all things are for the common good (*sympherei*)" (10:23), which deals with consideration toward the "weaker" brother at table fellowship (vv.28-29), and also prepares for 11:17-22, which deals with the same point. In all three cases, the issue of food is immaterial; what matters is the unity of the body of Christ, which is a metaphor for the oneness of the church despite the multiplicity of its members (1 Cor 12). This is precisely Paul's concern in 1 Corinthians 6:12-20.

---

[9] Fortunately after having translated *sympherei* as "helpful" in 1 Cor 6:12 and 10:23 RSV renders *pros to sympheron* in this case as "for the common good."

[10] "'Food is meant for the stomach and the stomach for food' – and God will destroy both one and the other."

Taking care of one's individual body will not forego its ultimate demise by God (v.13a) through the same action with which he brought to naught "things that are": "God chose what is low and despised in the world, even things that are not, to bring to nothing (*katargēsē*) things that are, so that no human being might boast in the presence of God" (1:28-29); "'Food is meant for the stomach and the stomach for food'—and God will destroy (*katargēsei*) both one and the other." (6:13a) It is important to notice the expression of absolute divine might reflected in the verb *katargeō*. Its last occurrence in the Corinthian correspondence is at the end of this same letter: "Then comes the end, when he delivers the kingdom to God the Father after destroying (*katargēsē*) every rule and every authority and power." (15:24) It is through his action against the mighty of this world to bring about salvation to the needy that God will destroy both food and stomach! Paul could not have been more radical in his condemnation of those who use the freedom granted to them by God for their own purpose.

The body that matters is not one's individual body that is bound to destruction; it is rather the body of the Lord Jesus Christ, which is not to be dedicated to harlotry, but to the Lord himself (6:13b).[11] It is precisely in view of that entire body being punished due to one man's harlotry that the immoral man was to be excised (5:1-8). If the members of that body maintain themselves in obedience to God, then God will raise them beyond destruction just as he raised the Lord, the head of that body (6:14; see later 1 Cor 15 as well as Romans 6). The believers' individual bodies are indeed members of Christ, the

---

[11] My readers are reminded that, in scripture, harlotry is the metaphor for the ultimate expression of sin: disobedience to God by turning your back to him and following the will of other deities and kings (Ezek 16; 23). See also my comments earlier on 1 Cor 5:1-5.

head of their community (1 Cor 6:15a; see also 12:27 and Rom 12:5). The members are not at liberty to behave as harlots, contrary to the head's will (6: 15b). In order to make his point more stringent, after the rhetorical "Never!" (*mē genoito*; God forbid!) at the end of v.15b, Paul pursues the metaphor of scriptural harlotry by pushing to the extreme its sexual connotations after the manner of his predecessor Ezekiel (chapters 16 and 23). To up the pressure he quotes scripture itself concerning the two partners engaging in sex becoming one flesh (Gen 2:24 in 1 Cor 6:16b) where the verb "glue" (Hebrew *dabaq*; Greek *proskollaomai*) is used to speak of the man's "cleaving to his wife." Paul uses the same verb *kollaomai* and applies it not only to the union with the harlot (6:16a) but even to that with the Lord himself (v.17) in order to underscore the close correspondence![12] However, the result is totally opposite. When united with the harlot, another human, the immoral man remains what he is, a human body (v.16a) bound to decay (v.13a). When united to Christ, man comes under the aegis of God's spirit that was revealed in the gospel concerning Christ (3:1-17) and thus becomes "one spirit with the Lord" (6:17).

Consequently one is to unconditionally flee scriptural harlotry (v.18a). The reason is that any other sin a human falls into is ultimately redeemable since it does not necessarily entail a change of allegiance; one's body is still a member of the body of Christ and thus his sin is "outside the body," that is, does not affect his allegiance to God and, thus, does not pertain to God's congregation (v.18b). The harloting person, on the other hand, switches allegiance from God to other deities, and this is

---

[12] One ought not be scandalized since the third instance in the Pauline corpus is clearly metaphorical: "Let love be genuine, hating what is evil, holding fast (*kollōmenoi*; gluing yourselves) to what is good." (Rom 12:9)

punishable with bodily excision or excommunication from God's congregation.[13] Harloting is a sin against one's own body, that is, against one's self (v.18c). By harloting, one becomes unglued, so to speak, from the foundation which is Christ the Lord. I purposely mention "foundation" (3:10-11) since in 6:19a Paul uses the imagery of temple of the spirit. The believers are part of this temple (3:16), which is God's building, in the same way they are part of his field (v.9); they do not belong to themselves, but are the property of God (6:19b). Indeed, they were purchased for a price, the way slaves were in the Roman markets, and thus became "slaves in the household of God" (Rom 6:22) and, as such, whatever they do should be for the glory of their new master (1 Cor 6:20b), as Ezekiel eloquently taught.

Before moving to the following chapter I should like to point out a common misreading of 1 Corinthians 6:19-20 that developed under the influence of mysticism and led to disastrous consequences. Often the singular "body" in these two verses is taken literally to mean that each individual body is the temple of the Holy Spirit. This would not only contradict 3:16 but also be blasphemy since, in scripture, God has only one temple. A multiplication of temples would be tantamount to harlotry. The dilemma of a second temple, let alone many, is the subject of an entire chapter in the Book of Joshua (34 verses), a matter that almost created a split among the tribes (Josh 22). In Greek, whenever addressing a multitude of people regarding a singular bodily organ (mouth, face, heart), one has the choice to use the singular (1 Cor 6:19 and 20), as used in French for instance, or the plural (v.15), as is usually the case in English. Thus, the intention of vv.19-20 is that each believer is a member of

---

[13] See earlier my comments on 5:1-5.

Christ's *one* body (v.15), or a stone, if you like, in God's *one* temple (3:16).

Chapter 7

Vv. 1-7 ¹Περὶ δὲ ὧν ἐγράψατε, καλὸν ἀνθρώπῳ γυναικὸς μὴ ἅπτεσθαι· ² διὰ δὲ τὰς πορνείας ἕκαστος τὴν ἑαυτοῦ γυναῖκα ἐχέτω καὶ ἑκάστη τὸν ἴδιον ἄνδρα ἐχέτω. ³ τῇ γυναικὶ ὁ ἀνὴρ τὴν ὀφειλὴν ἀποδιδότω, ὁμοίως δὲ καὶ ἡ γυνὴ τῷ ἀνδρί. ⁴ ἡ γυνὴ τοῦ ἰδίου σώματος οὐκ ἐξουσιάζει ἀλλὰ ὁ ἀνήρ, ὁμοίως δὲ καὶ ὁ ἀνὴρ τοῦ ἰδίου σώματος οὐκ ἐξουσιάζει ἀλλὰ ἡ γυνή. ⁵ μὴ ἀποστερεῖτε ἀλλήλους, εἰ μήτι ἂν ἐκ συμφώνου πρὸς καιρόν, ἵνα σχολάσητε τῇ προσευχῇ καὶ πάλιν ἐπὶ τὸ αὐτὸ ἦτε, ἵνα μὴ πειράζῃ ὑμᾶς ὁ σατανᾶς διὰ τὴν ἀκρασίαν ὑμῶν. ⁶ τοῦτο δὲ λέγω κατὰ συγγνώμην οὐ κατ' ἐπιταγήν. ⁷ θέλω δὲ πάντας ἀνθρώπους εἶναι ὡς καὶ ἐμαυτόν· ἀλλὰ ἕκαστος ἴδιον ἔχει χάρισμα ἐκ θεοῦ, ὁ μὲν οὕτως, ὁ δὲ οὕτως.

> ¹Now concerning the matters about which you wrote. It is well for a man not to touch a woman. ²But because of the temptation to immorality, each man should have his own wife and each woman her own husband. ³The husband should give to his wife her conjugal rights, and likewise the wife to her husband. ⁴For the wife does not rule over her own body, but the husband does; likewise the husband does not rule over his own body, but the wife does. ⁵Do not refuse one another except perhaps by agreement for a season, that you may devote yourselves to prayer; but then come together again, lest Satan tempt you through lack of self-control. ⁶I say this by way of concession, not of command. ⁷I wish that all were as I myself am. But each has his own special gift from God, one of one kind and one of another.

"You (plural) wrote" (*egrapsate*) is a unique instance in the New Testament. However, one should not take it literally, but rather as a way to draw the hearer's attention to the seriousness of the matter about to be discussed, namely, the scriptural attitude toward marriage. This is reflected in the number of verses (40) allocated to it. The reason for this is that the mores in the Roman empire were quite loose and threatened the inner fabric of the household family. Besides becoming a potential social plague, such a loose attitude toward conjugal commitment would threaten "the church of God" that Paul was doing his utmost to implant and build (1 Cor 3:6-17) in each and every Roman household. In other words, for Paul the social "immorality" could easily become a scriptural one (*porneias*; 7:2). This is precisely what he was fighting against in the previous two chapters. Indeed, instead of maintaining the oneness of the "body" or "temple," immorality would end up dividing and eventually dismantling it. Thus, in chapter 7, Paul did not open a new independent topic, but is dealing with another aspect of his main concern throughout 1 Corinthians. The unity of God's church in Corinth is the thread that holds together the entire epistle.

The statement "It is well (*kalon*; a good thing) for a man (*anthrōpō*) not to touch a woman (*gynaikos*)" (7:1b) is clearly construed as an *inclusio* with v.7a: "I wish that all were as I myself am," meaning "unmarried" (v.8).[1] The *inclusio* is actually corroborated by the vocabulary. Given that the passage is discussing the relation between a (male) man (*anēr-andros*) and a woman (*gynē-gynaikos)*, one would have expected Paul to use *andros* instead of *anthrōpō* (human being [in general]) in conjunction with *gynaikos* in v.1b. Obviously, the use of *anthrōpō* is intentional in view of the conclusion which would

---

[1] Discussing the issue as to whether he was widowed (or, for that matter, as some may surmise, had left his wife voluntarily) or had always been a celibate is beyond the scope of the letter's context.

apply to *pantas anthrōpous* (all; all human beings) in v.7.[2] This is further evident in v.8 where Paul uses the same *kalon* (well; a good thing) to speak of his being unmarried. However, Paul explains immediately that celibacy and marriage are not to be pitted against one another, for neither, as such, is a reference. Paul is not interested in discussing what is more ethical, since in scripture, there are no "moral philosophy" per se—whether defining the "good" and the "evil" or the "moral" and the "immoral"—as is clear from Genesis 2-3. The "good" (*kalon*) is simply God's commandment to do his will, as Paul confirms in Romans:

> The very commandment which promised life proved to be death to me. For sin, finding opportunity in the commandment, deceived me and by it killed me. So the law is holy, and the commandment is holy and just and good (*agathē*). Did that which is good (*agathon*), then, bring death to me? By no means! (7:10-13)[3]

The point of reference for an individual to decide for celibacy or marriage is "immorality" (*porneias*; 1 Cor 7:2) because it is the sin of harlotry that severs us from God's congregation.

In order to handle the seriousness of the matter Paul goes into detail not found elsewhere in the New Testament. He individualizes the addressees into "(male) man" and "woman," and stresses the responsibility of each in the marital relationship (vv.2-4); the individualization is intended to equalize the two in

---

[2] This may well be the reason behind the use of the plural *tas porneias* ([the] immoralities) instead of the singular *tēn porneian* ([the] immorality) which he has been using until now (5:1 [twice]; 6:13, 18).

[3] Later in Rom 7, *agathon* is used interchangeably with *kalon* (vv.18-21). Also, while in v.12 the commandment is *agathē* (good), in v.16 the Law is said to be *kalos* (good). See my comments in *C Rom*.

terms of duties. This is evident in that (1) the common *hekastos* (each [in the grammatical masculine gender]) is individualized into *hekastos* (each [masculine]) and *hekastē* (each [feminine]), the latter being a unique instance in the New Testament,[4] and (2) whereas the commands in vv.2 and 3 start with the man and then address the woman, the statement in v.4 begins with the woman and then deals with the man.

The first command given to avoid the sin of "immorality" concerns the oneness of the consort, which recalls Genesis 2:24 quoted a few verses earlier (1 Cor 6:16) precisely in conjunction with Paul's discussion of "immorality." It is the (male) man who is addressed since his inadmissible consort is the *pornē* ([female] harlot). This corresponds to the Genesis text where the main addressee is the man: "Therefore a (male) man leaves his father and his mother and cleaves to his wife, and they become one flesh." However, in 1 Corinthians 7:3 each of the consorts is commanded to abide by the "duty" with which each is "indebted." The meaning of the Greek *opheilēn* is "debt, indebtedness, something due." This term is very forceful to a Greco-Roman ear since it recalls the duties one owes to one's master. This is corroborated in that v.4 unequivocally states that each of the partners does not have full authority (*exousiazei*)[5] over one's own body; rather the one partner is under the full authority of the other partner. This is clearly an extreme metaphor; however, it is intended to underscore that the one partner may not indulge in offering one's body to someone other than the marriage partner. Otherwise, the partner will be committing the "immorality" (*porneia*) against God and his

---

[4] This may be another reason for the plural *tas porneias* ([the] immoralities) instead of the singular *tēn porneian* ([the] immorality).

[5] See earlier my comments on that verb in 6:12.

Christ, which is the epitome of sin in scripture.[6] The rule applies no less to the wife than it does to the husband.

Why is "the prayer" referred to in v.5? The usual assumption is that it refers to a prayer of a personal nature, whatever the reason given: a lengthy time for devotional prayer or prayer associated with the study of scripture due to the use of the verb *skholasēte*. Such an understanding is reflected in the addition "fasting" before or after "prayer" extant in some late manuscripts. A similar addition is found in Mark 9:29. This latter instance and other occurrences of "prayer" in the Gospels, as well as in Romans 12:12 and Colossians 4:2, refer to the congregational meeting and not to personal prayer.[7] It would indeed be strange if a spouse were to ask permission from the consort every time he or she wanted to say a prayer at home. A question that would come to mind in this day and age is, "Why would one ask permission from the other to go to church?" or "Why would not both go together to church?" The situation was totally different in those times as is clear from the following passage (1 Cor 7:8-16) where we hear of a believer spouse married to an unbeliever and where Paul puts the burden on the former. Verse 5 is actually dealing with such a situation. Add to this that the churches were house churches. Thus the table fellowships held in a household whose paterfamilias was a believer were, ipso facto, church gatherings. So the case assumed in v.5 is that of a married believer visiting a colleague in another household where such church gathering was held. Paul is requesting that the believer not take advantage and lengthen the stay or multiply the visits to such church gatherings since he or she could meet other friends and be tempted by Satan through *akrasian* (indulgence or lack of

---

[6] See earlier my comments on 1 Cor 5 and 6.
[7] See my comments in *NTI₁* 192.

self-control). Unless such visits are taken (1) with the unbelieving spouse's approval, (2) for a short time, that is, the time of the gathering without further lingering, and (3) at a church gathering where the believing spouse would be edified through the hearing of scripture and the teaching related to it, then those visits would be "robbing" (*apostereite*)[8] one's spouse, and Paul has just requested that the believer "be robbed" rather than "rob" (6:7-8).[9] That is why, at the end of his strict request, Paul adds the reason behind it: "but then come together (*epi to avto*) again." The importance of the phrase *epi to avto* lies in that it is identical to that used to speak of the church gatherings themselves later in the letter (11:20; 14:23).[10] The conjugal relationship, which is the basis of the "household church," is as sacred as the church gathering itself as Paul just explained in 6:12-20. The latter may not be used as an opportunity to allow Satan to tempt the believer into betraying the former.

Such is a suggestion, says Paul, not an order; it is done by way of *syngnōmēn* which is best translated as "with permission, should this sound agreeable to the spouses involved." In other words, all Paul is interested in is that the believer shun the sin of "immorality" (*porneia*). That fact forms an *inclusio* surrounding his requirements in 7:2-5. Indeed, these verses begin with "because of the temptation to immorality" and end with "lest Satan tempt you through lack of self-control."[11] For all practical purposes, this means that the believer has to take seriously his marriage even—if not more so—when the spouse is an

---

[8] RSV translates this verb into "refuse" in 1 Cor 7:5.
[9] The link is corroborated in that these are the only three instances of the verb *apostereō* in the Pauline corpus.
[10] See further Acts 1:15; 2:1, 44, 47; 4:26.
[11] Notice how RSV enhances the *inclusio* by adding in v.2a "the temptation to" (not found in the original) before "immorality."

unbeliever, which is the main point of the following passage (vv.8-16). That is why Paul concludes by saying he wished all were unmarried like him (v.7a). However, each one has received his "special gift" (*idion kharisma*) from the Lord himself (v.7b). Thus, by using the term *charisma* with which he started his letter (1:7a)[12] and which is going to be the key word in chapter 12 where he will develop the metaphor of the oneness of all in one body, Paul preempts any thought on the hearers' part that the celibate state is superior to being married. He could not afford to have the members of his community divorcing their unbelieving spouses and thus wreaking havoc in his churches! This is precisely the matter he will turn to in the following verses.

Vv. 8-16 ⁸ Λέγω δὲ τοῖς ἀγάμοις καὶ ταῖς χήραις, καλὸν αὐτοῖς ἐὰν μείνωσιν ὡς κἀγώ· ⁹ εἰ δὲ οὐκ ἐγκρατεύονται, γαμησάτωσαν, κρεῖττον γάρ ἐστιν γαμῆσαι ἢ πυροῦσθαι. ¹⁰ Τοῖς δὲ γεγαμηκόσιν παραγγέλλω, οὐκ ἐγὼ ἀλλὰ ὁ κύριος, γυναῖκα ἀπὸ ἀνδρὸς μὴ χωρισθῆναι, ¹¹ -ἐὰν δὲ καὶ χωρισθῇ, μενέτω ἄγαμος ἢ τῷ ἀνδρὶ καταλλαγήτω,- καὶ ἄνδρα γυναῖκα μὴ ἀφιέναι. ¹² Τοῖς δὲ λοιποῖς λέγω ἐγὼ οὐχ ὁ κύριος· εἴ τις ἀδελφὸς γυναῖκα ἔχει ἄπιστον καὶ αὕτη συνευδοκεῖ οἰκεῖν μετ' αὐτοῦ, μὴ ἀφιέτω αὐτήν· ¹³ καὶ γυνὴ εἴ τις ἔχει ἄνδρα ἄπιστον καὶ οὗτος συνευδοκεῖ οἰκεῖν μετ' αὐτῆς, μὴ ἀφιέτω τὸν ἄνδρα. ¹⁴ ἡγίασται γὰρ ὁ ἀνὴρ ὁ ἄπιστος ἐν τῇ γυναικὶ καὶ ἡγίασται ἡ γυνὴ ἡ ἄπιστος ἐν τῷ ἀδελφῷ· ἐπεὶ ἄρα τὰ τέκνα ὑμῶν ἀκάθαρτά ἐστιν, νῦν δὲ ἅγιά ἐστιν. ¹⁵ εἰ δὲ ὁ ἄπιστος χωρίζεται, χωριζέσθω· οὐ δεδούλωται ὁ ἀδελφὸς ἢ ἡ ἀδελφὴ ἐν τοῖς τοιούτοις· ἐν δὲ εἰρήνῃ κέκληκεν ὑμᾶς ὁ θεός. ¹⁶ τί γὰρ οἶδας, γύναι, εἰ τὸν ἄνδρα σώσεις; ἢ τί οἶδας, ἄνερ, εἰ τὴν γυναῖκα σώσεις;

⁸To the unmarried and the widows I say that it is well for them to remain single as I do. ⁹But if they cannot exercise self-control, they should marry. For it is better to marry than to be aflame

---

[12] See my comments on that verse.

with passion. ⁱ⁰To the married I give charge, not I but the Lord, that the wife should not separate from her husband ¹¹(but if she does, let her remain single or else be reconciled to her husband)—and that the husband should not divorce his wife. ¹²To the rest I say, not the Lord, that if any brother has a wife who is an unbeliever, and she consents to live with him, he should not divorce her. ¹³If any woman has a husband who is an unbeliever, and he consents to live with her, she should not divorce him. ¹⁴For the unbelieving husband is consecrated through his wife, and the unbelieving wife is consecrated through her husband. Otherwise, your children would be unclean, but as it is they are holy. ¹⁵But if the unbelieving partner desires to separate, let it be so; in such a case the brother or sister is not bound. For God has called us to peace. ¹⁶Wife, how do you know whether you will save your husband? Husband, how do you know whether you will save your wife?

Paul begins here by restating his preference, especially to those who are not yet married or are widowed, that is to say, those who still have the choice. However, he immediately adds that such is not a trivial matter. If one is not ready for that difficult kind of life, though a "good" (*kalon*; v.8) thing, still it is "better" (*kreitton*)[13] to marry than to be aflame with passion (v.9). The reason is obvious: divorce is not allowed, not only by the Apostle, but actually by the scriptural God himself (v.10). The rule is so strict that the alternatives to separation are either remaining single or reconciliation (v.11a), and again, what applies to one gender applies also to the other (v.11b). Paul then goes into specific detail concerning the non-admissibility of divorce even in the case where the partner is an unbeliever. The

---

[13] *kreitton* is the comparative of *agathon*, the equivalent of *kalon*. See above my comments on these two adjectives.

question should not even arise if both are believers. That, however, was not the common situation in Paul's times since the choice was individual and did not necessarily involve the other partner, let alone the rest of the family.

Paul is dealing here with the case when one partner has trusted the gospel preaching and has become a somewhat regular attendee of the church table fellowships. In this case, it is the believing partner that opted for a different kind of life than when the marriage began and both partners were heathen. Thus it is the believing partner who would have reneged on the initial understanding. It is then understandable that the other partner may find in that a reason for divorce and actually insist on divorcing; in this case, says Paul, the believing partner should not object out of fairness. However, the believer is bound to the scriptural rule and *may not* under any circumstance initiate the divorce (vv.12-13). This is a classic text showing that the burden is on the believer and not the non-believer, a teaching that will culminate in the Matthean injunction: "Do not resist one who is evil. But if any one strikes you on the right cheek, turn to him the other also; and if any one would sue you and take your coat, let him have your cloak as well; and if any one forces you to go one mile, go with him two miles." (Mt 5:39-41)

Giving the excuse that the unholy may contaminate the holy will not do since holiness is not sacramental, as it came to be understood in classical theology. Holiness is behavioral. Indeed, the holiness of the believer is reflective of the holiness of God who, through the believer, lords over the family to the extent that even the unbaptized children are under his aegis and become holy in his presence. One is not to understand this as a magical happening. The unbaptized children, as well as the unbelieving parent, would face daily the "holy" behavior of the believer; in other words, such behavior becomes part and parcel of the family's daily life, and thus it may influence the others to act in a similar manner that would sanctify them and eventually lead them to salvation (1 Cor 7:14-16). Only God can sanctify and save; the believing partner is just the means for God to act in the family the way he acts through Paul in his churches, that is, through teaching (4:16-17) and, whenever possible, through example (11:1; Phil 1:30; 3:17). On the other hand, the ultimate expression of salvation is the peace of the Kingdom to which God calls all believers.[14] Such peace is to be reflected in the life of the family (1 Cor 7:15) as much as in the life of the church (14:33). By mentioning our calling in 7:15 Paul is deftly preparing to expand on this in the following parenthetical passage (vv.17-24).

Vv. 17-24 ¹⁷ Εἰ μὴ ἑκάστῳ ὡς ἐμέρισεν ὁ κύριος, ἕκαστον ὡς κέκληκεν ὁ θεός, οὕτως περιπατείτω. καὶ οὕτως ἐν ταῖς ἐκκλησίαις πάσαις διατάσσομαι. ¹⁸ περιτετμημένος τις ἐκλήθη, μὴ ἐπισπάσθω· ἐν ἀκροβυστίᾳ κέκληταί τις, μὴ περιτεμνέσθω. ¹⁹ ἡ περιτομὴ οὐδέν ἐστιν καὶ ἡ ἀκροβυστία οὐδέν ἐστιν, ἀλλὰ τήρησις ἐντολῶν θεοῦ. ²⁰ ἕκαστος ἐν τῇ κλήσει ᾗ ἐκλήθη, ἐν ταύτῃ μενέτω. ²¹ δοῦλος ἐκλήθης, μή σοι μελέτω· ἀλλ' εἰ καὶ δύνασαι ἐλεύθερος γενέσθαι, μᾶλλον χρῆσαι. ²² ὁ γὰρ ἐν κυρίῳ κληθεὶς δοῦλος ἀπελεύθερος κυρίου ἐστίν, ὁμοίως ὁ ἐλεύθερος κληθεὶς δοῦλός ἐστιν Χριστοῦ. ²³ τιμῆς ἠγοράσθητε· μὴ γίνεσθε δοῦλοι ἀνθρώπων. ²⁴ ἕκαστος ἐν ᾧ ἐκλήθη, ἀδελφοί, ἐν τούτῳ μενέτω παρὰ θεῷ.

¹⁷Only, let every one lead the life which the Lord has assigned to him, and in which God has called him. This is my rule in all the churches. ¹⁸Was any one at the time of his call already circumcised? Let him not seek to remove the marks of circumcision. Was any one at the time of his call uncircumcised?

---

[14] See my comments earlier on 1:3.

> *Let him not seek circumcision. ^{19}For neither circumcision counts for anything nor uncircumcision, but keeping the commandments of God. ^{20}Every one should remain in the state in which he was called. ^{21}Were you a slave when called? Never mind. But if you can gain your freedom, avail yourself of the opportunity. ^{22}For he who was called in the Lord as a slave is a freedman of the Lord. Likewise he who was free when called is a slave of Christ. ^{23}You were bought with a price; do not become slaves of men. ^{24}So, brethren, in whatever state each was called, there let him remain with God.*

In this passage Paul elaborates on the fact that no given state—married or unmarried, slave or free man—is better than the other; the reason being that everything depends on God's calling and that calling aims not at the individual, but on the household of Christ, as he explains repeatedly in 3:10-17; 4:6-8; 6:1-11 and 12-20. Indeed, the verb *emerisen* (has assigned, has divided) is used only five times in the New Testament, three of which have God as the subject (Rom 12:3; 1 Cor 7:17; 2 Cor 10:13). The last case speaks of God's assignment of specific areas of activity to the apostles, which is reminiscent of the Jerusalem agreement (Gal 2:7-8). The instance in Romans (12:3) corresponds to what we have here in 1 Corinthians and, more specifically, occurs in a passage that speaks of the believers' being members of Christ's body, a metaphor that pervades 1 Corinthians (6:12-20 and 12:12-30). It is not farfetched to assume that in 7:17-24 Paul has this same metaphor in mind. Furthermore, the aim of God's calling is to invite the believer to "walk" (v.17b), which refers to a way of life and confirms the reason behind Paul's prohibition of divorce for the believer. Moreover, the new way of life is not a passing injunction to the Corinthians, but a general rule to all the churches (v.17c).

Still, the question that remains is why Paul digresses and suddenly speaks of circumcision-uncircumcision, a topic that is not at all within the Apostle's purview in the Corinthian correspondence. One can even push the issue further by questioning the freedman-slave reference in a context where the matter at hand is the choice between a married or unmarried state. The answer lies in the conclusion drawn at the end of the verses dealing with these pairings: "Every one should remain in the state in which he was called" (v.20); "So, brethren, in whatever state each was called, there let him remain with God." (v.24) This is precisely what Paul was driving at in vv.8-16 and will further stress in vv.25-36 where he will give the reason behind his request. Here he appeals to two basic examples of his teaching, circumcision versus uncircumcision and free versus slave. Both of these issues are at the heart of his primary writing, the epistle to the churches of Galatia. In these two matters, Paul did not bow to the pressure of the Jerusalemite leadership. So the hearers could not miss the level of seriousness with which Paul is requesting them to abide in whatever state they happen to be in, whether married or celibate. What is even more important is that Paul is putting all three matters on the same highest possible level, that of God's calling, which is the rallying cry that controls the entire letter: "God is faithful, by whom you were called into the fellowship of his Son, Jesus Christ our Lord." (1 Cor 1:9) Besides this opening statement, the verb "call" (*kaleō*) that refers to God's calling of the Corinthians occurs only in 7:15-24, and no less than nine times.[15] If God found it appropriate to issue his call to the Corinthians *as they were*, disregarding their status, be it lowly and despised (1:26-31), then one is not to take this

---

[15] The other two occurrences deal with either a believer invited to a meal hosted by an unbeliever (10:27) or Paul's calling to the apostolate (15:9). Even the noun "call" (*klēsis*) is found only in 1 Cor 1:26 and in 7:20.

matter lightly and "improve" on God's choice and will. To do so would belittle God's "folly" in that choice (v.21), and God's folly is wiser than human wisdom (v.25). So, in order to put the ultimate pressure on the Corinthians in the matter of marriage versus celibacy, Paul forces them to view it in the same way he taught all the churches to view circumcision-uncircumcision and freeman-slave.

Paul's reference to the most classical pair, circumcision-uncircumcision (7:18), is immediately followed by a statement confirming that: "… neither circumcision counts for anything nor uncircumcision, *but keeping the commandments of God.*" (v.19)[16] The presence of the scriptural God in family or church life is neither magical nor mystical-sacramental; it is a matter of abiding by God's will expressed in his commandments that are strict rules for a new way of life.[17] So from the perspective of God's will for those whom he calls, Paul is insisting that divorce, which is a change in marital status, should not be considered and is as much forbidden as a change in one's state of circumcision or uncircumcision. This is no trivial matter, especially for the Jew.

In order to fully understand what Paul is prohibiting in v.18, one is to take into consideration his tense relationship with the Jerusalemite leadership as well as the Greco-Roman social setting. In regard to the former, Paul strictly prohibited circumcision to his Gentile following; he dismissed it as unnecessary and even detrimental (Gal 5:2-4), and concluded that his opponents were using it for their own glory (6:12-13) as well as to "enslave" the Gentiles (4:21-5:1). Here in 1 Corinthians he repeats his caveat: "You were bought with a

---

[16] Unfortunately very often we linger on what does *not* count, forgetting that the main point of that verse is what *does* count.
[17] See my comments on Rom 6:4; 8:1-8; 12:1-3 in *C-Rom*.

price; do not become slaves of men." (7:23) By the same token, Paul is not about to allow his Jewish following to use his teaching regarding circumcision as an excuse to undo circumcision through an operation consisting of pulling over the foreskin in order to conceal circumcision (*epispasthō*; v.18a). This would have been done to avoid shame in the public baths where circumcision was viewed as a mutilation of the body, an abhorrence to Greco-Romans. To do this would be a flagrant misuse of the Pauline gospel for one's own egotistic purpose, and would be as condemnable as the attitude of the Jerusalem leadership that Paul criticized in Galatians 6:12-13.

In continuation with his interest in household life, Paul discusses in more detail the free-slave relationship (1 Cor 7:21-23). Here again Paul uses another example of a practical impossibility to underscore his stand against divorce. The general rule in the Roman empire is that one is either born free (*eleutheros*) or slave (*doulos*). A slave when freed becomes not a free person, but a freedman (*apeleutheros*; v.22). Since slaves were branded bodily, freed slaves would have to show a proof of their liberation. If the first example of circumcision-uncircumsion is a case of "one must not," the second example of free-slave is the more forceful case of "one cannot." Yet whether slave or free, one is "called" and as such the free man becomes "the slave of Christ" and the slave becomes "the Lord's freedman." In either case, one who is called ends up as a member of the household (body) of Christ.

Vv. 25-40 ²⁵ Περὶ δὲ τῶν παρθένων ἐπιταγὴν κυρίου οὐκ ἔχω, γνώμην δὲ δίδωμι ὡς ἠλεημένος ὑπὸ κυρίου πιστὸς εἶναι. ²⁶ Νομίζω οὖν τοῦτο καλὸν ὑπάρχειν διὰ τὴν ἐνεστῶσαν ἀνάγκην, ὅτι καλὸν ἀνθρώπῳ τὸ οὕτως εἶναι. ²⁷ δέδεσαι γυναικί, μὴ ζήτει λύσιν· λέλυσαι ἀπὸ γυναικός, μὴ ζήτει γυναῖκα. ²⁸ ἐὰν δὲ καὶ γαμήσῃς, οὐχ ἥμαρτες, καὶ ἐὰν γήμῃ ἡ παρθένος, οὐχ ἥμαρτεν· θλῖψιν δὲ τῇ σαρκὶ ἕξουσιν οἱ τοιοῦτοι, ἐγὼ δὲ ὑμῶν φείδομαι. ²⁹ Τοῦτο δέ φημι, ἀδελφοί, ὁ καιρὸς συνεσταλμένος ἐστίν· τὸ λοιπόν, ἵνα καὶ οἱ ἔχοντες γυναῖκας ὡς μὴ ἔχοντες ὦσιν ³⁰καὶ οἱ κλαίοντες ὡς μὴ κλαίοντες καὶ οἱ χαίροντες ὡς μὴ χαίροντες καὶ οἱ ἀγοράζοντες ὡς μὴ κατέχοντες, ³¹ καὶ οἱ χρώμενοι τὸν κόσμον ὡς μὴ καταχρώμενοι· παράγει γὰρ τὸ σχῆμα τοῦ κόσμου τούτου. ³² Θέλω δὲ ὑμᾶς ἀμερίμνους εἶναι. ὁ ἄγαμος μεριμνᾷ τὰ τοῦ κυρίου, πῶς ἀρέσῃ τῷ κυρίῳ· ³³ ὁ δὲ γαμήσας μεριμνᾷ τὰ τοῦ κόσμου, πῶς ἀρέσῃ τῇ γυναικί, ³⁴ καὶ μεμέρισται. καὶ ἡ γυνὴ ἡ ἄγαμος καὶ ἡ παρθένος μεριμνᾷ τὰ τοῦ κυρίου, ἵνα ᾖ ἁγία καὶ τῷ σώματι καὶ τῷ πνεύματι· ἡ δὲ γαμήσασα μεριμνᾷ τὰ τοῦ κόσμου, πῶς ἀρέσῃ τῷ ἀνδρί. ³⁵ τοῦτο δὲ πρὸς τὸ ὑμῶν αὐτῶν σύμφορον λέγω, οὐχ ἵνα βρόχον ὑμῖν ἐπιβάλω ἀλλὰ πρὸς τὸ εὔσχημον καὶ εὐπάρεδρον τῷ κυρίῳ ἀπερισπάστως. ³⁶ Εἰ δέ τις ἀσχημονεῖν ἐπὶ τὴν παρθένον αὐτοῦ νομίζει, ἐὰν ᾖ ὑπέρακμος καὶ οὕτως ὀφείλει γίνεσθαι, ὃ θέλει ποιείτω, οὐχ ἁμαρτάνει, γαμείτωσαν. ³⁷ ὃς δὲ ἕστηκεν ἐν τῇ καρδίᾳ αὐτοῦ ἑδραῖος μὴ ἔχων ἀνάγκην, ἐξουσίαν δὲ ἔχει περὶ τοῦ ἰδίου θελήματος καὶ τοῦτο κέκρικεν ἐν τῇ ἰδίᾳ καρδίᾳ, τηρεῖν τὴν ἑαυτοῦ παρθένον, καλῶς ποιήσει. ³⁸ ὥστε καὶ ὁ γαμίζων τὴν ἑαυτοῦ παρθένον καλῶς ποιεῖ καὶ ὁ μὴ γαμίζων κρεῖσσον ποιήσει. ³⁹ Γυνὴ δέδεται ἐφ᾽ ὅσον χρόνον ζῇ ὁ ἀνὴρ αὐτῆς· ἐὰν δὲ κοιμηθῇ ὁ ἀνήρ, ἐλευθέρα ἐστὶν ᾧ θέλει γαμηθῆναι, μόνον ἐν κυρίῳ. ⁴⁰ μακαριωτέρα δέ ἐστιν ἐὰν οὕτως μείνῃ, κατὰ τὴν ἐμὴν γνώμην· δοκῶ δὲ κἀγὼ πνεῦμα θεοῦ ἔχειν.

²⁵*Now concerning the unmarried, I have no command of the Lord, but I give my opinion as one who by the Lord's mercy is trustworthy.* ²⁶*I think that in view of the present distress it is well for a person to remain as he is.* ²⁷*Are you bound to a wife? Do not seek to be free. Are you free from a wife? Do not seek marriage.* ²⁸*But if you marry, you do not sin, and if a girl marries she does not sin. Yet those who marry will have worldly troubles, and I would spare you that.* ²⁹*I mean, brethren, the appointed time has grown very short; from now on, let those who*

have wives live as though they had none, ³⁰and those who mourn as though they were not mourning, and those who rejoice as though they were not rejoicing, and those who buy as though they had no goods, ³¹and those who deal with the world as though they had no dealings with it. For the form of this world is passing away. ³²I want you to be free from anxieties. The unmarried man is anxious about the affairs of the Lord, how to please the Lord; ³³but the married man is anxious about worldly affairs, how to please his wife, ³⁴and his interests are divided. And the unmarried woman or girl is anxious about the affairs of the Lord, how to be holy in body and spirit; but the married woman is anxious about worldly affairs, how to please her husband. ³⁵I say this for your own benefit, not to lay any restraint upon you, but to promote good order and to secure your undivided devotion to the Lord. ³⁶If any one thinks that he is not behaving properly toward his betrothed, if his passions are strong, and it has to be, let him do as he wishes: let them marry—it is no sin. ³⁷But whoever is firmly established in his heart, being under no necessity but having his desire under control, and has determined this in his heart, to keep her as his betrothed, he will do well. ³⁸So that he who marries his betrothed does well; and he who refrains from marriage will do better. ³⁹A wife is bound to her husband as long as he lives. If the husband dies, she is free to be married to whom she wishes, only in the Lord. ⁴⁰But in my judgment she is happier if she remains as she is. And I think that I have the Spirit of God.

Having impressed upon his hearers that a change in status is not as beneficial as it looks, Paul returns to the issue of marriage versus celibacy, this time giving the reason for this discussion: "It is well (*kalon*) for a man (*anthrōpō*) not to touch a woman" (7:1b). Indeed, the link between vv.1-16 and vv.25-40 is evident in that Paul begins his argument in the latter passage with a similar statement: "it is well (*kalon*) for a person (*anthrōpō*) to remain as he is." (v.26b) Since he does not have a command from the Lord, as in the case of divorce (v.10), and he has only an opinion, Paul makes sure to bolster the value of that opinion by putting pressure on the Corinthians to heed it as though it were a command from the Lord. Indeed, he begins with the term *gnōmēn* (opinion) which he used in 1:10 and is translated there as "judgment." The actual meaning of that term is "opinion after deliberation," "educated opinion," and thus "view with discernment, judgment." Its importance lies in that it brackets as an *inclusio* Paul's argument: "I give my opinion (*gnōmēn*) as one who by the Lord's mercy is trustworthy ... it is well for a person to remain as he is" (7:25-26); "But in my judgment (*gnōmēn*) she is happier if she remains as she is. And I think that I have the Spirit of God." (v.40). The only other instance of *gnōmē* in our letter is found in 1:10: "I appeal to you, brethren, by the name of our Lord Jesus Christ, that all of you agree and that there be no dissensions among you, but that you be united in the same mind and the same judgment (*gnōmē*)." It is clear that such union is not based on a democratic agreement among the Corinthians—for how could this be possible since they are only babes and fleshly, that is, not according to God's spirit?—but inasmuch as they follow Paul's directives. So, upon hearing the phrase "I give my opinion (*gnōmēn*; judgment)" in 7:25, the addressees are prompted to submit to it. This is confirmed in that Paul bolsters his *gnōmēn* in both vv.25-26 and 40 with a reference to the fact that he is giving it *as an apostle*. In v.25 he introduces himself as "one who by the Lord's mercy is trustworthy," which recalls what we heard earlier concerning his apostleship: "This is how one should regard us, as servants of Christ and stewards of the mysteries of God. Moreover it is required of stewards that they be found trustworthy." (4:1-2) In

7:40 he refers to himself as "having the Spirit of God," which corresponds to what he wrote earlier regarding himself in 2:10-16.

Thus, with the backing of his apostolic authority, Paul presents the ultimate reference for his suggestion: the Lord's coming and the foregoing state of *anankēn* translated here as "distress" (7:26). It is noticeable that, outside vv.25-40, the noun *anankēn* occurs only once more in this letter, in conjunction with Paul's apostolic ministry: "For if I preach the gospel, that gives me no ground for boasting. For necessity (*anankē*) is laid upon me. Woe to me if I do not preach the gospel!" (9:16) Such necessity is linked to the fact that Paul is bound to fulfill the commission entrusted to him even "if not of my own will" (v.17). Consequently, the distress Paul is speaking of in 7:26 is a *necessary* distress one cannot evade: the Lord is coming and all his "slaves" are accountable to him, and only to him, as to whether or not they have been faithful *to him*. This is precisely what Paul is trying to make the Corinthians aware of: all of their other "anxieties" (vv.32-33) are to be subordinated to the "anxiety" concerning their service (slavery) to the Lord (v.34). Once more, since the Lord is coming soon (v.29a), one is not to change one's state (v.27). And again, Paul is not forbidding anyone from marrying, however he is trying to spare them the extra worry related to marital duties (v.28). To underscore the shortness of time until the Lord's coming and of the swift "passing form of this world" (v.31b), Paul uses hyperbolic language suggesting no change in whatever state one is in (vv.29b-31a). Then he reverts to the state of marriage, which is to be taken very seriously. Earlier he underscored this seriousness by strictly forbidding divorce (vv.8-16). Here, he goes one step further by stressing the fact that married life is not a trivial matter that one can "handle" effortlessly; rather, it requires a commitment similar to one's commitment to the Lord (vv.32-34). However, as in the case of a Roman household, a slave's foremost undivided attention is to the master rather to one's spouse (v.35), and it is precisely this that creates "anxiety."

Since the text is meant to be heard, it would be worthwhile to delve into the actual phraseology of v.35. RSV's "benefit" is the Greek *symphoron*, the meaning of which I discussed in conjunction with 6:12 where the Greek verb *sympherei* is used. I explained the meaning of the Greek root as related to the "common good" and not one's own individual benefit. In a Roman household the one who makes the ultimate decision concerning the common good of the household is the paterfamilias, sole master of the house. Since the individual family of every slave is an integral part of the patrician's household, a given slave may not put the "good" of his own personal family over that of the "common good" which includes the other families within the household. This is precisely what Paul is addressing in v.35a.

What is interesting, however, is the Greek phraseology of v.35b "*alla pros to evskhēmon kai evparedron tō kyriō aperispastōs.*" RSV's "but to promote good order and to secure your undivided devotion to the Lord" does not allow the wordplay of the original, which is essential as an introduction to vv.36-40. The two nominalized adjectives that parallel *symphoron* are *evskhēmon* and *evparedron*. The first is from the same root as the noun *skhēma* that was part of the phrase "the form (*skhēma*) of this world" in v.31. So the addressees are hearing that the "good order" is also "in good shape," yet not according to the rules of this (Roman) world but rather according to the scriptural God's commandments (v.19). Indeed, the shape of this world is passing (v.31) and thus about to be no more. For the believer, there is a "new order." As reflected in the Greek *evparedron* this new order is centered around table fellowship where the scriptural words are imparted as the true bread of life. The verb *paredrevō* means literally "sit (at table) besides, in the company of" as is clear from its use later in the letter: "Do you not know that those who are employed in the temple service get their food from the temple, and those who serve (*paredrevontes*) at the altar share in the sacrificial offerings?" (9:13) The only other instance of that root is *evparedron* (7:35) which means "the good order related to table fellowship," where the lordship of the paterfamilias is at its clearest: he sits at the head of the table and controls the conversation associated with it. Hence Paul's ending with the adverb *aperispastōs* meaning "without distraction, without side worries."[18]

What is also important to note is that *evskhēmon* in v.35b prepares the way for the verb *askhēmonein* (behaving in an unbefitting [without the proper form]) at the beginning of v.36. The required "good order" (*evskhēmon*) may be broken by "irreverence, unorderly behavior" (*askhēmonein*) toward a fellow believer, more specifically toward one's betrothed. Here Paul applies the rule he suggested earlier: "To the unmarried and the widows I say that it is well (*kalon*) for them to remain single as I do. But if they cannot exercise self-control, they should marry. For it is better (*kreitton*) to marry than to be aflame with passion." (vv.8-9) In the case of those betrothed, if either's "passions are strong (aflame),"[19] then they should go ahead and get married (v.36). If, however, there is no necessity (*ananke*) whatsoever that would surpass the necessity linked to the Lord's coming, and if the betrothed has full authority (*exousian*) over

---

[18] RSV has "to secure your undivided devotion."
[19] The original Greek *hyperakmos* (aflame with passion) can apply to either gender.

the situation and can exercise his own will (*tou idiou thelēmatos*), and he is determined (*hedraios*; firmly established) in his heart that such is the right thing to do, then he may remain betrothed and not marry (v.37).

By translating *exousian de ekhei peri tou idiou thelēmatos* as "but having his desire under control" RSV does not take into consideration that *exousian* usually means "full authority" similar to that exercised by a Roman patrician and thus refers to exercising one's "*own* will" (*tou* idiou *thelēmatos*) *without any possible objection*. Consequently, Paul is not dealing here with control of one's libido, but rather with a legal matter involving the legal duties of a betrothed.[20] His conclusion repeats the rule he issued in vv.8-9 regarding the "good" (*kalōs*) and the "better" (*kreisson*) (v.38).

Lastly, Paul revisits the case of the widows by appealing to the Law which allows widows to remarry (v.39a). However, instead of saying the widow may remarry whomever she would like, he suggests the restriction that the new husband preferably be "in the Lord" (v.39b), meaning a co-believer. The obvious aim is to save her from the burden he discussed in vv.8-16. And once again he exercises his "judgment" (*gnōmēn*) *as an apostle* to suggest that she would be "more blessed" (*makariōtera*) if she remained unmarried (v.40a).[21] The apostolic authority is evident in the ending "And I think that I have the Spirit of God" (v.40b).

Paul used the noun *gnōmē* (judgment; educated opinion), which brackets the passage vv.25-40, to introduce his "opinion"

---

[20] Notice the repetition of "his *own* betrothed" in vv.37 and 38. Again, by eliminating "own" (*heavtou*) in both cases RSV does not reflect at all the legal connotation.
[21] See above my comments on v.25.

regarding matters not covered in scripture. He did so to stress that his apostolic authority is on par with God's scriptural commandments. One can make a similar case for the adverb *aperispastōs* (without distraction, without side worries) at the end of v.35. This adverb is from the same root as the verb *epispasthō* used in v.18a: "Was any one at the time of his call already circumcised? Let him not *seek to remove the marks of circumcision* (*epispasthō*)." Both stem from the verb *spaomai* (draw; stretch) but begin with a different preposition—*peri* (round; around) and *epi* (over). *Epispaomai* would mean "stretch over" and thus stretch the circumcised skin into a foreskin to cover the circumcision, and *perispaomai* would mean "be drawn around, be stretched in all directions" and thus be totally distracted. Since the basic verb *spaomai* is not found anywhere else in the entire Pauline corpus, it stands to reason that its double use here is intentional. The hearer could not have possibly missed the connection especially since the verbs occur merely a few verses apart and discuss the same topic. The first instance (*epispasthō* in v.18a) is a case of absolute prohibition to reverse circumcision, which parallels the absolute prohibition of circumcising a male Gentile (v.18b), and both are apostolic "rules" (*diatassomai*) valid in all the Pauline churches (v.17b). In opting for the adverb *aperispastōs* from the cognate verb *perispaomai* Paul wanted his hearers to perceive his "judgment" concerning the remarriage of a widow (vv.39-40) on the same level of seriousness as that of the prohibition of covering up the marks of circumcision. In other words, it is not simply a common opinion but that of the sole authoritative apostle in the church of Corinth.

Chapter 8

Vv. 1-13 ¹Περὶ δὲ τῶν εἰδωλοθύτων, οἴδαμεν ὅτι πάντες γνῶσιν ἔχομεν. ἡ γνῶσις φυσιοῖ, ἡ δὲ ἀγάπη οἰκοδομεῖ· ² εἴ τις δοκεῖ ἐγνωκέναι τι, οὔπω ἔγνω καθὼς δεῖ γνῶναι· ³ εἰ δέ τις ἀγαπᾷ τὸν θεόν, οὗτος ἔγνωσται ὑπ' αὐτοῦ. ⁴ Περὶ τῆς βρώσεως οὖν τῶν εἰδωλοθύτων, οἴδαμεν ὅτι οὐδὲν εἴδωλον ἐν κόσμῳ καὶ ὅτι οὐδεὶς θεὸς εἰ μὴ εἷς. ⁵ καὶ γὰρ εἴπερ εἰσὶν λεγόμενοι θεοὶ εἴτε ἐν οὐρανῷ εἴτε ἐπὶ γῆς, ὥσπερ εἰσὶν θεοὶ πολλοὶ καὶ κύριοι πολλοί, ⁶ ἀλλ' ἡμῖν εἷς θεὸς ὁ πατὴρ ἐξ οὗ τὰ πάντα καὶ ἡμεῖς εἰς αὐτόν, καὶ εἷς κύριος Ἰησοῦς Χριστὸς δι' οὗ τὰ πάντα καὶ ἡμεῖς δι' αὐτοῦ. ⁷ Ἀλλ' οὐκ ἐν πᾶσιν ἡ γνῶσις· τινὲς δὲ τῇ συνηθείᾳ ἕως ἄρτι τοῦ εἰδώλου ὡς εἰδωλόθυτον ἐσθίουσιν, καὶ ἡ συνείδησις αὐτῶν ἀσθενὴς οὖσα μολύνεται. ⁸ βρῶμα δὲ ἡμᾶς οὐ παραστήσει τῷ θεῷ· οὔτε ἐὰν μὴ φάγωμεν ὑστερούμεθα, οὔτε ἐὰν φάγωμεν περισσεύομεν. ⁹ βλέπετε δὲ μή πως ἡ ἐξουσία ὑμῶν αὕτη πρόσκομμα γένηται τοῖς ἀσθενέσιν. ¹⁰ ἐὰν γάρ τις ἴδῃ σὲ τὸν ἔχοντα γνῶσιν ἐν εἰδωλείῳ κατακείμενον, οὐχὶ ἡ συνείδησις αὐτοῦ ἀσθενοῦς ὄντος οἰκοδομηθήσεται εἰς τὸ τὰ εἰδωλόθυτα ἐσθίειν; ¹¹ ἀπόλλυται γὰρ ὁ ἀσθενῶν ἐν τῇ σῇ γνώσει, ὁ ἀδελφὸς δι' ὃν Χριστὸς ἀπέθανεν. ¹² οὕτως δὲ ἁμαρτάνοντες εἰς τοὺς ἀδελφοὺς καὶ τύπτοντες αὐτῶν τὴν συνείδησιν ἀσθενοῦσαν εἰς Χριστὸν ἁμαρτάνετε. ¹³ διόπερ εἰ βρῶμα σκανδαλίζει τὸν ἀδελφόν μου, οὐ μὴ φάγω κρέα εἰς τὸν αἰῶνα, ἵνα μὴ τὸν ἀδελφόν μου σκανδαλίσω.

¹*Now concerning food offered to idols: we know that "all of us possess knowledge." "Knowledge" puffs up, but love builds up.* ²*If any one imagines that he knows something, he does not yet know as he ought to know.* ³*But if one loves God, one is known by him.* ⁴*Hence, as to the eating of food offered to idols, we know that "an idol has no real existence," and that "there is no God but one."* ⁵*For although there may be so-called gods in heaven or on earth—as indeed there are many "gods" and many "lords"—* ⁶ *yet for us there is one God, the Father, from whom are all*

things and for whom we exist, and one Lord, Jesus Christ, through whom are all things and through whom we exist. ⁷However, not all possess this knowledge. But some, through being hitherto accustomed to idols, eat food as really offered to an idol; and their conscience, being weak, is defiled. ⁸Food will not commend us to God. We are no worse off if we do not eat, and no better off if we do. ⁹Only take care lest this liberty of yours somehow become a stumbling block to the weak. ¹⁰For if any one sees you, a man of knowledge, at table in an idol's temple, might he not be encouraged, if his conscience is weak, to eat food offered to idols? ¹¹And so by your knowledge this weak man is destroyed, the brother for whom Christ died. ¹²Thus, sinning against your brethren and wounding their conscience when it is weak, you sin against Christ. ¹³Therefore, if food is a cause of my brother's falling, I will never eat meat, lest I cause my brother to fall.

In chapters 8-10 Paul uses rhetorical dialogue profusely to interject probable objections to his statements. This makes his writing more lively to the hearer who thus feels engaged in the debate. The most noted form of this literary diatribe was used by the Stoics. In the New Testament, diatribe is found extensively in Romans, where the presumed addressee is openly spoken to (Rom 2:1, 3, 17; 9:20) and even provided with putative questions (3:1, 9, 27; 4:1; 6:1, 15; 7:7; 8:31; 9:19). The device used here in 1 Corinthians is more subtle in that the objections are imbedded within the writer's presentation; nevertheless the hearer can sense in the debate that the writer is correcting false assumptions through the frequently used adversative conjunction "but" (*alla*).[1]

---

[1] See on this matter the detailed and outstanding study on 1 Cor 8-10 by John Fotopoulos, *Food Offered to Idols in Roman Corinth. A Social-Rhetorical Reconsideration*

Chapter 8

Chapter 7 clearly established that in the community life of the household church, none is lord and thus unequivocally none is free except God and his house manager, Christ. All believers are either slaves or freedmen (7:22). If they are not to become "slaves of (other) men" it is because they have been "bought with a price" (v.23), which makes them members of a new household (6:20a). Thus, they are not to do as they please, but as pleases the head of the new household (v.20b; see also the entire passage vv.12-20). This teaching has a bearing on their "personal" lives not only within the household (7:1-40) but also in open society (6:1-11), as we shall see in chapters 8 through 10. What will soon become clear is that in open society the scriptural God is non-iconic, that is to say, he does not exist in the way the other deities exist, as temple statues that "have mouths but do not speak"(Ps 115:5; 135:16-17). The scriptural God utters his law through a set of strict commandments (1 Cor 7:19) that boil down to the love for the needy neighbor as the prophets taught (Is 1:10-20) and as Paul iterated (Rom 12:8-10; Gal 5:14). Thus the test of obedience to such a God is not what is done *toward* him, but rather what is done *for* him. In other words, the real test of allegiance to him is not demonstrated at altars or sacrificial tables, but in behavior toward the less fortunate neighbor. The ultimate expression of this reality will be expressed in 1 John, a late writing of the Pauline school:[2] "If any one says, 'I love God,' and hates his brother, he is a liar; for he who does not love his brother *whom he has seen*, cannot love God *whom he has not seen*." (4:20)

---

of 1 Corinthians 8:1-11:1. Wissenschaftliche Untersuchungen zum Neuen Testament 2. Reihe. Tübingen: Mohr Siebeck, 2003.
[2] See *NTI₃* 269.

The entire dilemma "concerning food offered to idols" (1 Cor 8:1a) lies in that their consumption took place in temple dining areas. Why would Corinthian believers go there? The reasons are multiple, though they have a common denominator: invitations by friends or colleagues to social events such as births, weddings, and especially thanksgiving meals for healings from illnesses, all of which would be celebrated in the "presence" of the deity. In the temple dining areas it is expected that most of the food served, especially the meat, would be from the offerings to the temple's deity. Thus the theoretical question that poses itself is, "Should a believer partake of food offered to idols?" Paul's entire argumentation dismisses the theory of the matter and concentrates rather on its practicality. The question then becomes, "Would the 'brother' be hurt or negatively affected by my behavior?" Paul thus dismisses *gnōsis* (intellectual knowledge) as a false premise in favor of the factual love for the "brother."[3]

The assumed stand of the arrogant is that "all of us possess knowledge" (8:1a). Before addressing this statement in v.7a (However, not all possess this knowledge), Paul confounds the arrogant in the presumed correctness of their stand. Knowledge is not an end in itself. The fullness of the knowledge imparted by Paul is God's will inscribed in his law (Col 1:9-10),[4] and God's aim is building his church (1 Cor 3:9-17) through the command of love for the other (8:1b), which is the epitome of that law. Knowledge for its own sake puffs up (8:1) and creates discord (4:6) that dismantles that building. Thus, if one dismantles what God is trying to erect, then even if one thinks that he has already

---

[3] One cannot help but note here that Paul would be unhappy with what befell classic theology, which became eminently gnoseological (revolving around theoretical knowledge) rather than behavioral, especially since most of it uses his writings profusely!

[4] See my comments in *C-Col* 37-42.

reached a level of knowledge (*egnōkenai ti*), one obviously does not yet know as one should (8:2), meaning that one still has a long way to go before reaching full knowledge. And if one intends to hide behind his love for God over that due his fellow men, then one is mistaken. Love for God comes second to God having known you first and to have known you is to have a special care and concern for you; hence John's statement "We love, because he first loved us" (1 John 4:19). Thus the knowledge one acquires concerning the non-iconic scriptural God is made possible only after one has been acknowledged by God, and such happened in conjunction with the promulgation of the Law. So knowledge of God should build up and not puff up. Moreover, those who have been known by God have a special obligation to love those lesser then they since "He who does not love, does not know God" (1 John 4:7-12). True knowledge has the meaning of love. Indeed, when God intervened to save the wayward Jacob from the impasse he put himself in by going down to Egypt, we are told: "When Israel was a child, I *loved* him, and out of Egypt I *called* my son" (Hos 11:1). This call materialized in the giving of the Law as is clear from Exodus, namely, that the immediate purpose of bringing the Israelites out of Egypt was not to bring them into Canaan—actually the generation that left Egypt, including Moses, perished in the wilderness[5]—but to bring them to the mountain where God, through Moses, would give them his law:

> "And now, behold, the cry of the people of Israel has come to me, and I have seen the oppression with which the Egyptians oppress them. Come, I will send you to Pharaoh that you may bring forth my people, the sons of Israel, out of Egypt." But Moses said to God, "Who am I that I should go to Pharaoh, and bring the sons

---

[5] Paul will revisit this matter later in the letter (10:1-13).

of Israel out of Egypt?" He said, "But I will be with you; and this shall be the sign for you, that I have sent you: when you have brought forth the people out of Egypt, you shall serve God *upon this mountain*." (Ex 3:9-12)

Afterward Moses and Aaron went to Pharaoh and said, "Thus says the Lord, the God of Israel, 'Let my people go, *that they may hold a feast to me in the wilderness*.'" (5:1; see also 7:16)

On the third new moon after the people of Israel had gone forth out of the land of Egypt, on that day *they came into the wilderness* of Sinai. And when they set out from Rephidim and *came into the wilderness* of Sinai, they encamped in the wilderness; and there *Israel encamped before the mountain*. And Moses went up to God, and the Lord called to him *out of the mountain*, saying, "Thus you shall say to the house of Jacob, and tell the people of Israel: You have seen what I did to the Egyptians, and how I bore you on eagles' wings and *brought you to myself*. Now therefore, *if you will obey my voice and keep my covenant*, you shall be my own possession among all peoples; for all the earth is mine, and you shall be to me a kingdom of priests and a holy nation. *These are the words which you shall speak to the children of Israel.*" So Moses came and called the elders of the people, and set before them *all these words which the Lord had commanded him*. (19:1-7)

It is the Corinthians' contention that the Law teaches that "an idol has no real existence" and that "there is no God but one, although there may be so-called gods in heaven or on earth" (1 Cor 8:4b-5a). If this is so, they reason, why give any regard to the matter of "eating of food offered to idols" (v.4a). Paul reminds them that de facto "there are many 'gods' and many 'lords'" (v.5b). The dining areas where the Corinthians are feasting, as well as the occasions of those festivities, are under the aegis of such! So the reality is not as simplistic as the arrogant are presuming. Furthermore, not all the believers are on the same level of theoretical knowledge. For the strong, who do not believe in idols, the food offered to an idol is not sacred; it is merely ordinary food. Those who are weak, however, may consider that sharing a cultic sacrificial meal with those who believe in the idol is a way of honoring that deity and thus endorsing the reality of that deity, which is strictly forbidden by the Law[6] and thus "their conscience, being weak, is defiled" (v.7). Though the matter of food may not be an issue when standing before the judgment (*parastēsei*) of God, Paul warns that scandalizing (tripping) behavior (*proskomma*; stumbling block) toward the weaker brother will undergo scrutiny, so one should not abuse one's liberty (*exousia*; absolute authority). The behavior of those who oppose Paul will be subject to judgment as people who are destroying God's temple, which is the community of all believers (3:17). Paul deftly uses the verb "build (up)" in a negative sense to stress this: "For if any one sees you, a man of knowledge, at table in an idol's temple, might he not, if his conscience is weak, be encouraged (*oikodomēthēsetai*; built up) toward eating food offered to idols?" (8:10) By following the behavior of the more "knowledgeable" brother (8:11), the weaker brother, for whom Christ died, might be induced to build unwisely upon Paul's foundation, and his building material would be condemned to burning (3:10-15), and he himself would perish (be destroyed). Since the weaker brother is a member of Christ's body (6:15), the one who may have encouraged this behavior would be sinning not only against that brother, but also against Christ (8:12). Consequently, one should forego eating sacrificial meat entirely if it would cause a brother's downfall (v.13). Such is obviously hyperbole since it would mean, for all practical purposes, abstaining from public

---

[6] Paul's argument is forceful since the Law itself gives importance to the idols in that dealing with them is prohibited.

life! The intention is clearly to put pressure on the hearers not to take lightly the lordly command of love toward the supposedly "less knowledgeable" brother.

Chapter 9

Vv. 1-27 ¹Οὐκ εἰμὶ ἐλεύθερος; οὐκ εἰμὶ ἀπόστολος; οὐχὶ Ἰησοῦν τὸν κύριον ἡμῶν ἑόρακα; οὐ τὸ ἔργον μου ὑμεῖς ἐστε ἐν κυρίῳ; ² εἰ ἄλλοις οὐκ εἰμὶ ἀπόστολος, ἀλλά γε ὑμῖν εἰμι· ἡ γὰρ σφραγίς μου τῆς ἀποστολῆς ὑμεῖς ἐστε ἐν κυρίῳ. ³ Ἡ ἐμὴ ἀπολογία τοῖς ἐμὲ ἀνακρίνουσίν ἐστιν αὕτη. ⁴ μὴ οὐκ ἔχομεν ἐξουσίαν φαγεῖν καὶ πεῖν; ⁵ μὴ οὐκ ἔχομεν ἐξουσίαν ἀδελφὴν γυναῖκα περιάγειν ὡς καὶ οἱ λοιποὶ ἀπόστολοι καὶ οἱ ἀδελφοὶ τοῦ κυρίου καὶ Κηφᾶς; ⁶ ἢ μόνος ἐγὼ καὶ Βαρναβᾶς οὐκ ἔχομεν ἐξουσίαν μὴ ἐργάζεσθαι; ⁷ Τίς στρατεύεται ἰδίοις ὀψωνίοις ποτέ; τίς φυτεύει ἀμπελῶνα καὶ τὸν καρπὸν αὐτοῦ οὐκ ἐσθίει; ἢ τίς ποιμαίνει ποίμνην καὶ ἐκ τοῦ γάλακτος τῆς ποίμνης οὐκ ἐσθίει; ⁸ Μὴ κατὰ ἄνθρωπον ταῦτα λαλῶ ἢ καὶ ὁ νόμος ταῦτα οὐ λέγει; ⁹ ἐν γὰρ τῷ Μωϋσέως νόμῳ γέγραπται· οὐ κημώσεις βοῦν ἀλοῶντα. μὴ τῶν βοῶν μέλει τῷ θεῷ ¹⁰ ἢ δι᾽ ἡμᾶς πάντως λέγει; δι᾽ ἡμᾶς γὰρ ἐγράφη ὅτι ὀφείλει ἐπ᾽ ἐλπίδι ὁ ἀροτριῶν ἀροτριᾶν καὶ ὁ ἀλοῶν ἐπ᾽ ἐλπίδι τοῦ μετέχειν. ¹¹ εἰ ἡμεῖς ὑμῖν τὰ πνευματικὰ ἐσπείραμεν, μέγα εἰ ἡμεῖς ὑμῶν τὰ σαρκικὰ θερίσομεν; ¹² Εἰ ἄλλοι τῆς ὑμῶν ἐξουσίας μετέχουσιν, οὐ μᾶλλον ἡμεῖς; ἀλλ᾽ οὐκ ἐχρησάμεθα τῇ ἐξουσίᾳ ταύτῃ, ἀλλὰ πάντα στέγομεν, ἵνα μή τινα ἐγκοπὴν δῶμεν τῷ εὐαγγελίῳ τοῦ Χριστοῦ. ¹³ Οὐκ οἴδατε ὅτι οἱ τὰ ἱερὰ ἐργαζόμενοι [τὰ] ἐκ τοῦ ἱεροῦ ἐσθίουσιν, οἱ τῷ θυσιαστηρίῳ παρεδρεύοντες τῷ θυσιαστηρίῳ συμμερίζονται; ¹⁴ οὕτως καὶ ὁ κύριος διέταξεν τοῖς τὸ εὐαγγέλιον καταγγέλλουσιν ἐκ τοῦ εὐαγγελίου ζῆν. ¹⁵ Ἐγὼ δὲ οὐ κέχρημαι οὐδενὶ τούτων. Οὐκ ἔγραψα δὲ ταῦτα, ἵνα οὕτως γένηται ἐν ἐμοί· καλὸν γάρ μοι μᾶλλον ἀποθανεῖν ἤ- τὸ καύχημά μου οὐδεὶς κενώσει. ¹⁶ ἐὰν γὰρ εὐαγγελίζωμαι, οὐκ ἔστιν μοι καύχημα· ἀνάγκη γάρ μοι ἐπίκειται· οὐαὶ γάρ μοί ἐστιν ἐὰν μὴ εὐαγγελίσωμαι. ¹⁷ εἰ γὰρ ἑκὼν τοῦτο πράσσω, μισθὸν ἔχω· εἰ δὲ ἄκων, οἰκονομίαν πεπίστευμαι· ¹⁸ τίς οὖν μού ἐστιν ὁ μισθός; ἵνα εὐαγγελιζόμενος ἀδάπανον θήσω τὸ εὐαγγέλιον εἰς τὸ μὴ καταχρήσασθαι τῇ ἐξουσίᾳ μου ἐν τῷ εὐαγγελίῳ. ¹⁹ Ἐλεύθερος γὰρ ὢν ἐκ πάντων πᾶσιν ἐμαυτὸν ἐδούλωσα, ἵνα τοὺς πλείονας κερδήσω· ²⁰ καὶ ἐγενόμην τοῖς Ἰουδαίοις ὡς Ἰουδαῖος, ἵνα Ἰουδαίους κερδήσω· τοῖς ὑπὸ νόμον ὡς ὑπὸ νόμον, μὴ ὢν αὐτὸς ὑπὸ νόμον, ἵνα τοὺς ὑπὸ νόμον κερδήσω· ²¹ τοῖς ἀνόμοις ὡς ἄνομος, μὴ ὢν ἄνομος θεοῦ ἀλλ᾽ ἔννομος Χριστοῦ, ἵνα κερδάνω τοὺς ἀνόμους· ²² ἐγενόμην τοῖς ἀσθενέσιν ἀσθενής, ἵνα τοὺς ἀσθενεῖς κερδήσω· τοῖς πᾶσιν γέγονα πάντα, ἵνα πάντως τινὰς σώσω. ²³ πάντα δὲ ποιῶ διὰ τὸ εὐαγγέλιον, ἵνα συγκοινωνὸς αὐτοῦ γένωμαι. ²⁴ Οὐκ οἴδατε ὅτι οἱ ἐν σταδίῳ τρέχοντες πάντες μὲν τρέχουσιν, εἷς δὲ λαμβάνει τὸ βραβεῖον; οὕτως τρέχετε ἵνα καταλάβητε. ²⁵ πᾶς δὲ ὁ ἀγωνιζόμενος πάντα ἐγκρατεύεται, ἐκεῖνοι μὲν οὖν ἵνα φθαρτὸν στέφανον λάβωσιν, ἡμεῖς δὲ ἄφθαρτον. ²⁶ ἐγὼ τοίνυν οὕτως τρέχω ὡς οὐκ ἀδήλως, οὕτως πυκτεύω ὡς οὐκ ἀέρα δέρων· ²⁷ ἀλλὰ ὑπωπιάζω μου τὸ σῶμα καὶ δουλαγωγῶ, μή πως ἄλλοις κηρύξας αὐτὸς ἀδόκιμος γένωμαι.

¹Am I not free? Am I not an apostle? Have I not seen Jesus our Lord? Are not you my workmanship in the Lord? ²If to others I am not an apostle, at least I am to you; for you are the seal of my apostleship in the Lord. ³This is my defense to those who would examine me. ⁴Do we not have the right to our food and drink? ⁵Do we not have the right to be accompanied by a wife, as the other apostles and the brothers of the Lord and Cephas? ⁶Or is it only Barnabas and I who have no right to refrain from working for a living? ⁷Who serves as a soldier at his own expense? Who plants a vineyard without eating any of its fruit? Who tends a flock without getting some of the milk? ⁸Do I say this on human authority? Does not the law say the same? ⁹For it is written in the law of Moses, "You shall not muzzle an ox when it is treading out the grain." Is it for oxen that God is concerned? ¹⁰Does he not speak entirely for our sake? It was written for our sake, because the plowman should plow in hope and the thresher thresh in hope of a share in the crop. ¹¹If we have sown spiritual good among you, is it too much if we reap your material benefits? ¹²*If others share this rightful claim upon you, do not we still more? Nevertheless, we have not made use of this right, but we endure anything rather than put an obstacle in the way of the gospel of Christ.* ¹³*Do you not know that those who are employed in the temple service get their food from the temple, and those who serve at the altar share in the sacrificial offerings?* ¹⁴*In the same way, the Lord commanded that those who proclaim the gospel should get their living by the gospel.* ¹⁵*But I have made no use of any of these rights, nor am I writing this to secure any such provision. For I would rather die than have any one deprive me of my ground for boasting.* ¹⁶*For if I preach the gospel, that gives me no ground for boasting. For necessity is laid upon me. Woe to me if I do not preach the gospel!* ¹⁷*For if I do this of my own will, I have a reward; but if not of my own will, I am entrusted with a commission.* ¹⁸*What then is my reward? Just this: that in my preaching I may make the gospel free of charge, not making full use of my right in the gospel.* ¹⁹*For though I am free from all men, I have made myself a slave to all, that I might win the more.* ²⁰*To the Jews I became as a Jew, in order to win Jews; to those under the law I became as one under the law—though not being myself under the law—that I might win those under the law.* ²¹*To those outside the law I became as one outside the law—not being without law toward God but under the law of Christ—that I might win those outside the law.* ²²*To the weak I became weak, that I might win the weak. I have become all things to all men, that I might by all means save some.* ²³*I do it all for the sake of the gospel, that I may share in its blessings.* ²⁴*Do you not know that in a race all the runners compete, but only one receives the prize? So run that you may obtain it.* ²⁵*Every athlete exercises self-control in all things. They do it to receive a perishable wreath, but we an imperishable.* ²⁶*Well, I do not run aimlessly, I do not box as one beating the* *air; ²⁷but I pommel my body and subdue it, lest after preaching to others I myself should be disqualified.*

Although Paul used the first person singular pronoun in 8:13, he was clearly speaking in an instructive manner. It also allowed him the opportunity to open the subject of his own person. In chapter 9, he will show in detail how he, in no less than his authoritative capacity (*exousia*; vv.4, 5, 6, 12 [twice], 18) as apostle, has all along been forsaking his rights for the sake of the weak. The message is clear: if he, with all his authority, can and does forsake his rights for the sake of the others, then the Corinthians ought to do the same, if not more, for their "weak brother for whom Christ died" (8:11).

Paul's entire point in chapter 9 can be subsumed in what he wrote earlier: "Likewise he who was free when called is a slave of Christ." (7:22b) Indeed, he opens his argument with "Am I not free?" (9:1a) and ends with "For though I am free from all men, I have made myself a slave to all, that I might win the more" (v.19). One is to understand Paul's adducing his "having seen (*heōraka*) the Lord" as a sign of his being an apostle (9:1c) and as a reference to the risen Lord's appearing to him as he did to the other apostles (15:4-8). This is confirmed in that "appeared" (*ōphthē*) in those verses is actually the passive form (was seen) of the verb *horaō* (see) used in 9:1c and these instances account for all the occurrences of that verb in this letter.

Paul is a free Roman citizen (Acts 16:37-38; 22:25-29; 23:27) and as such has authority when compared to many of the Corinthians who were from a lower class (1 Cor 1:26-28) and presumably slaves (7:21). More importantly, he is an apostle with absolute divine authority over them (9:1b). In order to shut out any possible appeal to outside authorities, he makes sure to remind them, as he did in chapters 1 and 3, that every city and its surrounding area has one apostle (Rom 15:20; 2 Cor 10:15-16), the one who planted the seed or lay the foundation (1 Cor 3:6, 10). Thus, even if Paul were the apostle only to the Corinthians and to no one else (9:2a), they would still be his "work(manship)" in the Lord (v.1d). In this sense, their having received the gospel is the seal of confirmation that, "before God" on judgment day (1 Thess 2:19; Phil 4:1), Paul is indeed an apostle of God (1 Cor 9:2b), and if his apologia stands in the divine court, it is all the more valid in the lesser court of the Corinthians (v.3). The tone is clearly ironic since Paul uses the participle *anakrinousin* to describe the Corinthians as examiners and judges of his case, which is from the verb *anakrinō* that is reserved to the "spiritual man" (2:15), that is, Paul himself, and yet *anakrinō* is forbidden even to him (4:3), since final judgment pertains exclusively to God (4:4).

Paul then enumerates instances whereby he relinquished his apostolic "authority" (*exousian*; absolute right), by comparing himself to the other leaders. However, in spite of the apparent "enumeration," virtually all his examples and the scriptural references that back them up (9:7-13) revolve around his right to complimentary eating and drinking. This is evident in that reference to this subject brackets as an *inclusio* (vv.4 and 6, and 14) his argumentation in vv.7-13. One then must question the function and value of the argument concerning the "sister woman" in v.5 since it does not seem to fit the immediate context; actually that argument sounds quite odd given that, position-wise, it seems to be an unwarranted digression between the discussion of eating and drinking (v.4) and the idea of this being free of charge (v.6), that is, without the necessity of being earned through work which Paul will momentarily show is scripturally ordained (vv.13-14). Commentators over the centuries remained in the dark as to the meaning and value of the "sister woman." The solution lies in approaching the matter as functional *within* the larger context, that is, *within* and *in conjunction with* the larger argument concerning the apostle's right to complimentary eating and drinking (vv.3-14). The situation here is similar to that in 7:17-24 which functions *within* the larger subject of chapter 7 concerning marriage and marital relations. Taking 9:4-6 together as a basis, all three verses revolve around the same question, even in its wording, which sounds like a refrain: *ouk ekhomen exousian* (have we not the right [absolute authority])?

The strange position of v.5 is further complicated by its phraseology: leading around (*periagein*; having as travel companion) a "sister woman" (*adelphēn gynaika*). This phrase has been the object of much discussion and different interpretations as is reflected in its diverse translations: "to be accompanied by a wife" (RSV); "to lead about a sister, a wife" (KJV); "travel with a Christian wife" (Phillips); "to take a Christian wife about" (NEB); "to take along a Christian woman" (JB); "to be accompanied by a Christian wife" (NJB). Obviously the anachronistic "Christian" is intended as a translation of the original *adelphēn* (sister), which is a reference to a female member of the Pauline communities. Most of the explanations of "sister woman" usually end up begging the question since they approach v.5 as standing on its own. Instead of starting our investigation with "sister woman," it would behoove us to begin by figuring out the meaning of *periagein* that is unique in the Pauline corpus. It occurs five more times in the New Testament, four of which are in conjunction with the preaching activity of either Jesus (*periēgen*; Mt 4:23; 9:35; Mk 6:6) or his nemeses, the scribes and Pharisees (*periagete*; Mt 23:15): each party is described as "going around" preaching. The fifth instance (Acts

13:11) is in conjunction with Paul's missionary activity, however, it is used ironically to describe Paul's nemesis, Elymas the magician, who "withstood" Paul and Barnabas and was trying to "turn away (*diastrepsai*; mislead through perversion) from the faith the proconsul who was seeking to hear the word of God" preached by them (vv.7-8). Elymas' action is described as "perverting" (*diastrephōn*) the apostolic teaching (v.10) and thus de facto "counter-preaching." His punishment (v. 11) was intended to unveil his cunningness: instead of him "going around (leading)" (*periagōn*) preaching and teaching, he was shown to be "going around" (*periagōn*) "seeking people to lead him by the hand (*kheiragōgous*)." The wordplay is evident since both Greek terms are from the root *agō* (lead). The conclusion is inescapable: the verb *periagein* is always connected with a preaching and thus apostolic activity. Since the entire passage of 1 Corinthians 9:3-14 revolves specifically around eating and drinking, which are the *reaped* "material (matters)" (*ta sarkika*; the fleshly matters; v.11) necessary for living (v.14), it seems reasonable to understand v.5 within this frame. Additionally, chapter 9 is sandwiched between two chapters that deal with table fellowship. Within this lengthy discussion of matters pertaining to food and table fellowship, it would be quite odd to have a single verse that would refer to matters of marriage and sexual relations, especially in view of the fact that this was just discussed at length in chapter 7.

Thus the solution to understanding 9:5 correctly is to consider the "sister woman" a woman in the church household, where the apostle would be residing, who would be assigned to attend to his "living" needs, more specifically and above all, his food and drink. In order to make matters simpler, the woman who was assigned to serve him would be a "sister," that is to say, a believer. Consequently, to assume that the Greek *gynaika*, which could refer to either a woman or a wife, is meant here as "wife" is, at worst, an *eisegesis* and, at best, an educated guess since it would mean that only Paul and Barnabas[1] were unmarried while (all) *the* rest of apostles, (all) *the* brothers of the Lord, and Cephas were married. We do not know that all of them were indeed married and to conclude so from 1 Corinthians 9:5 would be a circular argument. The only acceptable case would be that of Cephas, whose mother-in-law is mentioned in the Gospels (Mk 1:30/Lk 4:38); however, it would be farfetched to take that to mean that all the others were married. Obviously, *gynaika* could well refer to "wife," *if* the named were married; in that case the intended apostle would be joined by his wife who would take care of him. So the phraseology of *adelphēn gynaika* is intended to cover either possibility. The woman in question would be acting as a "deacon"[2] and would take care of the table fellowship while the apostle would be freed of that charge in order to dedicate himself to the ministry of the word (Acts 6:1-4).

Since his topic is apostleship, why did Paul add "the brothers of the Lord and Cephas" after "the other apostles"? What is intended by that addition? The only other instance in the Pauline corpus where Cephas occurs in conjunction with the Lord's brother is in Galatians 1:18-19: "Then after three years I went up to Jerusalem to visit Cephas, and remained with him fifteen days. But I saw none of the other apostles except James the Lord's brother." From the immediate context (vv.11-24) it is obvious that Paul is intending to dismiss Cephas and James as a reference in regard to assessing his gospel. Such is corroborated

---

[1] The addition of Barnabas is not as unexpected as it appears since Barnabas was a close colleague of Paul in his apostolic mission (Gal 2; Acts 9-15).
[2] I used "deacon" instead of "deaconess" on purpose to reflect that, in Greek, the same noun *diakonos* is used of both genders.

in the following chapter where the same James and Cephas, together with the Jerusalem Jewish leadership, are shown to be, at best, equal to Paul concerning the matter of the gospel (2:1-10).[3] So here in 1 Corinthians 9 Paul is purposely including the highest authority beyond "the other apostles" in order to block any appeal by his hearers against his authoritative statement. This is similar to what he did in 1:10-17 and 3:21-23 and as he will do in a more encompassing manner in 15:1-11.

In 9:7 Paul provides three examples of livelihood to back up his point concerning free food and drink: the military (v.7a), the vinedresser (v.7b), and the shepherd (v.7c). Then he makes clear that he is not merely referring to human mores, but actually to the law of Moses, which reflects God's will (v.8). The obvious reason behind the choice of the seemingly outlandish quotation from Deuteronomy 25:4 is that it speaks of treading out (*aloōnta*; threshing), which is precisely the verb that Paul will build upon in the following verse: "… because the plowman should plow in hope and the thresher (*aloōn*) thresh[4] in hope of a share in the crop." (1 Cor 9:10) His interest in this agricultural example lies in its close connection with the picture of sowing and reaping (v.11), which is a classic Pauline metaphor that pervades 1 Corinthians (3:6-9; 9:11; 15:36-37, 42-44)[5] and is the point of the Deuteronomic quotation.

It seems strange at face value that Paul would choose from the entire scripture a text that speaks of an ox only for him to immediately ask the rhetorical question "Is it for oxen that God is concerned?" (9:9b). Is there anything in the original Deuteronomic passage that justifies Paul's reading? In

---

[3] See *Gal* 59-73.
[4] This verb is added by RSV; it does not appear in the original.
[5] The other instances are 2 Cor 9:6-10 and Gal 6:6-9.

Deuteronomy the proverb concerning the ox seems to be haphazardly thrown between two sections dealing with brothers, yet concerning two different topics:

> If there is a dispute between men, and they come into court, and the judges decide between them, acquitting the innocent and condemning the guilty, then if the guilty man deserves to be beaten, the judge shall cause him to lie down and be beaten in his presence with a number of stripes in proportion to his offense. Forty stripes may be given him, but not more; lest, if one should go on to beat him with more stripes than these, your brother be degraded in your sight. *You shall not muzzle an ox when it treads out the grain.* If brothers dwell together, and one of them dies and has no son, the wife of the dead shall not be married outside the family to a stranger; her husband's brother shall go in to her, and take her as his wife, and perform the duty of a husband's brother to her. And the first son whom she bears shall succeed to the name of his brother who is dead, that his name may not be blotted out of Israel. And if the man does not wish to take his brother's wife, then his brother's wife shall go up to the gate to the elders, and say, "My husband's brother refuses to perpetuate his brother's name in Israel; he will not perform the duty of a husband's brother to me." Then the elders of his city shall call him, and speak to him: and if he persists, saying, "I do not wish to take her," then his brother's wife shall go up to him in the presence of the elders, and pull his sandal off his foot, and spit in his face; and she shall answer and say, "So shall it be done to the man who does not build up his brother's house." And the name of his house shall be called in Israel, The house of him that had his sandal pulled off. (25:1-10)

The proverb clearly functions as an introduction to the following section since it speaks of threshing the scattered seeds into the ground with the hope that some of them would take root and grow. On the other hand, the progeny in scripture is referred to as the "seed" of the father which he, as husband, implants into his wife's womb by "going into her" *on hope* that the seed would bear fruit. In this sense, he would be enjoying some of his seed. Furthermore, the discussed case shows that the widow's quest is *on hope* that her brother-in-law would marry her. If he does not do so, then her children would not be of the deceased's family seed and would not bear the deceased's family name but that of the stranger. This being the case, the deceased would remain without "seed" or "name" to perpetuate his memory. Thus the Deuteronomic passage makes full sense: just as the threshing ox should be allowed to enjoy some of the seed it is treading as wages for its labor and, by the same token, so that it would have enough energy to continue that labor, so also the original husband should be allowed to enjoy the fruit of the seed he is sowing and shame on his brother should he not ensure that.

So Paul read and correctly used the original on three levels. First of all, the proverb of Deuteronomy 25:4 was indeed written "in view of us, human beings" (1 Cor 9:10 a). Second, the main points in both the proverb and the case discussed are, on the one hand, the hope of the fruitfulness of that labor (v.10b) and, on the other hand, the enjoyment of the benefits of one's labor (v.11). Third, and in a sense most importantly, the "first husband" is the first in line to be entitled to the fruits of the "seed." In our case, it is Paul who is the first husband as is clear from 9:2 (see also 3:6, 10 and 2 Cor 3:1-3): "If others share this rightful claim (*exousian*) upon you, do not we *still more?*" (1 Cor 9:12a) Yet, his conclusion is unexpected: he prefers to abstain from using his absolute right (v.12b) and be in straights (*stegomen*) in order not to put any obstacle (*enkopēn*; hurdle) in the way of Christ's gospel (v.12c).

It is worthwhile to note two things regarding terminology. On the one hand, in the entire New Testament, the verb *stegomen* occurs as a feature of true love ([love] that bears [*stegei*] all things; 13:7a) and is used only twice more in conjunction with Paul's apostolic activity (1 Thess 3:1, 5), which fits perfectly with what Paul is doing here: out of love for the Corinthians and commitment to the gospel cause, he is accepting to endure unnecessary hardship. On the other hand, the idea of "obstacle (hurdle, hindrance)" found three more times in the Pauline corpus, in the verbal form *enkoptō*, also concerns Paul's apostolic activity (Rom 15:22; Gal 5:7; 1 Thess 2:18). The last instance occurs three verses before *stegontes* in 1 Thess 3:1 and in conjunction with the same topic, Paul wanting to visit Thessalonica in order to check on the status of the Thessalonians' response to his preaching: "… because we wanted to come to you—I, Paul, again and again—but Satan hindered (*enekopsen*) us." (2:18)

In 1 Corinthians 9:13 Paul again refers to the Law in order to conclude that, as apostle, he has the right to food free of charge (v.14) only to underscore that he is intentionally abstaining from such right (v.15a). Usually repetition in a written document meant for public reading is a literary device for underscoring. However, repetition can, and often does, carry with it a different aspect of the same matter. As we have seen, the first quotation from Deuteronomy was intended to point out the aspect of planting and harvesting, which entails waiting in hope and thus the possibility of being unsuccessful at the end. In v.13 Paul appeals to a more straightforward rule from the Law (Lev 6:16, 26; Num 18:8, 31; Deut 18-1-3): "Do you not know that those who are employed in the temple service get their food from the temple, and those who serve at the altar share in the sacrificial offerings?" But how could he conclude that this same rule applies to "those who proclaim the gospel" (1 Cor 9:14)? The answer lies in that he viewed the apostle in the same vein as the Old Testament prophet that carried the word of the scriptural God who is in no need of a stone temple (Is 66:1-4). The apostle is the "priest" of the heavenly temple of the Jerusalem above.[6] As such he is entitled to reap *immediately* his due from "the offering (*prosphora*) of the nations (Gentiles)" (Rom 15:16) and the "libation upon the sacrificial offering of your (the Gentiles') faith" (Phil 2:17). However, he writes, "I have made no use of any of these rights, nor am I writing this to secure any such provision" (1 Cor 9:15a).

Paul insisted earlier that "God chose what is low and despised in the world, even things that are not, to bring to nothing things that are, so that no human being might boast in the presence of God" (1:28-29) and that "as it is written, 'Let him who boasts, boast of the Lord'" (v.31). However, this boasting cannot be effected except at the Lord's coming as Paul indicated elsewhere: "For what is our hope or joy or crown of boasting before our Lord Jesus at his coming? Is it not you (the Gentiles)?" (1 Thess 2:19) Any false boasting ahead of time would be as "empty" as the false teaching about the meaning of Christ's crucifixion: "For I would rather die than have any one deprive (empty; *kenōsei*) me of my ground for boasting" (1 Cor 9:15b); "... lest the cross of Christ be emptied (*kenōthē*) of its power." (1:17b). The close connection between these two statements is evident in that they contain the only two instances of the verb *kenoō* (empty) in the letter and both cases reference Paul's preaching the gospel: "For Christ did not send me to baptize but to preach the gospel (*evangelizesthai*) ..." (1:17a); "For if I preach the gospel

---

[6] See my detailed comments on Gal 4:21-28 in *Gal*, on Rom 12:1-3a and 15:15-16 in *C-Rom*, and on Phil 2:17 in *C-Phil*.

(*evangelizomai*), that gives me no ground for boasting." (9:16a) Such activity for Paul is a calling and a mission (Gal 1:15-16) and thus a "necessity" (*ananke*; something imposed; 1 Cor 9:16b). Consequently, Paul is under "woe" (curse) should he not carry out his mission (v.16c).

The metaphor behind these statements is that of house manager or overseer. Indeed, Paul refers to his apostleship as an *oikonomian* (v.17b), the duty of an *oikonomos* (4:1-2)[7] who is a slave assigned by the paterfamilias as his right hand man in matters of management of the household.[8] He is rewarded if he performs well and, more importantly, willingly (9:17a), and does not give any hardship to the paterfamilias. Even begrudgingly, he is still bound to his master's commissioning (v.17b). His reward, says Paul, is to accept the fact that his commission be done to a T in order for him to keep it, since the ultimate *exousia* (absolute authoritative power), which ensures his own livelihood, lies with the paterfamilias (v.18). In fact, neither the overseer's satisfaction nor that of those who are under his command is of any value. It is solely the satisfaction of the paterfamilias that matters, and the fewer complaints he hears from the household members, the better it is for the overseer.

That is why, although Paul, as overseer, was free from all his subalterns, he enslaved himself—acted as a slave—toward most of them in order to gain them to the cause of his commission (v.19). One should not assume from the series of examples in

---

[7] The close link between these two passages is further evident in the fact that the overseer is to be found *trustworthy* (*pistos*; 4:2) of the commission with which he is entrusted (*pepistevmai*; 9:17b).

[8] *oikonomos* is made out of the nouns *oikos* (house, household) and *nomos* (rule); thus the *oikonomos* is the one in charge to instate the house rules and oversee the right execution thereof.

vv.20-22a that Paul was a hypocrite or double-faced; such would contradict the entire tenor of his writings.⁹ Rather, the entire passage is a reflection of the effort Paul is making to use language and a level of understanding that each of his hearers could comprehend in order to convince them of his argument. This is similar to the earlier metaphor he used in 3:1-3a to refer to his hearers as babes and speaking to them at that level: "But I, brethren, could not address you as spiritual men, but as men of the flesh, as babes in Christ. I fed you with milk, not solid food; for you were not ready for it; and even yet you are not ready, for you are still of the flesh." He does this also in 1 Thessalonians where again the topic is his apostleship, exactly as is the case in 1 Corinthians 9, and, moreover, the phraseology is similar:

> For you yourselves know, brethren, that our visit to you was not in vain; but though we had already suffered and been shamefully treated at Philippi, as you know, we had courage in our God to declare to you the gospel of God in the face of great opposition. For our appeal does not spring from error or uncleanness, nor is it made with guile; but just as we have been approved by God *to be entrusted with the gospel*, so we speak, not to please men, but to please God who tests our hearts. For we never used either words of flattery, as you know, or a cloak for greed, as God is witness; *nor did we seek glory from men, whether from you or from others, though we might have made demands as apostles of Christ*. But we were gentle among you, *like a nurse taking care of her children*. So, being affectionately desirous of you, we were ready to share with you not only the gospel of God but also our own selves, because you had become very dear to us. For you remember our labor and toil, brethren; *we worked night and day, that we might not burden any of you, while we preached to you the gospel of God*. You are witnesses, and God also, how holy and righteous and blameless was our

---

⁹ Besides, no hypocrite admits, and so bluntly, to his hypocrisy.

behavior to you believers; for you know how, *like a father with his children*, we exhorted each one of you and encouraged you and charged you to lead a life worthy of God, who calls you into his own kingdom and glory. (1 Thess 2:1-12)

Notice the ending of the passage where it is clear that the intention behind his behavior is to teach his hearers, namely, to exhort, encourage, and charge them to lead a life worthy of God. If one hears 1 Corinthians 9:19-22a along the same lines, then his wanting to "gain" them with the intention to "save" them, which is precisely the aim of his gospel (1:18, 21; 15:1-2), makes sense. Still, salvation will depend on the Corinthians' response; that is why he is trying to "gain *as many as possible*" (9:19) with the view of "saving by all means (*pantōs*; at any cost) *some*" (9:22).

The conclusion in v.23 rejoins what he wrote earlier concerning not boasting before the Lord's coming. Indeed, all he does for the sake of the gospel is with the view of his sharing (*synkoinōnos*) in it, or in its blessings, as RSV has it. Indeed, as I explained in my comments on 1:9, *koinōnia* is the fellowship around the master of the house who provides all, including the chief steward (*oikonomos*), with necessary food, drink, and daily care for their living. The chief steward, above anyone else, is bound to full obedience to his master (9:16-18), which is his only way to remain within the latter's house fellowship. Thus, it stands to reason that Paul would write that, to the extent to which he does his commission, which is the preaching of the gospel (1:17), he has a share in that fellowship (9:23). Since ultimately his appraisal depends on the success of his mission among his addressees, he will have to proceed in his efforts until the end, until the Lord's coming (4:5). To speak of that process, Paul uses metaphors from the sports events of his time: racing

(9:24-26a), which is his classic example (see Gal 2:2; 5:7; Phil 2:16; 2 Tim 4:7; Heb 12:1) because it corresponds to the scriptural metaphor of "walking" according to God's will expressed in the Law,[10] and boxing (1 Cor 9:26b). Boxing allows Paul to use two verbs virtually unique in the New Testament[11] to speak of subjugating one's body, that is, oneself (v.27a). The first, *hypōpiazō* (pommel), means literally "beat, punch, or pommel, under the eye" and is clearly a specific boxing term. The second, *doulagōgeō* (subdue), means literally "lead as one would a slave; enslave; exert full control over," and would fit all sports, but pertains to boxing in a special way since a boxer has to receive and accept the opponent's pummeling. It is an interesting choice in that the Greek verb for subdue uses the root *doulos* (slave). The intention is that the chief steward is to remind himself constantly that he is no better than the other members of the household; they are all slaves who will have to answer to the master at the end, and each will have to make sure not to be found *adokimos* (failing the test; disqualified; v.27b) when fire will test (*dokimasei*) the work of each (3:13).[12]

In Luke 12:41-48 we have a unique parable that deals specifically with the *oikonomos* (chief steward) and his duty toward his colleagues and, more importantly, with the fact that his judgment by the master will hinge on the way he will have dealt with those colleagues. This shows that the duty of the chief steward is on the behavioral level—how he acts toward the other members of the household—as much as it is on the content level—the instructions he gives them to perform their duties. This sheds light on why the list of examples in 1 Corinthians

---

[10] See Rom 6:4; 8:4; Gal 5:16, 25; 6:16; 2:10; Eph 5:2, 8, 15.
[11] The first, *hypōpiazō* (pommel), occurs once more, obviously metaphorically, as "wear out" in Lk 18:5.
[12] This is the only instance of the root *dokim—* before 9:27.

9:20-22 ends with "To the weak I became weak, that I might win the weak" (v.22a), which does not correspond to the first three that are connected with the Law. Still, it fits perfectly with the phrase *ennomos Khristou* Paul deftly slipped in the previous example: "To those outside the law I became as one outside the law—not being without law toward God but *under the law of Christ* (*ennomos Khristou*)—that I might win those outside the law." The phrase "law of Christ" (*nomos Khristou*) was introduced in Galatians in conjunction with the behavior of seniors toward juniors: "Brethren, if a man is overtaken in any trespass, *you who are spiritual* should restore him in a *spirit of gentleness*. Look to yourself, lest you too be tempted. Bear one another's burdens, and so fulfill the law of Christ." (6:1-2)[13] A few verses earlier "gentleness" was mentioned as one of the facets of the fruit of the Spirit, love (5:22-23).[14] Whether Jews or Gentiles, those to whom Paul preached are his "weaker" brethren and his own salvation depends on *how* he will have led each of them.

---

[13] See my comments in *Gal* 309-13.
[14] See my comments in *Gal* 297-301.

Chapter 10

Vv. 1-13 ¹Οὐ θέλω γὰρ ὑμᾶς ἀγνοεῖν, ἀδελφοί, ὅτι οἱ πατέρες ἡμῶν πάντες ὑπὸ τὴν νεφέλην ἦσαν καὶ πάντες διὰ τῆς θαλάσσης διῆλθον ² καὶ πάντες εἰς τὸν Μωϋσῆν ἐβαπτίσθησαν ἐν τῇ νεφέλῃ καὶ ἐν τῇ θαλάσσῃ ³ καὶ πάντες τὸ αὐτὸ πνευματικὸν βρῶμα ἔφαγον ⁴ καὶ πάντες τὸ αὐτὸ πνευματικὸν ἔπιον πόμα· ἔπινον γὰρ ἐκ πνευματικῆς ἀκολουθούσης πέτρας, ἡ πέτρα δὲ ἦν ὁ Χριστός. ⁵ Ἀλλ' οὐκ ἐν τοῖς πλείοσιν αὐτῶν εὐδόκησεν ὁ θεός, κατεστρώθησαν γὰρ ἐν τῇ ἐρήμῳ. ⁶ Ταῦτα δὲ τύποι ἡμῶν ἐγενήθησαν, εἰς τὸ μὴ εἶναι ἡμᾶς ἐπιθυμητὰς κακῶν, καθὼς κἀκεῖνοι ἐπεθύμησαν. ⁷ μηδὲ εἰδωλολάτραι γίνεσθε καθώς τινες αὐτῶν, ὥσπερ γέγραπται· ἐκάθισεν ὁ λαὸς φαγεῖν καὶ πεῖν καὶ ἀνέστησαν παίζειν. ⁸ μηδὲ πορνεύωμεν, καθώς τινες αὐτῶν ἐπόρνευσαν καὶ ἔπεσαν μιᾷ ἡμέρᾳ εἴκοσι τρεῖς χιλιάδες. ⁹ μηδὲ ἐκπειράζωμεν τὸν κύριον, καθώς τινες αὐτῶν ἐπείρασαν καὶ ὑπὸ τῶν ὄφεων ἀπώλλυντο. ¹⁰ μηδὲ γογγύζετε, καθάπερ τινὲς αὐτῶν ἐγόγγυσαν καὶ ἀπώλοντο ὑπὸ τοῦ ὀλοθρευτοῦ. ¹¹ ταῦτα δὲ τυπικῶς συνέβαινεν ἐκείνοις, ἐγράφη δὲ πρὸς νουθεσίαν ἡμῶν, εἰς οὓς τὰ τέλη τῶν αἰώνων κατήντηκεν. ¹² Ὥστε ὁ δοκῶν ἑστάναι βλεπέτω μὴ πέσῃ. ¹³ πειρασμὸς ὑμᾶς οὐκ εἴληφεν εἰ μὴ ἀνθρώπινος· πιστὸς δὲ ὁ θεός, ὃς οὐκ ἐάσει ὑμᾶς πειρασθῆναι ὑπὲρ ὃ δύνασθε ἀλλὰ ποιήσει σὺν τῷ πειρασμῷ καὶ τὴν ἔκβασιν τοῦ δύνασθαι ὑπενεγκεῖν.

¹I want you to know, brethren, that our fathers were all under the cloud, and all passed through the sea, ²and all were baptized into Moses in the cloud and in the sea, ³and all ate the same supernatural food ⁴and all drank the same supernatural drink. For they drank from the supernatural Rock which followed them, and the Rock was Christ. ⁵Nevertheless with most of them God was not pleased; for they were overthrown in the wilderness. ⁶Now these things are warnings for us, not to desire evil as they did. ⁷Do not be idolaters as some of them were; as it is written, "The people sat down to eat and drink and rose up to dance." ⁸*We must not indulge in immorality as some of them did, and twenty-three thousand fell in a single day. ⁹We must not put the Lord to the test, as some of them did and were destroyed by serpents; ¹⁰nor grumble, as some of them did and were destroyed by the Destroyer. ¹¹Now these things happened to them as a warning, but they were written down for our instruction, upon whom the end of the ages has come. ¹²Therefore let any one who thinks that he stands take heed lest he fall. ¹³No temptation has overtaken you that is not common to man. God is faithful, and he will not let you be tempted beyond your strength, but with the temptation will also provide the way of escape, that you may be able to endure it.*

In 1 Corinthians 10:1-13 Paul increases the pressure on his hearers. In the previous chapter he appealed to the Law as the expression of God's authoritative will, and gave himself, their senior and chief steward, as the example for the Corinthians to heed and to follow. Here he pursues the matter further by appealing to the same Law (the five Books of Moses) to remind them that God's will is not suggestive, but imperative: those who do not abide by it are punished. The mistake of the Corinthians is classic—taking God's graciousness for granted[1]—and can be witnessed throughout the history of Judaism and Christianity. This attitude is reflected in both the beginning of God's story with man and its final chapter.

The story consigned in the Book of Exodus, which described the exodus from Egypt, revolved around "the mountain of God (the divine mountain)" in the wilderness where God appeared to Moses (Ex 3:1) and commissioned him thus: "But I will be with you; and this shall be the sign for you, that I have sent you: *when*

---

[1] See Rom 1-2 and 9-11 and my comments on those chapters in *C-Rom*.

you have brought forth the people out of Egypt, you shall serve God upon this mountain." (v.12) In other words, the reason behind God's intervention is *first* to bring Israel to that mountain *in order to* grant them his Law (Ex 19-Lev 27) that would secure safety, blessings, and long life in the land of the promise (Lev 26 and Deut 28). An often overlooked feature in the giving of the Law is that it is the expression of God's gracefulness toward Israel.

Israel perceived the exodus as the seal of God's beneficence and, consequently, equated having been taken out of Egypt with reaching the unshakable safety of the land of the promise. Yet the scriptural story of God's intervention on behalf of the scriptural Israel, which began with the exodus out of the land of bondage, ends in 2 Kings 25 with the exile of the same Israel into another land of bondage, the reason being that Israel did not heed God's commands while enjoying the land of the promise. Even the first generation of that same Israel, due to its disobedience, perished in the wilderness without ever reaching that land. Thus God's law becomes effective the moment it is promulgated. It is not the intention of the Law to bring about curses and death; it is disobedience to the law that forces the hand of the just judge into implementing the punishment.

In this passage Paul reminds the allegedly "spiritual" Corinthians that baptism and sharing in the Lord's table do not guarantee divine blessing and life eternal. In order to make his case, he appeals to the scriptural story of Israel in the wilderness. This is a classic text which corroborates my contention that the New Testament Apostle did not preach anything new content wise in comparison with the Old Testament Prophet; rather the Apostle shared with the nations the teaching that the Prophet imparted to Israel. Through Paul's preaching, the Corinthians have become "the church (congregation) of God."[2] The scriptural story addresses them inasmuch as they have become the children of the scriptural "fathers": "I want you to know, brethren, that *our fathers* were all under the cloud, and all passed through the sea." (1 Cor 10:1) Consequently, the story of the scriptural fathers who perished in the wilderness becomes "warnings for us, not to desire evil as they did" (v.6), just as the same story functioned as "a warning for the children of Israel."

When one hears vv.1-6 from this perspective, one does not fall into the trap of Gnosticism which led to the understanding of v.4b as though it were speaking of a pre-existent Christ. Literature is always to be heard in context and, in this case, the point Paul is making does not concern the "person" of Christ, let alone a discussion of such topic. The scriptural story of the wilderness functions as "instruction" as well as a "warning" to the Corinthians upon whom—*through the Christ preached by Paul*—the "end of the ages has come" (v.11), meaning that the "warning" of that story is more urgent for the Corinthians than it was for Israel!

In order to address the Corinthian situation more appropriately Paul "casts" the scriptural story of the wilderness in terms that apply directly to their situation. This device is evident in that he writes that "all were *baptized* into Moses in the cloud and in the sea" (v.2). Since the verb "baptize" is not found in conjunction with the exodus story in the Old Testament,[3] Paul's

---

[2] See my comments on 1 Cor 1:2.
[3] If the original in 1 Cor 10:2 is *ebaptisanto* (the aorist middle voice, meaning "baptized themselves, entered the waters, immersed themselves in the waters") instead of *ebaptisthēsan* (the aorist passive voice, meaning "were baptized, were immersed into the waters") as witnessed by many manuscripts, then Paul seems to have been aware of the fact that the middle voice occurs in three (2 Kg 5:14; Jdt 12:7; Sir 34:25) of the four Old Testament instances, the last one being in the active form describing

aim must have been to draw his hearers' attention to the parallelism between the situation of the scriptural Israel and that of the Corinthians.[4] This being the case, one should read vv.3-4, which deal with eating and drinking, along the same lines. To make the connection more pertinent for his hearers, Paul "casts" the scriptural story in terms that hit home by adding the adjective "supernatural" (*pnevmatikon*; spiritual) before both food and drink. When one takes into consideration that spirit in scripture pertains exclusively to God and his realm, then this adjective is pertinent to the scriptural story where Israel was fed with "manna from heaven" and drank water that, through God's will, gushed out of a rock (Ex 17:6; Num 20:8-11); both were divine gifts, a "grace" (*kharis*). Paul's wording is guided by the fact that "spiritual" is an integral part of his vocabulary throughout the letter starting with 2:4, and thus the Corinthians can readily apply it to their situation. Furthermore, it prepares for 10:14-33 where Paul discusses eating and drinking at temple meals or eating meat purchased at the market and, beyond that, for the passage that specifically concerns the Eucharistic table fellowship (11:17-34). The explanatory phrase "For they drank from the supernatural (*pnevmatikon*; spiritual) Rock which followed them, and the Rock was Christ" (10:4b) is not meant to refer to the (pre-existing) "person" of Christ, as was

---

"lawlessness immersing (encompassing) me" (Is 21:4) and thus not in conjunction with water. He thus would have used it on purpose. However, *ebaptisthēsan* seems to be the *lectio difficilior* (the reading more difficult to explain) and thus the original. Copyists would have intentionally changed it in order to differentiate between the baptism into (*eis*) Moses (1 Cor 10:2) and that into (*eis*) Christ (Rom 6:3; Gal 3:27).

[4] In either case one is baptized into the Law, either of Moses or of Christ (Gal 6:2). Regarding the Old Testament, I explained in my comments on 1 Cor 8 that the crossing of the Red (or Reed) Sea was performed *in order to* bring the people to the mountain of God where he would hand them his law through Moses. Similarly, the baptism into Christ is performed *so that* the baptized follow a new way of life (Rom 6:4, 12-23) according to the Law of the spirit of God (8:2).

misconstrued in subsequent theology, but rather to say that for the Corinthians Christ *functions* in a similar way as the rock *functioned* for Israel in the wilderness: he is the source of their life and the foundation of the "spiritual" temple of which they are a part (3:16). If this is so, then the fact that "with most of them God was not pleased; for they were overthrown in the wilderness" (10:5) *functions* as a "warning" to the believers "not to desire evil as they did" (v.6). The original Greek is clear in that it uses "types" (*typoi*) instead of "warnings." This, in turn, corroborates that the rock is functionally a "type" of Christ. A few verses later, Paul will reiterate, in a clearer fashion, what he wrote in v.6. What happened in the wilderness happened to Israel, not the Corinthians; however, the scriptural story is to function as a lesson for the Corinthians: "Now these things happened to them as a warning (*typikōs*; typologically; as a type), but they were written down for our instruction." (v.11)

As I explained in my comments on chapters 5 and 6, scriptural immorality (harlotry; fornication) is a metaphor for idolatry which consists in going after other deities instead of following the scriptural God and obeying his law. By mentioning idolatry (Do not be idolaters [*eidōlolatrai*] as some of them were; 10:7a) before immorality (We must not indulge in immorality as some of them did; v.8a), Paul is preparing for his argument in vv.14-33 that deals with heathen sacrificial meals and begins with a reference to the "worship of idols" (*eidōlolatrias*; idolatry, v.14). Such is evident in the scriptural quotation he uses to describe the Israelites' actions: "The people sat down to eat and drink and rose up to dance." (v.6b) The parallel quotation (v.7b) from Numbers 26:62 (twenty-three thousand fell in a single day) is intended to overwhelm, if not literally crush, the hearers since the members of a Roman household church would not amount to more than a few hundred at the most. Paul's message is, "If

God did not shy from letting twenty-three thousand be destroyed, take heed not to 'put the Lord[5] to the test'" (10:9a). The utmost seriousness of the matter is evident in that the initial prohibition (Do [you, in the plural] not; v.7) is followed by three parallel exhortations (We must not vv. 8, 9, 10).[6]

Before concluding this passage, Paul iterates in v.11 the importance of the scriptural lesson he pointed out in v.6, by adding that, unlike Israel who lived and died at the beginning of the scriptural story, the Corinthians stand at the tail end of that story: "Now these things happened to them as a warning, but they were written down for our instruction (*nouthesian*), *upon whom the end of the ages has come.*" (v.11) What lies before them is not another hurdle they have to overcome, but God's final judgment. That is why in the verses that follow Paul uses terminology pointing to the resurrection before that judgment, and in so doing, prepares for chapter 15: "Therefore let any one who thinks that he stands (*hestanai*) take heed lest he fall." (10:12) Indeed, the perfect infinitive *hestanai* is from the indicative *histēmi* which is used to describe Jesus' standing (*anestē*;[7] 1 Thess 4:14) after having been raised (*egēgertai*; 1 Cor 15:4, 12, 13, 14, 16, 17, 20) by God who raised (*ēgeiren*; v.15) him.[8] It is evident then that Paul is speaking of the Corinthians' fall after the final resurrection, that is to say, of their ultimate

---

[5] Some manuscripts have "Christ" instead of "Lord."
[6] The Greek *gongyzete* (murmur) in v.10 has "you (plural)" instead of "we" as the subject in the majority of the manuscripts.
[7] *anestē* (stood up; rose) is a construct from the verb *estē* (from *histēmi*) preceded by the preposition *ana* (upward)
[8] Notice also how Paul deftly kept the link with the original scriptural "type" by choosing a scriptural quotation that uses the same verb "rose up" to describe Israel's behavior in the wilderness: "The people *sat down* to eat and drink and rose up (*anestēsan*) to dance." (10:7)

condemnation to eternal death.⁹ However, in order to avoid leading them to utter despair, Paul ends his instruction on a positive note: "No temptation has overtaken you that is not common to man. God is faithful, and he will not let you be tempted beyond your strength, but with the temptation will also provide the way of escape, that you may be able to endure it." (10:13) After having threatened them with the rod—the "divine" rod this time—he ends, as a true father would, with a touch of gentleness—again "divine"—this time around! This parallelism with 4:14-21 is actually intended in that the Greek root *nouthe*— connoting instruction (warning admonition) in 10:11 occurs only once more in this letter in 4:14: "I do not write this to make you ashamed, but to admonish (*nouthetō[n]*) you as my beloved children."

Vv. 14-22 ¹⁴Διόπερ, ἀγαπητοί μου, φεύγετε ἀπὸ τῆς εἰδωλολατρίας. ¹⁵ ὡς φρονίμοις λέγω· κρίνατε ὑμεῖς ὅ φημι. ¹⁶ Τὸ ποτήριον τῆς εὐλογίας ὃ εὐλογοῦμεν, οὐχὶ κοινωνία ἐστὶν τοῦ αἵματος τοῦ Χριστοῦ; τὸν ἄρτον ὃν κλῶμεν, οὐχὶ κοινωνία τοῦ σώματος τοῦ Χριστοῦ ἐστιν; ¹⁷ ὅτι εἷς ἄρτος, ἓν σῶμα οἱ πολλοί ἐσμεν, οἱ γὰρ πάντες ἐκ τοῦ ἑνὸς ἄρτου μετέχομεν. ¹⁸ βλέπετε τὸν Ἰσραὴλ κατὰ σάρκα· οὐχ οἱ ἐσθίοντες τὰς θυσίας κοινωνοὶ τοῦ θυσιαστηρίου εἰσίν; ¹⁹ Τί οὖν φημι; ὅτι εἰδωλόθυτόν τί ἐστιν ἢ ὅτι εἴδωλόν τί ἐστιν; ²⁰ ἀλλ' ὅτι ἃ θύουσιν, δαιμονίοις καὶ οὐ θεῷ [θύουσιν]· οὐ θέλω δὲ ὑμᾶς κοινωνοὺς τῶν δαιμονίων γίνεσθαι. ²¹ οὐ δύνασθε ποτήριον κυρίου πίνειν καὶ ποτήριον δαιμονίων, οὐ δύνασθε τραπέζης κυρίου μετέχειν καὶ τραπέζης δαιμονίων. ²² ἢ παραζηλοῦμεν τὸν κύριον; μὴ ἰσχυρότεροι αὐτοῦ ἐσμεν;

¹⁴Therefore, my beloved, shun the worship of idols. ¹⁵I speak as to sensible men; judge for yourselves what I say. ¹⁶The cup of

---

⁹ The importance of this matter is further evident in that, before chapter 15, Paul will revisit it in conjunction with his discussion of the Corinthians' attitude during the Eucharistic table fellowship (11:17-34).

blessing which we bless, is it not a participation in the blood of Christ? The bread which we break, is it not a participation in the body of Christ? [17]Because there is one bread, we who are many are one body, for we all partake of the one bread. [18]Consider the people of Israel; are not those who eat the sacrifices partners in the altar? [19]What do I imply then? That food offered to idols is anything, or that an idol is anything? [20]No, I imply that what pagans sacrifice they offer to demons and not to God. I do not want you to be partners with demons. [21]You cannot drink the cup of the Lord and the cup of demons. You cannot partake of the table of the Lord and the table of demons. [22]Shall we provoke the Lord to jealousy? Are we stronger than he?

After his introductory remarks Paul goes directly to the problem at hand: heathen sacrificial meals. He flatly commands the Corinthians to shun (*phevgete,* flee from) idolatry (10:14) and proceeds to explain that, in practice, they should not participate in sacrificial meals at the temples of the different deities. Before proceeding, however, he cajoles his hearers to get their undivided attention. First, he appeals to them as "sensible men" (*phronimois*; v.15a). This adjective occurs only once more in this letter, in a context where Paul is using irony to shame them: "We are fools for Christ's sake, but you are wise (*phronimoi*) in Christ. We are weak, but you are strong. You are held in honor, but we in disrepute." (4:10) This is an evident connection to his earlier chiding and is meant to challenge them to make the effort not to be shamed again. The intention of Paul's remark is corroborated in 10:15b where he invites them to use their common sense to "judge" (*krinate*) for themselves the value of what he is saying. Paul used this same verb earlier when he shamed them for bringing their internal matters to Roman courts by reminding them that the least among them should be able to carry out such a task (6:1-11). So, after challenging them to be wise, he proceeds to ask them to act upon such wisdom and practice it. In reality, he is inviting them to follow *his* reasoning and *his* instruction which he will convey to them in the following verses.

Paul begins with the "sacrificial" meals he introduced at the Eucharistic gatherings around the Lord's instruction. The connotation of sacrifice is reflected in the reference to blood together with body, both in this instance (10:16) and later in 11:23-26. The inclusion of blood (shed) is to underscore that the body was actually "broken" (10:16; 11:24). One is to take care not to divide the two as though they were referring to two separate "actions." It is the breaking of the body that triggers the shedding of the blood. This is similar to drinking wine *together with* eating *at the one occasion*. Notice how the mention of blessing with the one item (wine) and the breaking with the other (bread) (10:16) are actions that take place in conjunction with the *one* meal. So Paul is not comparing sacrifice to sacrifice—since the believers' table fellowship does not entail an actual sacrifice—rather he is contrasting two kinds of table fellowship. Christ's sacrifice has already taken place (5:7) once and for all (Rom 6:3-4). At the Eucharistic table fellowship, the believers "recollect" the sacrifice of their teacher while they hear his teaching time and again (1 Cor 11:23-26). Consequently, "participation" (RSV) is a poor translation of the Greek *koinōnia* which means fellowship with others around the one leader.[10] Actually participation applies more appropriately to heathen sacrificial meals when slaughtered meat is the main ingredient. The Pauline table fellowship revolves around bread and wine. It is through partaking of (*metekhomen*; participating in) the one

---

[10] See earlier my comments on 1 Cor 1:7.

bread that we become part of the one table and the one teaching, that is to say, we become members of the one "body" (10:17; see 6:15), the one community around Christ.

So, wherein does the problem lie? It lies in the common understanding of ritual sacrifices, including those found in the Old Testament: "Consider Israel according to the flesh (*Israēl kata sarka*);[11] are not those who eat the sacrifices (*thysias*) partners (*koinōnoi*; participants) in the (sacrificial) altar (*thysiastēriou*)?" (10:18) Paul is drawing the attention of his hearers, especially those who are "strong" (1 Cor 8), to the fact that there are Jews among them whose mentality is still according to the flesh and thus view all sacrifices from the perspective that those who offer to the deity become partners (*koinōnoi*) in the fellowship of that deity (10:18). Paul is saying that partaking of the sacrifices offered to "demons" (fake deities) who are not God (v.20a) makes the participants "partners" (*koinōnous*) of demons (v.20b). The believers are not allowed to be partakers of two tables and two cups especially when one of those tables and one of those cups is the Lord's (v.21). No one is stronger than God, as Paul reminded them earlier when he wrote "the weakness of God is stronger than men" (1:25b); thus God should not be provoked to jealousy, as he forewarned in no uncertain terms:

> They have stirred me to jealousy with what is no god; they have provoked me with their idols. So I will stir them to jealousy with those who are no people; I will provoke them with a foolish nation. For a fire is kindled by my anger, and it burns to the depths of Sheol, devours the earth and its increase, and sets on fire the foundations of the mountains. And I will heap evils upon them; I will spend my arrows upon them; they shall be wasted

---

[11] By translating this phrase as "the people of Israel" RSV is missing Paul's point as will be reflected in my comments.

with hunger, and devoured with burning heat and poisonous pestilence; and I will send the teeth of beasts against them, with venom of crawling things of the dust. In the open the sword shall bereave, and in the chambers shall be terror, destroying both young man and virgin, the sucking child with the man of gray hairs. (Deut 32:21-25)

Such is not an idle threat when it comes from the same God who earlier in Numbers (1) in one day punished twenty-three thousand with death (Num 26:62; see 1 Cor 10:8), (2) "sent fiery serpents among the people, and they bit the people, so that many people of Israel died" (Num 21:6; see 1 Cor 10:9) and (3) allowed some fourteen thousand seven hundred grumblers to die by the plague (Num 16:41-49; see 1 Cor 10:10). In this manner, Paul is reminding the "strong" among his hearers to heed God who is "stronger" than they, and they should be very apprehensive about sharing in pagan sacrificial meals.

Vv. 23-33 ²³ Πάντα ἔξεστιν ἀλλ' οὐ πάντα συμφέρει· πάντα ἔξεστιν ἀλλ' οὐ πάντα οἰκοδομεῖ. ²⁴μηδεὶς τὸ ἑαυτοῦ ζητείτω ἀλλὰ τὸ τοῦ ἑτέρου. ²⁵ Πᾶν τὸ ἐν μακέλλῳ πωλούμενον ἐσθίετε μηδὲν ἀνακρίνοντες διὰ τὴν συνείδησιν· ²⁶ τοῦ κυρίου γὰρ ἡ γῆ καὶ τὸ πλήρωμα αὐτῆς. ²⁷ εἴ τις καλεῖ ὑμᾶς τῶν ἀπίστων καὶ θέλετε πορεύεσθαι, πᾶν τὸ παρατιθέμενον ὑμῖν ἐσθίετε μηδὲν ἀνακρίνοντες διὰ τὴν συνείδησιν. ²⁸ ἐὰν δέ τις ὑμῖν εἴπῃ· τοῦτο ἱερόθυτόν ἐστιν, μὴ ἐσθίετε δι' ἐκεῖνον τὸν μηνύσαντα καὶ τὴν συνείδησιν· ²⁹συνείδησιν δὲ λέγω οὐχὶ τὴν ἑαυτοῦ ἀλλὰ τὴν τοῦ ἑτέρου. ἱνατί γὰρ ἡ ἐλευθερία μου κρίνεται ὑπὸ ἄλλης συνειδήσεως; ³⁰ εἰ ἐγὼ χάριτι μετέχω, τί βλασφημοῦμαι ὑπὲρ οὗ ἐγὼ εὐχαριστῶ; ³¹ Εἴτε οὖν ἐσθίετε εἴτε πίνετε εἴτε τι ποιεῖτε, πάντα εἰς δόξαν θεοῦ ποιεῖτε. ³²ἀπρόσκοποι καὶ Ἰουδαίοις γίνεσθε καὶ Ἕλλησιν καὶ τῇ ἐκκλησίᾳ τοῦ θεοῦ, ³³ καθὼς κἀγὼ πάντα πᾶσιν ἀρέσκω μὴ ζητῶν τὸ ἐμαυτοῦ σύμφορον ἀλλὰ τὸ τῶν πολλῶν, ἵνα σωθῶσιν.

Chapter 10   185

V. 11:1 μιμηταί μου γίνεσθε καθὼς κἀγὼ Χριστοῦ.

²³"All things are lawful," but not all things are helpful. "All things are lawful," but not all things build up. ²⁴ Let no one seek his own good, but the good of his neighbor. ²⁵Eat whatever is sold in the meat market without raising any question on the ground of conscience. ²⁶For "the earth is the Lord's, and everything in it." ²⁷If one of the unbelievers invites you to dinner and you are disposed to go, eat whatever is set before you without raising any question on the ground of conscience. ²⁸(But if some one says to you, "This has been offered in sacrifice," then out of consideration for the man who informed you, and for conscience' sake— ²⁹I mean his conscience, not yours—do not eat it.) For why should my liberty be determined by another man's scruples? ³⁰If I partake with thankfulness, why am I denounced because of that for which I give thanks? ³¹So, whether you eat or drink, or whatever you do, do all to the glory of God. ³²Give no offense to Jews or to Greeks or to the church of God, ³³just as I try to please all men in everything I do, not seeking my own advantage, but that of many, that they may be saved.

11:1 Be imitators of me, as I am of Christ.

At this point, Paul reiterates his statement of 6:12a, namely, that the freedom granted by God through Christ is to be checked against what is beneficial for the common good rather than for the empowered individual. This time, however, he clearly explains that the common good is the building up of the community (10:23), which he will explicate in chapter 14. Therefore, one is not to look for his own good but for the good of the other; put otherwise, one is to put the needs of the neighbor over one's own needs (10:24). With this point in mind Paul proceeds to show how the dilemma of eating or not eating sacrificial meat can be readily solved. Anything purchased in the (meat) market (*makellō*) should be eaten without raising questions of conscience as to whether the purchased meat was sacrificial or not (v.25); the reason is that, scripturally, "the earth is the Lord's, and everything in it" (v.26), a statement found repeatedly in the Book of Psalms (24:1; 50:12; 89:11). Similarly, when a believer is invited to eat meat, he should do so in order not to offend the non-believer host (1 Cor 10:27). However, if one of the brethren points out that the meat being consumed is sacrificial, then the brother who is eating it should cease from doing so in order not to offend the conscience of that weaker brother (vv.28-29a). One might object, "Why should my liberty be determined by another man's scruples? Why would I be denounced if I partake with thankfulness?" (vv.29b-30). Such is a very strong objection since it uses the terminology of the Eucharistic (thanksgiving) table fellowship: if one thanks "the Lord of all the earth and everything in it," why would eating sacrificial meat be a wrong thing to do? Paul retorts by referring to the same God the objector is appealing to: not only eating and drinking, but *everything the believer does* is to be done "to the glory of God" (v.31), since he is the God of all the earth and will be judging all its inhabitants. Those who will have been introduced to his law will be judged according to whether or not they will have implemented it (Rom 2:12-13). That law is subsumed in the love for the weaker neighbor (13:8-10; Gal 5:13-15) and the lack of such love scandalizes that neighbor and makes him stumble. This is precisely why Paul is requesting that his hearers be *aproskopoi* (giving no offense; not scandalizing; not making someone else stumble) "to Jews or to Greeks or to the church of God," that is to say, *to anyone at all* (1 Cor 10:32). An overview of the other two occurrences of *aproskop—* in the New Testament will corroborate this.

The only other instance of *aproskopoi* is in Philippians:

And it is my prayer that *your love* may abound more and more, with knowledge and all discernment, so that you may approve what is excellent, and may be pure and *blameless* (*aproskopoi*) for *the day of Christ*, filled with the fruits of righteousness which come through Jesus Christ, *to the glory and praise of God*. (1:9-11)[12]

The parallelism is inescapable in that *aproskopoi* occurs in conjunction with "the glory of God." Yet in Philippians, the other two factors are love for others and judgment day. The other instance of *aproskop—* is found in Acts 24:16 where Paul speaks of his behavior, which corresponds fully to what he is doing also here in 1 Corinthians, that is, giving himself as the example to be followed in matter of putting the needs of others over one's own needs (10:33). Actually in Acts 24:16, which is a copy of 1 Corinthians 10:32, the adjective *aproskopon* (without making the other stumble) qualifies the noun "conscience": "So I always take pains to have a clear (*aproskopon*) conscience *toward God and toward men in everything* (*dia pantos*; in every way)."[13] It is also worthwhile to add here 2 Corinthians 6:3 where we find the single instance of the noun *proskopē* (stumbling block; obstacle) in the New Testament. Paul opens the long litany of his efforts for the sake of others (6:4b-10) with the statement: "We put *no* (*mēdemian*; no kind of) obstacle (*proskopēn*) *in any one's way* (*mēdeni*; in any way), so that no fault may be found with our ministry, but as servants of God we commend ourselves *in every way* (*en panti*; in everything)…" (vv.3-4a)

In the previous chapter (1 Cor 9:19-23) Paul gave himself as the archetype in matter of being "non offensive" toward all kinds

---

[12] See my comments on these verses in *C-Phil* 77-83.
[13] RSV omits translating the last phrase *dia pantos* (in everything)."

of human beings. The connection between 9:19-23 and 10:23-33 is intentional as is evident through the final "that they may be saved" at the end of 10:33 and "that I might by all means save some" (9:22). Paul concludes by inviting his hearers to go beyond him and imitate Christ himself (11:1). Two points are to be made regarding such a request. I explained in my commentary on Philippians that Paul's strategy was first to present himself as a "slave" (1:1) and then to up the ante by saying that such ought not surprise them since Christ himself acted as a "slave" (2:5-11);[14] in so doing he was asking the Philippians to "imitate him as he imitates Christ." Since neither the Philippians nor the Corinthians have ever met Christ, Paul's example is actually their only example. In other words, Christ is an example only through Paul's teaching. This is clear from what Paul wrote earlier in the letter: "I urge you, then, *be imitators of me*. Therefore I sent to you Timothy, my beloved and faithful child in the Lord, to remind you of *my ways in Christ, as I teach them* everywhere in every church." (1 Cor 4:16-17) So, ultimately, it is Paul's *hearers*, and not *viewers*, that are to follow his example—and that of Christ—as he *teaches* it. Thus just as Christ is taught through hearing (Eph 4:20-21) to be the primary example of *behavior* to follow (vv.17-19, 22-24), so is Paul himself. In Philippians he wrote: "Finally, brethren, whatever is true, whatever is honorable, whatever is just, whatever is pure, whatever is lovely, whatever is gracious, if there is any excellence, if there is anything worthy of praise, think about these things. What you have learned and received and heard and seen in me, do; and the God of peace will be with you." (4:8-9) Notice how not only the priority is given to the hearing over the seeing, but also the latter is mentioned after Paul used three verbs that reflect the aural

---

[14] See *C-Phil* 106-33.

factor in communicating his example of *behavior*. The value of this Pauline teaching lies in that his letters will still be valid after his demise. This precludes any cop out by subsequent generations who might assert that they are less lucky than those who lived in Paul's times and *eye witnessed* his behavior. No *hearer* of Paul's letters at any time and in any place is farther from him than the original *hearers*. This is witnessed to by those Roman addressees who never met Paul before having *heard* his letter addressed to them. Just as it is with the scriptural God and his Christ, Paul is seen *with the ear,* not the eye! Only idols made by human hands are seen with the eye.

Chapter 11

Vv. 2-16 ² Ἐπαινῶ δὲ ὑμᾶς ὅτι πάντα μου μέμνησθε καί, καθὼς παρέδωκα ὑμῖν, τὰς παραδόσεις κατέχετε. ³ Θέλω δὲ ὑμᾶς εἰδέναι ὅτι παντὸς ἀνδρὸς ἡ κεφαλὴ ὁ Χριστός ἐστιν, κεφαλὴ δὲ γυναικὸς ὁ ἀνήρ, κεφαλὴ δὲ τοῦ Χριστοῦ ὁ θεός. ⁴ πᾶς ἀνὴρ προσευχόμενος ἢ προφητεύων κατὰ κεφαλῆς ἔχων καταισχύνει τὴν κεφαλὴν αὐτοῦ. ⁵ πᾶσα δὲ γυνὴ προσευχομένη ἢ προφητεύουσα ἀκατακαλύπτῳ τῇ κεφαλῇ καταισχύνει τὴν κεφαλὴν αὑτῆς· ἓν γάρ ἐστιν καὶ τὸ αὐτὸ τῇ ἐξυρημένῃ. ⁶ εἰ γὰρ οὐ κατακαλύπτεται γυνή, καὶ κειράσθω· εἰ δὲ αἰσχρὸν γυναικὶ τὸ κείρασθαι ἢ ξυρᾶσθαι, κατακαλυπτέσθω. ⁷ Ἀνὴρ μὲν γὰρ οὐκ ὀφείλει κατακαλύπτεσθαι τὴν κεφαλὴν εἰκὼν καὶ δόξα θεοῦ ὑπάρχων· ἡ γυνὴ δὲ δόξα ἀνδρός ἐστιν. ⁸ οὐ γάρ ἐστιν ἀνὴρ ἐκ γυναικὸς ἀλλὰ γυνὴ ἐξ ἀνδρός· ⁹ καὶ γὰρ οὐκ ἐκτίσθη ἀνὴρ διὰ τὴν γυναῖκα ἀλλὰ γυνὴ διὰ τὸν ἄνδρα. ¹⁰ διὰ τοῦτο ὀφείλει ἡ γυνὴ ἐξουσίαν ἔχειν ἐπὶ τῆς κεφαλῆς διὰ τοὺς ἀγγέλους. ¹¹πλὴν οὔτε γυνὴ χωρὶς ἀνδρὸς οὔτε ἀνὴρ χωρὶς γυναικὸς ἐν κυρίῳ· ¹² ὥσπερ γὰρ ἡ γυνὴ ἐκ τοῦ ἀνδρός, οὕτως καὶ ὁ ἀνὴρ διὰ τῆς γυναικός· τὰ δὲ πάντα ἐκ τοῦ θεοῦ. ¹³ Ἐν ὑμῖν αὐτοῖς κρίνατε· πρέπον ἐστὶν γυναῖκα ἀκατακάλυπτον τῷ θεῷ προσεύχεσθαι; ¹⁴ οὐδὲ ἡ φύσις αὐτὴ διδάσκει ὑμᾶς ὅτι ἀνὴρ μὲν ἐὰν κομᾷ ἀτιμία αὐτῷ ἐστιν, ¹⁵ γυνὴ δὲ ἐὰν κομᾷ δόξα αὐτῇ ἐστιν; ὅτι ἡ κόμη ἀντὶ περιβολαίου δέδοται [αὐτῇ]. ¹⁶ Εἰ δέ τις δοκεῖ φιλόνεικος εἶναι, ἡμεῖς τοιαύτην συνήθειαν οὐκ ἔχομεν οὐδὲ αἱ ἐκκλησίαι τοῦ θεοῦ.

²I commend you because you remember me in everything and maintain the traditions even as I have delivered them to you. ³But I want you to understand that the head of every man is Christ, the head of a woman is her husband, and the head of Christ is God. ⁴Any man who prays or prophesies with his head covered dishonors his head, ⁵but any woman who prays or prophesies with her head unveiled dishonors her head—it is the

same as if her head were shaven. ⁶*For if a woman will not veil herself, then she should cut off her hair; but if it is disgraceful for a woman to be shorn or shaven, let her wear a veil. ⁷For a man ought not to cover his head, since he is the image and glory of God; but woman is the glory of man. ⁸(For man was not made from woman, but woman from man. ⁹Neither was man created for woman, but woman for man.) ¹⁰That is why a woman ought to have a veil on her head, because of the angels. ¹¹(Nevertheless, in the Lord woman is not independent of man nor man of woman; ¹²for as woman was made from man, so man is now born of woman. And all things are from God.) ¹³Judge for yourselves; is it proper for a woman to pray to God with her head uncovered? ¹⁴Does not nature itself teach you that for a man to wear long hair is degrading to him, ¹⁵but if a woman has long hair, it is her pride? For her hair is given to her for a covering. ¹⁶If any one is disposed to be contentious, we recognize no other practice, nor do the churches of God.*

In 1 Corinthians 11:2 Paul commends his hearers "because *you remember me in everything and maintain the traditions even as I have delivered them to you.*" To remember Paul is tantamount to remembering him *as apostle* (9:1-2). For the Corinthians, Paul's person is his teaching which they are to preserve in his presence among them and more so in his absence (Phil 2:12). Since the remainder of this letter consists of novel instructions regarding their house church gatherings, not all of which are commendations (see, e.g., 1 Cor 11:17-34), 11:2 functions as a *captatio benevolentiae* for them to heed the instructions he is about to give them. The novelty of the instructions is evident in the phraseology with which he introduces them: "I want you to understand (*eidenai;* know)" (11:3); "I do not want you to be uninformed (*agnoein;* be ignorant)" (12:1); "I want you to understand (*gnōrizō*)" (v.3); "And I will show you a still more excellent way" (v.31); "I want you to understand (*gnōrizō*)"[1] (15:1); "I tell you this ... Lo! I tell you a mystery" (vv.50-51); "Now concerning the contribution for the saints: as I directed the churches of Galatia, so you also are to do." (16:1)

The topic of this passage is the head cover or head veil of the praying or prophesying person. Since prayer and prophecy are mentioned together in both instances (11:4 and 5) one is to understand that Paul is talking about such during church gatherings. Indeed, even if prayer can be done individually, the setting of prophecy is always church gatherings as will be made clear in chapter 14: "He who prophesies is greater than he who speaks in tongues, unless some one interprets, so that the church may be edified." (v.5) Thus the prayer intended here is along the lines of what we hear later in that same chapter: "When you come together, each one has a hymn, a lesson, a revelation, a tongue, or an interpretation. Let all things be done for edification." (v.26) The handicap of traditional exegesis is its assumption that the passage is dealing with the general issue of a woman's head covering. Looking closely at our passage (11:2-16) one can notice two differences between the hierarchy in v.3 and that in vv.7-9. The latter draws on Genesis 1-2 and thus is the scriptural hierarchy, God-man-woman; furthermore it compares man with God using the Genesis terminology of "image" (v.7). The hierarchy of v. 3 adds "Christ" and uses the term "head," neither of which is found in Genesis 1-2. Furthermore, the addition of "Christ" is clearly underscored since, sequentially speaking, "the head of every man is Christ" should have been between "the head of a woman is her husband (the man)" and "the head of Christ is God." When one adds the fact that the

---

[1] RSV's "Now I would remind you" does not reflect the original which RSV translated as "I want you to understand" in 12:3.

statement in 1 Corinthians 11:3 is introduced with the apostolic "I want you to understand (*eidenai*; know)," then Paul's central teaching in this passage is that "the head of every man is Christ." The question then to be asked is, "How could this be the teaching in a passage that deals with a woman's head covering, especially when the mention of Christ completely disappears after its unexpected use in v.3?"

Paul's systematic and ultimate reference is the scripture of the Old Testament. Since the scriptural allusions in 11:2-16 are taken from Genesis 1-4, one ought to begin with what those chapters say of God, man, woman. Without being verbatim quotations, three of the allusions are express references, namely, that man is the image (*eikōn*) of God (1 Cor 11:7; see Gen 1:26-27); that woman was (made) for man (1 Cor 11:9; see Gen 2:18-20); that woman was created (*ektisthē*; built) from man (1 Cor 11:8; see Gen 2:21-23). When Genesis 1 and 2 are taken together there is clearly a three step hierarchy: God, man, woman.

In using "glory" (*doxa*) instead of "likeness" (*homoiōsis*; Gen 1:26) as a parallel to "image" in 1 Corinthians 11:7, Paul betrays both his precise knowledge of scriptural terminology and his mastery in using that terminology to bring home his point. The original meaning of the Hebrew *kabod* (glory) is the statue[2] of the deity and thus its image or likeness whereby one recognizes the deity, be it Baal or Marduk, Bel or Nebo. Thus "glory," as a reflection of the original, is lesser than that original which would be in a primary position to or (at the) "head" of its reflection. This stands to reason since a given deity is the blueprint for

---

[2] The Hebrew *kabod* actually means "weightiness and, thus, importance," which reality is reflected in the heavy and majestic statues of the deity.

statues that are built in its image. So man is a "lesser" rendition of God according to Genesis 1:26-27. In turn, woman is *built* from (*ek*; out of) man (2:22)[3] and thus is his "glory" (1 Cor 11:7). Still, in tune with the rest of the story, Paul writes that, although woman is *from* man (v.12a), man is *through* (*dia*) woman (v.12): Eve is "the *mother* of all living (human) beings" (Gen 3:20) and conceived the first "sons of man (Adam)" (human beings), Cain and Abel (4:1-2). As "mother" she is in a primary position to the extent that every "man" is to "honor (*kibbed*)[4] his father *and mother*" (Ex 20:12; Deut 5:16). Still, what is beyond and more important than woman being from man and man through woman, is that "both[5] are *from* God" (1 Cor 11:12c) who formed Adam (Gen 2:7) *and* built Eve (v.22). From that perspective man and woman are on the same footing. However, in the scriptural story, man's contravention of God's command resulted in the following divine decision: "To the woman he [the Lord God] said, 'I will greatly multiply your pain in childbearing; in pain you shall bring forth children, yet your desire shall be for your husband, and he shall rule over you.'" (3:16)

As we saw in 1 Corinthians 7, through the intermediacy of God's Christ, Paul equalized the status of woman with that of man just as he did the status of the slave with that of the free person. However, as we discover in Colossians and Philemon, Paul does not implement this equalization through a forceful

---

[3] RSV translates the original Hebrew "built" into "made." See my comments on that verse in *C-Gen*.
[4] From the same root as *kabod*, and thus its literal meaning is "give glory, weightiness, importance to."
[5] RSV translates *ta panta* as "all things," which does not make much sense in this context. See my defense of *ta panta* as meaning "both of whom (the mentioned immediately before)" in *Gal* 157-9.

revolution, but rather through persuasion of all parties, especially the patricians.[6] Here also in 1 Corinthians he uses the same approach of persuasion by putting greater pressure on man rather than woman. He does so by introducing Christ between God and man, making the relation between man and God a relative instead of an absolute one. Instead of God being directly the head of man, who is the image and glory of God (11:7), God is the head of man via Christ: "But I want you to understand that the head of every man is Christ, the head of a woman is her husband, and the head of Christ is God." (v.3) In other words, man is "belittled." Why did Paul opt for such a solution instead of "promoting" woman to equality with man as he did in chapter 7? The reason is that the matter in chapter 7 was a marital issue between two individuals. Here in chapter 11 the matter is ecclesial and thus more incendiary. In his Gentile churches Paul actually brought about equality of woman with man at the highest possible level: standing in the community to pray on its behalf to God and to address it with God's exhortation (11:5). In so doing, he introduced a practice that was not the one followed in the synagogues.

Later in chapter 14, we shall hear about a serious ado in the church gatherings linked to the functions of prophecy and speaking in tongues. Paul could not afford such mayhem because it would give reason for his opponents in Jerusalem to criticize his Gentile mission and curtail it. That is why he had to intervene and not allow the women prophets in his congregations to take the opportunity to be ostentatious when their counterparts, the Jewish women, were not even allowed to speak publicly in the synagogues. To do so, he stresses the scriptural hierarchy God-man-woman while demeaning the man

---

[6] See Col 4:1 and Philem and my comments thereon in *C-Col* 90-1 and 109-27.

to a level below the original by inserting Christ between him and God. Thus he reminds everyone that, in the church of God, the only one who represents God *directly* is neither the man nor the woman, but solely Christ. It is through him, the sole high priest, that the assignee for the day, whether man or woman, can function as "speaker" in the congregation. Therefore, a woman in such a position ought not to behave as though she is freed by the gospel to do as she pleases, but rather she is to please her new "lord," the Messiah of Israel. As a prophetess she may not use the freedom granted by God through Christ "as an opportunity for the flesh" (Gal 5:13b) to "edify oneself rather than the church" (1 Cor 14:4) and not to "be servants of one another" (Gal 5:13c).

In order to solve what has proven to be a *crux interpretum* as to the basis for Paul's ruling, one ought to begin with 1 Corinthians 11:14-15, which is the main point of reference for his injunction. Indeed, after a somewhat lengthy scriptural discussion, Paul seems to go on a tangent in appealing to "nature" (v.14). He then includes this unexpected argument in the overall discussion by using the term "glory" (*doxa*; v.15a). However, the appeal to "nature" immediately precedes his authoritative conclusion with which he shuts out any further debate of the matter: "If any one is disposed to be contentious, *we recognize no other practice, nor do the churches of God.*" (v.16)

Hairdo and hairdressing has been an age long part of the feminine appearance and meant to reflect a "glorious" (*doxa*) look. Men, by comparison, do not show off their hair, at least in the Greco-Roman setting. It would be "degrading" (*atimia*; dishonor, disgrace, shame) for them to worry about their hairdo and hair gear (v.14). As for a woman, her shame would be to have her hair cut short or shaven, with which shame Paul threatens a woman who prophesies without her hair covered (vv.5-6).

By using the term "glory" (*doxa*) Paul is pointing out that woman should not draw attention to her "glorious look" since she is the "glory" of her husband who, in turn, is the "glory" of God. To the contrary, in her function as prophetess in the church of God, she is to draw attention to God and his teaching. The Old Testament prophets have taught time and again that glory befits God exclusively and that anyone or anything that would appear "glorious" and haughty" shall be brought down.[7] This understanding is corroborated by the use of "covering" (*peribolaiou*; v.15b) as parallel to "glory." The noun *peribolaion* occurs only once more in the New Testament in Hebrews 1:12 which is actually a quotation from Ps 102(LXX 103):27. So the sole New Testament original instance of *peribolaion* occurs in 1 Corinthians 11:15b. Thus, the basis of its parallelism with "glory" is to be sought in its use in the Septuagint. There, except for Exodus 22:26 and Deuteronomy 22:12, where it refers to a human being's garment or cloak, all its other occurrences speak either of ornate garments of powerful or wealthy people (Judg 8:26; Is 59:17; Jer 15:12;[8] Ezek 16:13; 27:7) or in reference to cosmic entities as the deep (Ps 103[LXX 104]:6; Job 26:6) or the heavens (Is 50:3).

Throughout this passage in 1 Corinthians, Paul's aim is to control the potential arrogance of both man and woman. He takes care of man by inserting Christ between him and God. Concerning the woman he insists on keeping the order of the classical Roman household, as he does elsewhere (Eph 5:22-23;

---

[7] See especially Isaiah and Ezekiel.
[8] The original reads *ei gnōthēsetai sidiros kai peribolaion khalkoun*.

Col 3:18). Still, since there is only one Lord, the man does not lord it over the woman; indeed, Paul prefaces his "Wives, be subject (sub-ordained) to your husbands, as to the Lord" (Eph 5:22) with "Be subject (sub-ordained) *to one another* out of reverence for Christ" (v.21). Conversely, in Colossians, he concludes his house rules with the following statement addressed to the men: "Masters (*Hoi kyrioi*; Lords), treat your slaves justly and fairly, knowing that you also have a Master (*kyrion*; Lord) in heaven." (4:1) Here in 1 Corinthians, Paul goes to great length to show that, in the Lord, there is no congenital superiority of man over woman: "Nevertheless, *in the Lord* woman is not independent of man nor man of woman; for as woman was made from man, so man is now born of woman. *And both are from God*." (11:11-12)

So how is one to understand v. 10 ("That is why a woman ought [*opheilei*; is indebted] to have a veil[9] [*exousian*; authority] on her head, because of the angels")? This conclusion (That is why…) follows the related statements in vv.7-9 that begin with "For a man ought (*opheilei*; is indebted) not to cover his head, since he is the image and glory of God; but woman is the glory of man" (v.7) which are backed up scripturally. When it comes to behavior in a household ecclesial setting as is the case here in chapter 11 as well as in Ephesians and Colossians, the Roman traditional order—which is also the scriptural order reflected in Genesis (1 Cor 11:7-9)—is to be honored. Paul is not intending to subvert this; rather he seeks to tame it under obedience to the gospel by subordinating the absolute lordship of the paterfamilias to that of Christ and, through him, to that of the scriptural God.[10] This intention is clear through the mixing of

---

[9] RSV opts for veil (*kalymma*) which is the less supported reading.
[10] See my *C-Phil*, *C-Rom*, and *C-Col* where I repeatedly underscore that point.

"head" and "glory" terminology: Christ is the head of man who is the head of his wife whereas man is the glory of God and woman is man's glory. That God, and not Christ, is the ultimate reference can be seen in the *inclusio* "the head of every man is Christ, the head of a woman is her husband, and the head of Christ is *God* (11:3) … And both (man and woman) are from *God* (v.12)." The vocabulary of "indebtedness" together with "authority" was encountered earlier in 7:4-5 where Paul kept man and woman on a totally equal footing in matters of conjugal duties.

In scripture God is first and foremost as well as essentially the judge (Ps 82) and, as such, he presides over the divine council, among whose members are the angels. Here in 1 Corinthians 11:10 the mention of angels brings to mind the setting of God presiding over his house church (*ekklēsia*), just as in scripture he presided over Israel's congregation (*ekklēsia*) which he punished severely whenever it revolted against his will (10:5). A few verses later Paul will apply the same tenet to his Gentile *ekklēsia* (11:30). Here in v.10 and before appealing to his hearers' common sense in conjunction with the "natural" order (vv.13-15), Paul puts the ultimate pressure on them by appealing to the setting of divine council and thus irrevocable judgment.

Vv. 17-34 ¹⁷ Τοῦτο δὲ παραγγέλλων οὐκ ἐπαινῶ ὅτι οὐκ εἰς τὸ κρεῖσσον ἀλλὰ εἰς τὸ ἧσσον συνέρχεσθε. ¹⁸ πρῶτον μὲν γὰρ συνερχομένων ὑμῶν ἐν ἐκκλησίᾳ ἀκούω σχίσματα ἐν ὑμῖν ὑπάρχειν καὶ μέρος τι πιστεύω. ¹⁹ δεῖ γὰρ καὶ αἱρέσεις ἐν ὑμῖν εἶναι, ἵνα [καὶ] οἱ δόκιμοι φανεροὶ γένωνται ἐν ὑμῖν. ²⁰ Συνερχομένων οὖν ὑμῶν ἐπὶ τὸ αὐτὸ οὐκ ἔστιν κυριακὸν δεῖπνον φαγεῖν· ²¹ ἕκαστος γὰρ τὸ ἴδιον δεῖπνον προλαμβάνει ἐν τῷ φαγεῖν, καὶ ὃς μὲν πεινᾷ ὃς δὲ μεθύει. ²² μὴ γὰρ οἰκίας οὐκ ἔχετε εἰς τὸ ἐσθίειν καὶ πίνειν; ἢ τῆς ἐκκλησίας τοῦ θεοῦ καταφρονεῖτε, καὶ καταισχύνετε τοὺς μὴ

ἔχοντας; τί εἴπω ὑμῖν; ἐπαινέσω ὑμᾶς; ἐν τούτῳ οὐκ ἐπαινῶ.
²³ Ἐγὼ γὰρ παρέλαβον ἀπὸ τοῦ κυρίου, ὃ καὶ παρέδωκα ὑμῖν, ὅτι ὁ κύριος Ἰησοῦς ἐν τῇ νυκτὶ ᾗ παρεδίδετο ἔλαβεν ἄρτον ²⁴ καὶ εὐχαριστήσας ἔκλασεν καὶ εἶπεν· τοῦτό μού ἐστιν τὸ σῶμα τὸ ὑπὲρ ὑμῶν· τοῦτο ποιεῖτε εἰς τὴν ἐμὴν ἀνάμνησιν. ²⁵ ὡσαύτως καὶ τὸ ποτήριον μετὰ τὸ δειπνῆσαι λέγων· τοῦτο τὸ ποτήριον ἡ καινὴ διαθήκη ἐστὶν ἐν τῷ ἐμῷ αἵματι· τοῦτο ποιεῖτε, ὁσάκις ἐὰν πίνητε, εἰς τὴν ἐμὴν ἀνάμνησιν. ²⁶ ὁσάκις γὰρ ἐὰν ἐσθίητε τὸν ἄρτον τοῦτον καὶ τὸ ποτήριον πίνητε, τὸν θάνατον τοῦ κυρίου καταγγέλλετε ἄχρι οὗ ἔλθῃ. ²⁷ Ὥστε ὃς ἂν ἐσθίῃ τὸν ἄρτον ἢ πίνῃ τὸ ποτήριον τοῦ κυρίου ἀναξίως, ἔνοχος ἔσται τοῦ σώματος καὶ τοῦ αἵματος τοῦ κυρίου. ²⁸ δοκιμαζέτω δὲ ἄνθρωπος ἑαυτὸν καὶ οὕτως ἐκ τοῦ ἄρτου ἐσθιέτω καὶ ἐκ τοῦ ποτηρίου πινέτω· ²⁹ ὁ γὰρ ἐσθίων καὶ πίνων κρίμα ἑαυτῷ ἐσθίει καὶ πίνει μὴ διακρίνων τὸ σῶμα. ³⁰ διὰ τοῦτο ἐν ὑμῖν πολλοὶ ἀσθενεῖς καὶ ἄρρωστοι καὶ κοιμῶνται ἱκανοί. ³¹ εἰ δὲ ἑαυτοὺς διεκρίνομεν, οὐκ ἂν ἐκρινόμεθα· ³² κρινόμενοι δὲ ὑπὸ [τοῦ] κυρίου παιδευόμεθα, ἵνα μὴ σὺν τῷ κόσμῳ κατακριθῶμεν. ³³ Ὥστε, ἀδελφοί μου, συνερχόμενοι εἰς τὸ φαγεῖν ἀλλήλους ἐκδέχεσθε. ³⁴ εἴ τις πεινᾷ, ἐν οἴκῳ ἐσθιέτω, ἵνα μὴ εἰς κρίμα συνέρχησθε. τὰ δὲ λοιπὰ ὡς ἂν ἔλθω διατάξομαι.

¹⁷But in the following instructions I do not commend you, because when you come together it is not for the better but for the worse. ¹⁸For, in the first place, when you assemble as a church, I hear that there are divisions among you; and I partly believe it, ¹⁹for there must be factions among you in order that those who are genuine among you may be recognized. ²⁰When you meet together, it is not the Lord's supper that you eat. ²¹For in eating, each one goes ahead with his own meal, and one is hungry and another is drunk. ²²What! Do you not have houses to eat and drink in? Or do you despise the church of God and humiliate those who have nothing? What shall I say to you? Shall I commend you in this? No, I will not. ²³For I received from the Lord what I also delivered to you, that the Lord Jesus on the night when he was betrayed took bread, ²⁴and when he had given thanks, he broke it, and said, "This is my body which is for you. Do this in remembrance of me." ²⁵In the same way also the cup, after supper, saying, "This cup is the new covenant in my blood. Do this, as often as you drink it, in remembrance of me." ²⁶For as often as you eat this bread and drink the cup, you proclaim the Lord's death until he comes. ²⁷Whoever, therefore, eats the bread or drinks the cup of the Lord in an unworthy manner will be guilty of profaning the body and blood of the Lord. ²⁸Let a man examine himself, and so eat of the bread and drink of the cup. ²⁹For any one who eats and drinks without discerning the body eats and drinks judgment upon himself. ³⁰That is why many of you are weak and ill, and some have died. ³¹But if we judged ourselves truly, we should not be judged. ³²But when we are judged by the Lord, we are chastened so that we may not be condemned along with the world. ³³So then, my brethren, when you come together to eat, wait for one another ³⁴—if any one is hungry, let him eat at home—lest you come together to be condemned. About the other things I will give directions when I come.

After having praised the Corinthians, Paul moves to an outright condemnation of the way they gather as church congregation (*synerkhesthe* [v.17]; *synerkhomenōn hymōn en ekklēsia* [v.18]). The reason is that their attitude in those gatherings creates divisions (*skhismata*; v.19), which is the main reason why Paul is writing the letter (1:10). Dissensions (*aireseis*) are bound to happen and their function is to bring to light those who prove to be genuine (*dokimoi*) (1 Cor 11:19) in their view after the test; *dokimoi* is from the same root as the verb *dokimasei* in 3:13: "... each man's work will become manifest; for the Day will disclose it, because it will be revealed with fire, and the fire will test (*dokimasei*) what sort of work each one has done."

Hence the *dokimoi* are those who will have passed the test and thus will have a better chance on judgment day. However, the problem lies in that the gatherings, which are meant to bring all *epi to avto* (into one place; into the same state of mind; in unison),[11] end up being divisive. The reason for this is that the Corinthians are not taking seriously the rules of table fellowship.

The supper provided at these gatherings is the property of the host in the sense that everyone is fed from his table where only food provided by him is consumed. To bring one's own food is an outright insult to the host. It is as though one would be consuming one's own food, in which case one might as well have stayed at home. If a guest does brings along a gift of food, that gift is put aside in order to be used at a future occasion when it would be considered the host's property and served at a dinner not attended by the one who had brought the gift. Furthermore, the food and drink are consumed at the host's bidding when all the main guests are present so that all would consume from the "common" table of the one lord of the house. To eat or drink at one's own leisure, especially before the other guests are gathered, would be irreverent to them and, more importantly, to the host. On the other hand, the one presiding over the meal, and thus de facto the lord of that occasion, need not be the household lord himself. When one of the guests is senior to the host, as in the case of the emperor, a senator, or a governor, then the house itself, let alone the table spread, literally becomes that of the senior and not the host. In the Middle East, the classic welcome greeting to a visiting senior is "the house is yours."[12] This is

---

[11] RSV dismisses completely this phrase from its translation. See earlier my comments on *epi to avto* in 7:5.
[12] This is more than the Spanish "mi casa es su casa," which corresponds to the English "consider my house yours" or "make yourself at home." In both these cases the house

precisely what Paul is saying in 11:20-22. Those who are interested in eating and drinking should do so in their own homes (22a); however, the gathering they come to is "the church of God" where the Lord Jesus presides. Thus the Corinthians' disregard toward those who have nothing and the latter's ensuing humiliation is tantamount to despising God's church, and this is no cause for praise on the Apostle's part (v.22b).

Then Paul goes to explain in which sense the Lord Jesus is the actual host of the supper. Unfortunately, translations do not reflect that v.23 forms an *inclusio*: "For I received (*parelabon*; took what was handed over) from the Lord what I also delivered (*paredōka*) to you, that the Lord Jesus on the night when he was betrayed (*paradideto* [from the same verb *paradidōmi* as *paredōka*]; was being betrayed, handed over[13]) took (*elabon*, from the same root *lambanō* as the verb *parelabon*) bread." The intentionality is blatant. Jesus, the host, is being "betrayed" while he is holding the bread with which he is about to feed the Corinthians, that is, they are betraying Paul's teaching which he "delivered" to them and with which he is feeding them. Indeed, since at the Lord's supper the Corinthians are to commemorate the Lord's death (v.26), he could not possibly be present with them. In his absence, however, the Lord is present through Paul, his representative as chief household steward (*oikonomos*), who delivers the master's injunctions in his remembrance (*anamnēsin*; vv.24 and 25). In Paul's absence, it is Timothy who will preside, and his mission is "to remind (*anamnēsei*) you of my ways in Christ, as *I teach* them everywhere in every church" (4:17). Since the Corinthians can eat in their own homes (v.22), when they

---

is still my property and thus remains *shared* between the guest and me. Thus technically speaking the host still has a share in the decision making during mealtime.

[13] The verb *paradideto* is in the imperfect denoting a continuous action in the past; hence my translation into "*was being* betrayed, handed over."

are gathered as God's church they are to be fed with the teaching of the gospel which Paul "received" from the Lord (Gal 1:12; see also Acts 20:24) and which the Corinthians would be betraying should they perpetrate divisions among themselves (1 Cor 11:18). Actually the entire letter was triggered by the news of such divisions (1:10-11).

So how should one understand 1 Corinthians 11:24-26 in the larger context of Paul's criticism of his addressees' behavior at the Lord' supper? Misreading of those verses is due to the heavily sacramental understanding of the Eucharistic gathering which pervaded later classical theology and continues to our own times. Instead of hearing those verses within the entire argument of the passage, which is essentially dealing with the behavior of the attendees at such gatherings, vv.24-26 are viewed as self-standing and then used to discuss the relation between the bread and Christ's physical body, on the one hand, and the wine and Christ's actual blood, on the other hand. The phraseology and structure of v.23 are intended to underscore the attitude of *betrayal* toward the Lord, entailed in the blasphemous behavior referred to in the preceding verses (21-22). The statement of v.23 is only part of the sentence that continues in v.24, therefore, the latter verse should be taken in the same vein. Further, v.25 is closely linked to v.24 in that it is introduced with "in the same way," and the action referred to is to be done "in remembrance of me" just as that of v.24. On the other hand, the matter of betrayal is so serious that those who commit such are liable to divine judgment (v.34); indeed, some are already suffering divine punishment (v.30). This explains why the conclusion (So then, Therefore [*hōste*]; v.33) of the entire passage is not a request to believe in the so-called "real presence" of the Lord in the "elements" of the bread and wine, but rather "when you come together to eat, *wait for one another—if any one is hungry, let him eat at home*—lest you come together to be condemned (unto judgment)" (vv.33-34).

Why did Paul refer to the "night" when the Lord was betrayed?[14] The obvious reason lies in that the meal referred to in v.21 is a supper or dinner (*deipnon*), which was the main meal in a Roman household, especially when the gathering was formal or festive. In stressing night as the time of the Lord's betrayal, Paul was bringing "home" his message: the Lord is being betrayed by the Corinthians just as he was betrayed unto punishment by death, which their gathering was supposed to commemorate (v.26). Still, Paul could have used "day," which would have been appropriate as well as more common since "day" encompasses the twenty-four hour period and has the same general connotation as "time" or "hour" as is evident from Romans 13:11-12a: "Besides this you know what hour it is, how it is full time now for you to wake from sleep. For salvation is nearer to us now than when we first believed; the night is far gone, the day is at hand." Therefore, the choice of night was obviously intentional. "Day" functions in Paul as shorthand for "day of the Lord," which is judgment day:

> They show that what the law requires is written on their hearts, while their conscience also bears witness and their conflicting thoughts accuse or perhaps excuse them on that day when, according to my gospel, God judges the secrets of men by Christ Jesus. (Rom 2:15-16)

> ... each man's work will become manifest; for the Day will disclose it, because it will be revealed with fire. (1 Cor 3:13)

---

[14] Appeal to the Gospels in order to shed light on this matter amounts to begging the question since those books were written *after* the Pauline epistles and, consequently, the information in them builds up on that found in Paul's letters.

> But I am not ashamed, for I know whom I have believed, and I am sure that he is able to guard until that Day what has been entrusted to me ... may the Lord grant him to find mercy from the Lord on that Day (2 Tim 1:12, 18)

> Henceforth there is laid up for me the crown of righteousness, which the Lord, the righteous judge, will award to me on that Day, and not only to me but also to all who have loved his appearing. (2 Tim 4:8)

> Let us hold fast the confession of our hope without wavering, for he who promised is faithful; and let us consider how to stir up one another to love and good works, not neglecting to meet together, as is the habit of some, but encouraging one another, and all the more as you see the Day drawing near. (Heb 10:23-25)

Thus "night" becomes functional as the period preceding that day and, by the same token, refers to that time of trial just before the end:

> Besides this you know what hour it is, how it is full time now for you to wake from sleep. For salvation is nearer to us now than when we first believed; the night is far gone, the day is at hand. Let us then cast off the works of darkness and put on the armor of light; let us conduct ourselves becomingly as in the day, not in reveling and drunkenness, not in debauchery and licentiousness, not in quarreling and jealousy. But put on the Lord Jesus Christ, and make no provision for the flesh, to gratify its desires. (Rom 13:11-14)

The equivalence of night and darkness, on the one hand, and of day and light, on the other hand, in conjunction with the divine judgment is at its clearest in 1 Thessalonians:

> But as to the times and the seasons, brethren, you have no need to have anything written to you. For you yourselves know well that

the day of the Lord will come like a thief in the night. When people say, "There is peace and security," then sudden destruction will come upon them as travail comes upon a woman with child, and there will be no escape. But you are not in darkness, brethren, for that day to surprise you like a thief. For you are all sons of light and sons of the day; we are not of the night or of darkness. So then let us not sleep, as others do, but let us keep awake and be sober. For those who sleep sleep at night, and those who get drunk are drunk at night. But, since we belong to the day, let us be sober, and put on the breastplate of faith and love, and for a helmet the hope of salvation. For God has not destined us for wrath, but to obtain salvation through our Lord Jesus Christ, who died for us so that whether we wake or sleep we might live with him. (5:1-10)

Looking closely at the last two passages, one notices that, just as is the case in 1 Corinthians 11, the issue is a matter of behavior. Furthermore, in both cases, drunkenness is specifically mentioned and, in 1 Thessalonians, it is actually presented as *the* behavior to be avoided. So the setting of the metaphor of night is a festive meal where wine is provided in abundance. What is of import for our discussion, however, is that drunkenness takes a central place in 1 Corinthians in a way that betrays intentionality. Indeed, since the opposite of being hungry is eating (11:34) one would have expected in v.21 "is filled, is sate, is satisfied" (*empimplēmi; empiplō*) as in Luke 1:53; 6:25; John 6:12; Acts 14:17 and Romans 15:24,[15] instead of "is drunk," as the reverse of "is hungry." The conclusion is unavoidable: being drunk is not a way to behave at the table of the Lord. In order to recognize the Lord at his coming (*parousia*; presence) among us, it is not enough to be awake; one is to be sober (1 Thess 5:6-8)!

---

[15] The original for RSV's "I have enjoyed your company" is "I have been filled (*emplēsthō*) with [by, through] your company."

So, Paul's purview here is not a dogmatic teaching concerning the "how" of such presence, but rather *that* such presence entails divine judgment of our behavior. The "how" is assumed: the Lord is, or rather becomes, present through Paul's teaching (1 Cor 4:14-21) which he received from the Lord (11:23; see also Gal 1:12). Betraying that teaching is tantamount to betraying the Lord himself and "handing" him "over" to the powers that condemned him to shameful death by crucifixion (1 Cor 2:6-8).

The imperfect tense "was being betrayed" (*paradideto*; 11:23) in the original Greek, which RSV translates as "was betrayed," is unexpected since Paul could have more readily, and actually more à propos, used the aorist "was betrayed" (*paredothē*) as he did in Romans 4:25.[16] I strongly believe that Paul had in mind the Antioch episode where Cephas betrayed the oneness of table fellowship: "For before certain men came from James, he ate with the Gentiles; but when they came he was drawing back (*hypestellen*) and separating (*aphōrizen*) himself, fearing the circumcision party." (Gal 2:12) There also the two imperfect tenses are intentional since they are immediately followed by two aorists: "And with him the rest of the Jews acted insincerely (*synypekrithēsan*), so that even Barnabas was carried away (*synapēkhthē*) by their insincerity." (v.13) In my Commentary on Galatians, I explained the imperfect tense was used to underscore that Cephas' decision was taken over a period of time and thus was intentional.[17] This understanding of 1 Corinthians 11:23 is borne out by the fact that, in the letter, Cephas is Paul's prominent nemesis (1:12; 3:22; 9:5; 15:5[18]). Cephas' betrayal of the Jerusalem agreement, which stressed the oneness of the

---

[16] RSV has the loose translation of "was put to death."
[17] See *Gal* 75-9.
[18] See later my comments on 1 Cor 15:1-11.

gospel (Gal 2:7-8), split the one church gathered around the one table fellowship in Antioch. Here also the Corinthians' behavior is putting at risk the oneness of the Corinthian church and, by the same token, is "breaking" up the one "body" of Christ (1 Cor 10:16-17). Paul is pointing out that, in so doing, they are reversing what the Lord did. He "broke" his body "for your sake" (*hyper hymōn*; 11:24) in order to unify Jew and Gentile, the free and the slave, the have and the have-not; in turn and at no less an occasion where they are supposed to "remember" his sacrifice, they are tearing apart this same "body."

This reading of v.24 is corroborated in the way v.25 is phrased: "*In the same way* also the cup, *after supper*, saying, 'This cup is the new covenant in my blood. Do this, as often as you drink it, in remembrance of me.'" The breaking of the bread and the blessing of the cup (10:16) are at the same time linked (in the same way) yet separated in time (after supper). Consequently they are two independent moments referring to the same remembrance, that of the Lord's death, as is clear from 11:26: the one through the action of "breaking" and the other through the mention of the (spilled) blood. In other words, the two actions are not to be taken together as though they are aiming at the body *and* the blood of the Lord; rather they are *independently* referring to the *one and the same* sacrifice. The question that then arises is why there are two commemorations of the Lord's sacrifice, one at the beginning[19] of the supper and the other at the end? The answer is twofold. On the one hand, by having the two commemorations bracket the meal, Paul is underscoring

---

[19] I opted for "the beginning" rather than "during" the supper because bread was the main ingredient of any meal and, unless it was broken and divided among the commensals, the meal could not start. But even if we took the breaking of the bread as happening during the meal, the same discrepancy in time would still obtain since the blessing of the cup is said to have taken place *after* the supper.

that the *entire* (time of the) meal is the supper of the Lord who is thus present *throughout* the meal. The corollary is that the guests are to behave according to his will from the moment they enter the house until the end of the supper; at no moment are they allowed to assume that he is not present.[20] On the other hand, and more importantly for Paul, since the blessing of the cup is to take place *after the supper*, then the guests are not to drink—let alone get drunk—during, or worse before, the supper as some were doing (11:21).

The conclusion is inescapable. As an authoritative apostle who has "the spirit of the Lord" (7:40) and "the mind of Christ" (2:16), Paul devised his phraseology ad hoc in order to emphasize his point. The house church gatherings take place around the Lord who is present, not in person, but through the apostle's words of teaching that ensure that the Lord is remembered. As for the Lord himself, he "was put to death (*paredothē*; was delivered, was handed over) for our trespasses" (Rom 4:25). The gatherings are in remembrance of that death and are to remain so "until he comes" (1 Cor 11:26). Furthermore, since Paul established that the gospel "word" of his teaching revolved around the Lord's crucifixion (1:18), the common meal of remembrance functioned at the same time as a "proclamation" of that gospel (11:26). Indeed, the verb "you proclaim" (*katangellete*) found here was used twice earlier and, in both cases, to speak of Paul's preaching: "When I came to you, brethren, I did not come proclaiming (*katangellōn*) to you the testimony of God in lofty words or wisdom" (2:1); "In the same way, the Lord commanded that those who proclaim

---

[20] This is far cry from the common, if not traditional, understanding that the Lord becomes *really* present among those who are gathered at the so-called "words of institution."

(*katangellousin*) the gospel should get their living by the gospel." (9:14) Common meals, especially the festive ones, were and still are the classic venues where people would exchange views. Such Greco-Roman gatherings were known as *symposia* (festive encounters where wine was served) whence our symposia (conferences). In case of the presence of a guest of honor, such as the emperor or a senator or a governor, then that person would steal the show by becoming the main speaker. Put otherwise, Paul was establishing his churches as synagogues where the word of the Lord was imparted to the one community of Jews and Gentiles, freemen and slaves, gathered as one around the one table. However, the behavior of some Corinthians was disturbing that order.

The sacramentalism that took hold of Christian theology became so pervasive that it imposed the classic misunderstanding of 11:27. It assumed the unworthiness referred to was either a state of unpreparedness through lack of prayer, fasting, and repentance, or a lack of dogmatic comprehension that the bread and wine were the "real" body and blood of the Lord. Such could not be farther from Paul's intention. Indeed the adverb *anaxiōs* (in an unworthy manner) is found elsewhere in the Pauline corpus in its positive form *axiōs* (worthily) in conjunction with *behaving* according to the gospel teaching:

> I commend to you our sister Phoebe, a deaconess of the church at Cenchreae, that you may receive her in the Lord as befits (*axiōs*) the saints. (Rom 16:1-2)

> I therefore, a prisoner for the Lord, beg you to lead a life worthy (*axiōs*) of the calling to which you have been called. (Eph 4:1)

> Only let your manner of life be worthy (*axiōs*) of the gospel of Christ, so that whether I come and see you or am absent, I may

hear of you that you stand firm in one spirit, with one mind striving side by side for the faith of the gospel. (Phil 1:27)

... to lead a life worthy (*axiōs*) of the Lord, fully pleasing to him, bearing fruit in every good work. (Col 1:10)

... to lead a life worthy (*axiōs*) of God, who calls you into his own kingdom and glory. (1 Thess 2:12)[21]

The one who misbehaves is said to be *enokhos* (guilty), which is a judicial term indicating legal liability as is clear from its other occurrences (Mt 5:21, 22; 26:66; Mk 3:29; 14:64). In other words, the one who misbehaves is not taking into consideration the Lord who is seated at the head of the table and who is also the judge. Further unequivocal corroboration is found in the rest of the passage (1Cor 11:28-34) that is replete with legal terminology: the noun *krima* (judgment) as well as the verb *krinō* (judge) and its cognates *diakrinō* (discern) and *katakrinō* (condemn).

In view of the very serious legal liability, Paul recommends that each person examine himself before approaching the bread and the cup (1 Cor 11:28). The reason given is that, should one not discern the "body," then one would be eating and drinking one's own judgment. Some manuscripts have "the body of the Lord" instead of "the body." This is evidently an emendation on the part of the scribe who wanted to clarify what "the body" meant.[22] Be that as it may, the real dilemma is actually reflected

---

[21] See also "This is evidence of the righteous judgment of God, that you may be made worthy (*kataxiōthēnai*) of the kingdom of God, for which you are suffering" (2 Thess 1: 5) and "To this end we always pray for you, that our God may make you worthy (*axiōsē*) of his call, and may fulfil every good resolve and work of faith by his power" (v.11).

[22] This is a clear cut case of the rule *lectio difficilior potior* (the reading that is more difficult to explain is more plausibly the original).

in that after having mentioned twice the bread and the cup (vv.27a and 28), after having used the couple "the body and blood of the Lord" (v.27b), and after having referred to "eating and drinking" four times, two of which in v.29, Paul ends (in Greek) that same verse by writing "without discerning the body (of the Lord)" without mention of "the blood." The only plausible explanation is that he wanted to make sure that the hearers would understand that he intended "the body (of the Lord)" to mean the community of believers, rather than the commemorative table fellowship which he expressed as "the body and blood of the Lord." In other words, what the hearers are to consider when assessing their behavior is not their own personal needs but rather the needs and the good of the house church (6:12; 10:23). This is precisely what Paul will be commenting on in chapters 12-14.[23]

Paul then compounds the pressure by saying that many have already failed the test (11:30) just as Israel did in the wilderness (10:5). Indeed, "many of you are weak and ill, and some have died." This argument hit home since, as I indicated in my comments on 10:1-5, the Corinthians relied on the "magic" powers of the "spiritual" food they ate and the "spiritual" drink they drank (vv.3b-4a). They forgot that the real Christ, the "spiritual" *rock* in their lives (v.4b), is not a magical potion but is rather present among them through his law (Gal 6:2), which is none other than "the law of the Spirit of life in Christ Jesus" that "has set me free from the law of sin and death" (Rom 8:2). A sure sign that the Corinthians, through their misbehavior, are contravening the law of the Spirit of *life* is the fact underscored

---

[23] Paul uses often this device of introducing terms or thoughts that seem sudden or unexpected, yet whose function is to draw his hearer's attention to the topic he is about to tackle, a "teaser" as we would say nowadays.

by Paul that not only "many of you are weak and ill" but also "some have *died*" (1 Cor 11:30). Had they enacted correctly the discernment (*diekrinomen*), they would not have been judged (*ekrinometha*) by the Lord (v.31). Yet, there is hope for the Corinthians who have not died if they take seriously the educational chastening (*paidevometha*) in order that they be corrected and not undergo the final condemnation (*katakrithōmen*) with the world (v.32). Having put extreme pressure on them, Paul ends with an exhortation aimed at the correct handling as well as understanding of the house church gathering, which is the theme of the entire passage (11:17-18):[24] "So then (*hōste*; therefore), my brethren, when you come together (*synerkhomenoi*) to eat, wait for one another—if any one is hungry, let him eat at home—lest you come together (*synerkhēsthe*) to be condemned (*eis krima*; unto judgment)." (vv.33-34a) Then, lest the Corinthians think that this is the end of the story and assume that they can relax now that they mentally comprehend what Paul is saying, he points out that he will give them directions regarding other matters when he comes to them (v.34b). They are not off the hook yet! Paul's reference to his coming is clearly a rhetorical device, similar to the one he used in 4:21 when he was coming to them through Timothy, the bearer of his letter (v.17). Here also, Paul is about to "visit" the Corinthians regarding "the other things (matters)" that he will discuss in the following chapters (12:1-16:4).

---

[24] "But in the following instructions I do not commend you, because when you come together (*synerkhesthe*) it is not for the better but for the worse. For, in the first place, when you assemble (*synerkhomenōn*; come together) as a church, I hear that there are divisions among you; and I partly believe it."

Chapter 12

Vv. 1-11 ¹Περὶ δὲ τῶν πνευματικῶν, ἀδελφοί, οὐ θέλω ὑμᾶς ἀγνοεῖν. ² Οἴδατε ὅτι ὅτε ἔθνη ἦτε πρὸς τὰ εἴδωλα τὰ ἄφωνα ὡς ἂν ἤγεσθε ἀπαγόμενοι. ³ διὸ γνωρίζω ὑμῖν ὅτι οὐδεὶς ἐν πνεύματι θεοῦ λαλῶν λέγει· Ἀνάθεμα Ἰησοῦς, καὶ οὐδεὶς δύναται εἰπεῖν· Κύριος Ἰησοῦς, εἰ μὴ ἐν πνεύματι ἁγίῳ. ⁴ Διαιρέσεις δὲ χαρισμάτων εἰσίν, τὸ δὲ αὐτὸ πνεῦμα· ⁵ καὶ διαιρέσεις διακονιῶν εἰσιν, καὶ ὁ αὐτὸς κύριος· ⁶ καὶ διαιρέσεις ἐνεργημάτων εἰσίν, ὁ δὲ αὐτὸς θεὸς ὁ ἐνεργῶν τὰ πάντα ἐν πᾶσιν. ⁷ ἑκάστῳ δὲ δίδοται ἡ φανέρωσις τοῦ πνεύματος πρὸς τὸ συμφέρον. ⁸ ᾧ μὲν γὰρ διὰ τοῦ πνεύματος δίδοται λόγος σοφίας, ἄλλῳ δὲ λόγος γνώσεως κατὰ τὸ αὐτὸ πνεῦμα, ⁹ ἑτέρῳ πίστις ἐν τῷ αὐτῷ πνεύματι, ἄλλῳ δὲ χαρίσματα ἰαμάτων ἐν τῷ ἑνὶ πνεύματι, ¹⁰ ἄλλῳ δὲ ἐνεργήματα δυνάμεων, ἄλλῳ [δὲ] προφητεία, ἄλλῳ [δὲ] διακρίσεις πνευμάτων, ἑτέρῳ γένη γλωσσῶν, ἄλλῳ δὲ ἑρμηνεία γλωσσῶν· ¹¹ πάντα δὲ ταῦτα ἐνεργεῖ τὸ ἓν καὶ τὸ αὐτὸ πνεῦμα διαιροῦν ἰδίᾳ ἑκάστῳ καθὼς βούλεται.

¹Now concerning spiritual gifts, brethren, I do not want you to be uninformed. ²You know that when you were heathen, you were led astray to dumb idols, however you may have been moved. ³Therefore I want you to understand that no one speaking by the Spirit of God ever says "Jesus be cursed!" and no one can say "Jesus is Lord" except by the Holy Spirit. ⁴Now there are varieties of gifts, but the same Spirit; ⁵and there are varieties of service, but the same Lord; ⁶and there are varieties of working, but it is the same God who inspires them all in every one. ⁷To each is given the manifestation of the Spirit for the common good. ⁸To one is given through the Spirit the utterance of wisdom, and to another the utterance of knowledge according to the same Spirit, ⁹to another faith by the same Spirit, to another gifts of healing by the one Spirit, ¹⁰to another the working of miracles, to another prophecy, to another the ability to distinguish between spirits, to another various kinds of tongues, to another the interpretation of tongues. ¹¹*All these are inspired by one and the same Spirit, who apportions to each one individually as he wills.*

In the following three chapters Paul will continue to discuss matters related to the church gatherings. He intentionally broaches the subject by referring to the "spiritual." The reason is that the Corinthians did not understand that being "spiritual" meant *behaving* according to the will of God's spirit. They considered the spirit granted to them through their acceptance of Paul's preaching a possession that allowed them unbridled freedom to do as they pleased. The gifts bestowed through God's spirit were being used to *enjoy* the power associated with those gifts, forgetting that the purpose of those gifts was to build up and sustain the *one* temple of the Spirit, the *one* body of Christ, the *one* congregation of God. It is this problem that will occupy Paul for no less than three full chapters.[1]

As he does elsewhere,[2] Paul begins by reminding his hearers that, scripturally speaking, they were once heathens, led astray and controlled by dumb idols (1 Cor 12:2). Those who submit to the idols cannot comprehend how someone who was condemned to an ignominious death could be indeed a lord, let alone *the* Lord (v.3). Now, however, they are led by the Spirit to the right confession of the Lord. One should not imagine that God's spirit is a force that acts magically on its recipients and

---

[1] The opening *pnevmatikōn* (spiritual) in 12:1 is an adjective plural in the genitive case. Since the genitive plural in Greek has the same form in all three grammatical genders (masculine, feminine, and neuter) it is not readily clear whether "spiritual" in 12:1 is intended to refer to persons or to *kharismatōn* (spiritual gifts; v.4). On the other hand, since the problem is linked to the *use* of those gifts by their respective recipients, deciding the matter is irrelevant to the general argument.

[2] See e.g. Gal 4:8; Eph 2:11; 1 Thess 1:9.

leads them independently without regard to any previous teaching or instruction. To the contrary, as Paul made clear earlier in 2:10-3:4, it is *always and consistently through him* that the Spirit is imparted to the Corinthians. It is Paul who implanted in their minds that the "gods" they used to worship are no more than mere idols (12:2) with no intrinsic value as deities (Gal 4:8).

"I do not want you to be uninformed (*agnoein*)" (1 Cor 12:1) is a statement that introduces a teaching about to be conveyed. Clearly, Paul was not referring to something the Corinthians already knew, but rather he was drawing their undivided attention to what he was about to *teach* them, as he has been doing all along in this letter. Paul begins by stating the source of the diverse gifts: "Now there are varieties of gifts (*kharismatōn*), but the same Spirit; and there are varieties of service (*diakoniōn*; table fellowship services [ministries]), but the same Lord; and there are varieties of working (*energēmatōn*; outcomes), but it is the same God who inspires (*energōn*; works out, sets in motion) them all in every one." (vv.4-6) Notice that all three pairs use corresponding terms. The Spirit is the agent of divine grace (*kharis*) that produces the gifts (*kharismata*); the table ministries (*diakoniai*) are under the aegis of the lord, the paterfamilias, and God works out (*energei*; energizes, produces) the outcomes (*energēmata*; products). The intention is evident: all things and products (*ta panta*) have one divine source and the recipients of the gifts are just media through whom God implements *his* will. After having established that God is the one who decides what is to be done, v.7 clarifies that the individual is not his ultimate concern, but rather "the common good" (*to sympheron*). Paul referred to this previously in 6:12 and 10:23 to contend with the believers' tendency toward individualism.

The list of the "spiritual" gifts in 12:8-11 is interesting for the following reasons. First, we are repeatedly told—thrice in the main enumeration and once in the conclusion—that each and every one of those gifts is dispensed by the one and same Spirit. The hearers of the letter cannot possibly miss this central message, especially since it repeats what has just been said in v.4. It is as though Paul wants to drill this into their ears and minds so they would never forget it. Second, prophecy and speaking in tongues, the two contenders for primary importance in the minds of the Corinthians, are intentionally relegated to the bottom of the list; in this manner Paul is deflating their importance for his hearers. Still, one can sense Paul's own preference for the gifts linked to the "word." Indeed, the first two gifts listed are "the utterance (*logos*; word) of wisdom" and "the utterance (*logos*; word) of knowledge." Both wisdom and knowledge were intimately connected earlier in the letter with the word of the gospel. Thus Paul is drawing attention to the priority of those gifts that pertain to communicating the gospel message through the medium used by Paul himself, that is, intelligible human discourse (14:18-19). His preference is also reflected in the structure of the list's ending: "to another prophecy, to another the ability to distinguish (discern; *diakriseis*) between spirits, to another various kinds of tongues, to another the interpretation of tongues." (12:10) As will be explicated in chapter 14, the gift of "tongues" is not self-sufficient since it requires another gift, that of the interpretation of what is uttered in tongues; in this sense it is a "lesser" kind of gift. Paul treats the gift of prophecy similarly, although in an oblique manner. Although the gift of prophecy is self-standing, it is nevertheless to be checked by other prophets who would discern whether the prophet who is speaking actually has the "right" spirit: "Let two or three prophets speak, and let the others weigh (discern; *diakrinetōsan*) what is said." (14:29)³ I shall forego discussing in detail the different "kinds" of gifts as is done in conventional commentaries that view the scriptural books as philosophical treatises rather than "persuasive literature." The function of the lengthy enumeration is to overwhelm the hearer with the fact that the *one* Spirit is manifested (12:7) through *so many* different channels, the result being that no one channel has any kind of supremacy, let alone monopoly. Conversely, the testing of those manifold manifestations does not lie in advocating the "correct" mental understanding as to what the Spirit is all about, as unfortunately was and still is done in classical theology. The real compass is the "common good" (v.7b), and this is precisely what Paul will expound on in the rest of chapter 12.

Vv. 12-31 ¹²Καθάπερ γὰρ τὸ σῶμα ἕν ἐστιν καὶ μέλη πολλὰ ἔχει, πάντα δὲ τὰ μέλη τοῦ σώματος πολλὰ ὄντα ἕν ἐστιν σῶμα, οὕτως καὶ ὁ Χριστός· ¹³καὶ γὰρ ἐν ἑνὶ πνεύματι ἡμεῖς πάντες εἰς ἓν σῶμα ἐβαπτίσθημεν, εἴτε Ἰουδαῖοι εἴτε Ἕλληνες εἴτε δοῦλοι εἴτε ἐλεύθεροι, καὶ πάντες ἓν πνεῦμα ἐποτίσθημεν. ¹⁴Καὶ γὰρ τὸ σῶμα οὐκ ἔστιν ἓν μέλος ἀλλὰ πολλά. ¹⁵ ἐὰν εἴπῃ ὁ πούς· ὅτι οὐκ εἰμὶ χείρ, οὐκ εἰμὶ ἐκ τοῦ σώματος, οὐ παρὰ τοῦτο οὐκ ἔστιν ἐκ τοῦ σώματος; ¹⁶ καὶ ἐὰν εἴπῃ τὸ οὖς· ὅτι οὐκ εἰμὶ ὀφθαλμός, οὐκ εἰμὶ ἐκ τοῦ σώματος, οὐ παρὰ τοῦτο οὐκ ἔστιν ἐκ τοῦ σώματος; ¹⁷ εἰ ὅλον τὸ σῶμα ὀφθαλμός, ποῦ ἡ ἀκοή; εἰ ὅλον ἀκοή, ποῦ ἡ ὄσφρησις; ¹⁸ νυνὶ δὲ ὁ θεὸς ἔθετο τὰ μέλη, ἓν ἕκαστον αὐτῶν

---

³ Concerning the "deceitful spirits" and the duty of testing them see 2 Cor 11:4; 1 Tim 4:1; and especially 1 Thess 5:19-21a where spirit and prophecy are mentioned in tandem: "Do not quench the Spirit, do not despise prophesying, but test (*dokimazete*) everything." The closeness in meaning and function between the verbs *dokimazō* and *diakrinō* was pointed out in my discussion of 1 Cor 11:28-29: "Let a man examine (*dokimazetō*) himself, and so eat of the bread and drink of the cup. For any one who eats and drinks without discerning (*diakrinōn*) the body eats and drinks judgment upon himself."

ἐν τῷ σώματι καθὼς ἠθέλησεν. ¹⁹ εἰ δὲ ἦν τὰ πάντα ἓν μέλος, ποῦ τὸ σῶμα; ²⁰ νῦν δὲ πολλὰ μὲν μέλη, ἓν δὲ σῶμα. ²¹ οὐ δύναται δὲ ὁ ὀφθαλμὸς εἰπεῖν τῇ χειρί· χρείαν σου οὐκ ἔχω, ἢ πάλιν ἡ κεφαλὴ τοῖς ποσίν· χρείαν ὑμῶν οὐκ ἔχω· ²² ἀλλὰ πολλῷ μᾶλλον τὰ δοκοῦντα μέλη τοῦ σώματος ἀσθενέστερα ὑπάρχειν ἀναγκαῖά ἐστιν, ²³ καὶ ἃ δοκοῦμεν ἀτιμότερα εἶναι τοῦ σώματος τούτοις τιμὴν περισσοτέραν περιτίθεμεν, καὶ τὰ ἀσχήμονα ἡμῶν εὐσχημοσύνην περισσοτέραν ἔχει, ²⁴ τὰ δὲ εὐσχήμονα ἡμῶν οὐ χρείαν ἔχει. ἀλλὰ ὁ θεὸς συνεκέρασεν τὸ σῶμα τῷ ὑστερουμένῳ περισσοτέραν δοὺς τιμήν, ²⁵ ἵνα μὴ ᾖ σχίσμα ἐν τῷ σώματι ἀλλὰ τὸ αὐτὸ ὑπὲρ ἀλλήλων μεριμνῶσιν τὰ μέλη. ²⁶ καὶ εἴτε πάσχει ἓν μέλος, συμπάσχει πάντα τὰ μέλη· εἴτε δοξάζεται [ἓν] μέλος, συγχαίρει πάντα τὰ μέλη. ²⁷ ὑμεῖς δέ ἐστε σῶμα Χριστοῦ καὶ μέλη ἐκ μέρους. ²⁸ Καὶ οὓς μὲν ἔθετο ὁ θεὸς ἐν τῇ ἐκκλησίᾳ πρῶτον ἀποστόλους, δεύτερον προφήτας, τρίτον διδασκάλους, ἔπειτα δυνάμεις, ἔπειτα χαρίσματα ἰαμάτων, ἀντιλήμψεις, κυβερνήσεις, γένη γλωσσῶν. ²⁹ μὴ πάντες ἀπόστολοι; μὴ πάντες προφῆται; μὴ πάντες διδάσκαλοι; μὴ πάντες δυνάμεις; ³⁰ μὴ πάντες χαρίσματα ἔχουσιν ἰαμάτων; μὴ πάντες γλώσσαις λαλοῦσιν; μὴ πάντες διερμηνεύουσιν; ³¹ ζηλοῦτε δὲ τὰ χαρίσματα τὰ μείζονα. Καὶ ἔτι καθ' ὑπερβολὴν ὁδὸν ὑμῖν δείκνυμι.

¹²*For just as the body is one and has many members, and all the members of the body, though many, are one body, so it is with Christ.* ¹³*For by one Spirit we were all baptized into one body— Jews or Greeks, slaves or free—and all were made to drink of one Spirit.* ¹⁴*For the body does not consist of one member but of many.* ¹⁵*If the foot should say, "Because I am not a hand, I do not belong to the body," that would not make it any less a part of the body.* ¹⁶*And if the ear should say, "Because I am not an eye, I do not belong to the body," that would not make it any less a part of the body.* ¹⁷*If the whole body were an eye, where would be the hearing? If the whole body were an ear, where would be the sense of smell?* ¹⁸*But as it is, God arranged the organs in the*

body, each one of them, as he chose. ¹⁹If all were a single organ, where would the body be? ²⁰As it is, there are many parts, yet one body. ²¹The eye cannot say to the hand, "I have no need of you," nor again the head to the feet, "I have no need of you." ²²On the contrary, the parts of the body which seem to be weaker are indispensable, ²³and those parts of the body which we think less honorable we invest with the greater honor, and our unpresentable parts are treated with greater modesty, ²⁴which our more presentable parts do not require. But God has so composed the body, giving the greater honor to the inferior part, ²⁵that there may be no discord in the body, but that the members may have the same care for one another. ²⁶If one member suffers, all suffer together; if one member is honored, all rejoice together. ²⁷Now you are the body of Christ and individually members of it. ²⁸And God has appointed in the church first apostles, second prophets, third teachers, then workers of miracles, then healers, helpers, administrators, speakers in various kinds of tongues. ²⁹Are all apostles? Are all prophets? Are all teachers? Do all work miracles? ³⁰Do all possess gifts of healing? Do all speak with tongues? Do all interpret? ³¹But earnestly desire the higher gifts. And I will show you a still more excellent way.

Paul capitalizes on the metaphor of the one body and the many members, which he introduced in 6:15, then elaborated on in 10:16-17, and brought up once more in 11:29. The way 12:12 is formulated corroborates that Paul very often used the term "Christ (messiah)" to refer to the church as messianic community.[4] That the writer had in mind Galatians is evident from v.13 which is unexpected and sounds like a marginal note; the mention of baptism in conjunction with "all" (*pantes*) and "Jews and Greeks, slaves and free" occurs elsewhere in the New

---

[4] See my comments on Gal 3:24-29 in *C-Gal* 133-88.

Testament only in Galatians 3:26-28. Still, the combination of baptism and drinking in conjunction with the Spirit perfectly fits 1 Corinthians since it harks back to what we heard earlier in chapter 10:

> I want you to know, brethren, that our fathers were all under the cloud, and *all* passed through the sea, and *all* were *baptized* into Moses in the cloud and in the sea, and *all* ate the same supernatural (*pnevmatikon*; spiritual) food and *all drank* the same supernatural (*pnevmatikon*; spiritual) *drink*. For they *drank* from the supernatural (*pnevmatikēs*; spiritual) Rock which followed them, and the Rock was Christ. Nevertheless with most of them God was not pleased; for they were overthrown in the wilderness. Now these things are warnings for us, not to desire evil as they did … We must not indulge in immorality (*pornevōmen*) as some of them did (indulge in immorality (*epornevsan*);[5] and twenty-three thousand fell in a single day. (vv.1-6; 8a)

By drawing the hearers' attention to that previous passage, Paul is trying to remind them of the consequences should they not hearken to what he is about to tell them. He is not simply describing a static or ontological reality; he is trying to impress upon them how they ought to behave and, if they do not heed his warning, they are liable to experience what happened to the scriptural Israel in the wilderness!

Having established in the minds of his hearers the seriousness of the matter, Paul goes on to draw practical conclusions from the metaphor of the body (12:14-17). As to why each member is what it is and functions the way it does is not a matter of biology or nature but rather "as it is, *God* arranged (*etheto*; appointed) the organs in the body, each one of them, as *he* chose (*ēthelēsen*;

---

[5] Both these verbs *pornevōmen* and *epornevsan* are from the same root as *porneia* (harlotry).

willed)" (v.18). If Paul, the planter of the seed and the builder of the body, is himself what he is according "to the will of God" (1:1), how much more so is the body and its members. Hence, it does not help for anyone to question God's will and wisdom. Should God have allowed the believers to choose what they wanted to be, the body might have ended with just one member; in which case, it would not be the body in which God is ultimately interested (12:19-20). Furthermore, the members need one another so that there is no room for being puffed up and boasting (v.21; see also 4:6 and 8:1). Nature, which Paul already appealed to in 11:14-15, is such that "the parts of the body which seem to be weaker are indispensable, and those parts of the body which we think less honorable we invest with the greater honor, and our unpresentable (*askhēmona*; shameful) parts are treated with greater modesty (*evskhēmosynēn*; decorum, propriety), which our more presentable (*evskhēmona*) parts do not require" (12:22-24a). Again, it is God that "has so composed the body, giving the greater honor to the inferior part, that there may be no discord (*skhisma*; division; split) in the body, but *that the members may have the same care for one another*" (vv.24b-25). The use of *skhisma* clearly harks back to 1:10 and 11:18 and confirms that anything that threatens the oneness of the table fellowship and, by extension, of God's (one) church in Corinth (1:2) is a blasphemy against God and his will (1:1; 12:18). Indeed, God's ultimate aim is to invite all into his kingdom where his glory will shine and all will share in his joy. In the meantime, and in order to attain that glory and joy, all members are to share in the joy and suffering of the community: "If one member suffers, all suffer together; if one member is honored, all rejoice together." (12:26) Suffering with the other members and sharing in their glorification is tantamount to sharing this with Christ himself, through whom God consummates his plan: "…

and if children, then heirs, heirs of God and fellow heirs with Christ, provided we suffer with him in order that we may also be glorified with him." (Rom 8:17)

The entire discussion concerning the metaphor of the human body (1 Cor 12:12-26) is in view of the conclusion regarding the spiritual gifts (vv.27-30). This is clear from the following features:

1. The same phrase *etheto ho Theos* (God appointed, arranged) occurs in both passages (vv.18 and 28) to underscore the central point of the entire chapter, namely, the oneness of the origin of God's grace in spite of its multiple faces, as evidenced in the introductory vv.1-11.

2. In v.18 the complement noun of the verb *etheto* (arranged, appointed) is the "(body) members" whereas in v.28 it is the different recipients of God's spiritual gifts. By the same token, the "body" of v.18 becomes the "body of Christ" in v.28, which is specifically identified as the church community (v.29).

3. In the original Greek the second person plural "you" referring to Paul's addressees, which is used twice at the beginning (vv.1 [*hymas*] and 2 [*hymin*]), disappears thereafter only to reappear in v.27 (*hymeis*).[6]

The list of gifts is repeated twice, once in a positive manner (v.28) and the other time in a series of rhetorical questions

---

[6] And also v.31 (*hymin*).

(vv.29-30). This repetition is obviously intended to underscore the message. A close look at these two sections will evidence that Paul is already preparing for his preference of prophecy over speaking in tongues. In comparison with the first list (vv.8-10), where both gifts appear toward the end, in vv.28-30 prophecy is "promoted" to second position only after apostleship while speaking in tongues is kept at the tail end of both lists (v.28; vv.29-30). Moreover, in v.28, the first three gifts (apostles, prophets, and teachers) are specifically introduced with the ordinals "first," "second," and "third," while the rest of the gifts are then simply enumerated one after the other. Speaking in tongues is at the end of four gifts introduced *en bloc* with a single "then." Furthermore, two extra gifts—"helpers" (*antilēmpseis*) and "administrators" (*kybernēseis*)— not found in the other lists (vv.8-10 and 29-30) and unique in the New Testament, are listed before speaking in tongues. Finally, unlike the other two lists, v.28 ends with speaking in tongues without reference to the gift of interpretation, which addition would have placed the speaking in tongues in the penultimate rather the ultimate position.

The hierarchy of apostles, prophets, and teachers are all gifts that use the "intelligible word" which will be the main point in Paul's argument in chapter 14. It is precisely the church that is God's concern in 12:28, so it stands to reason then that a church prophet is second only to the apostle. In the latter's absence, an eventuality that Paul prepares his hearers for time and again in his letters, the prophets will carry on the apostolic teaching within the official gatherings of their respective churches. In counterpart, the teachers, whose authoritative reference is also the apostolic teaching based on scripture,[7] will work with individuals or small groups outside the official gatherings, whenever necessity arises.

However, before defending his preference for prophecy and in order not to allow the prophets to think that they are personally "better" than the speakers in tongues, Paul offers to show the Corinthians "a still more excellent way" (v.31b). His use of "way" brings to mind the only other instance of that noun in this letter:

> For though you have countless guides in Christ, you do not have many fathers. For I became your father in Christ Jesus through the gospel. I urge you, then, be imitators of me. Therefore I sent to you Timothy, my beloved and faithful child in the Lord, to remind you of my ways in Christ, as I teach them everywhere in every church. (4:15-17)

The example then of "a still more excellent way" is Paul himself. Such a conclusion is not farfetched given that, in chapter 14, we hear: "I thank God that I speak in tongues more than you all; nevertheless, in church I would rather speak five words with my mind, in order to instruct others, than ten thousand words in a tongue." (vv.18-19) Earlier in chapter 7 Paul wrote "I wish that all were as I myself am" (v.7a), and in chapter 9 Paul wrote

---

[7] See Romans where the duty of the teacher (*didaskōn*; instructor) is the teaching (*didaskalia*; instruction) (12:7) which is later explicated in the following words: "For whatever was written in former days was written for our instruction (*didaskalian*), that by steadfastness and by the encouragement of the scriptures we might have hope." (15:4) Hence the teaching of Paul's opponents is said to be merely *didaskalias tōn anthrōpōn* (teaching [instruction] of men; RSV has "human doctrines"; Col 2:22) which is earlier referred to as *tēn paradosin tōn anthrōpōn* (the tradition of men) in contradistinction to Paul's apostolic tradition: "Now we command you, brethren, in the name of our Lord Jesus Christ, that you keep away from any brother who is living in idleness and not in accord with *the tradition* (*tēn paradosin*) that you received from us." (2 Thess 3:6)

extensively of the sacrifices he put up with for the sake of his churches. Regardless of the gift, all are to be used to help the needy and less fortunate members of God's church and even the outsiders. As Paul made clear earlier: "Give no offense to Jews or to Greeks or to the church of God, just as I try to please all men in everything I do, not seeking my own advantage (*mē zētōn to hemavtou symphoron*), but that of many, that they may be saved. Be imitators of me, as I am of Christ." (10:32-11:1)

Chapter 13

Vv. 1-3 ¹Ἐὰν ταῖς γλώσσαις τῶν ἀνθρώπων λαλῶ καὶ τῶν ἀγγέλων, ἀγάπην δὲ μὴ ἔχω, γέγονα χαλκὸς ἠχῶν ἢ κύμβαλον ἀλαλάζον. ² καὶ ἐὰν ἔχω προφητείαν καὶ εἰδῶ τὰ μυστήρια πάντα καὶ πᾶσαν τὴν γνῶσιν καὶ ἐὰν ἔχω πᾶσαν τὴν πίστιν ὥστε ὄρη μεθιστάναι, ἀγάπην δὲ μὴ ἔχω, οὐθέν εἰμι. ³ κἂν ψωμίσω πάντα τὰ ὑπάρχοντά μου καὶ ἐὰν παραδῶ τὸ σῶμά μου ἵνα καυχήσωμαι, ἀγάπην δὲ μὴ ἔχω, οὐδὲν ὠφελοῦμαι.

> ¹*If I speak in the tongues of men and of angels, but have not love, I am a noisy gong or a clanging cymbal.* ²*And if I have prophetic powers, and understand all mysteries and all knowledge, and if I have all faith, so as to remove mountains, but have not love, I am nothing.* ³*If I give away all I have, and if I deliver my body to be burned, but have not love, I gain nothing.*

Paul begins his remarks by belittling speaking in tongues. Without love, not only speaking in human tongues but even speaking in the tongues of angels, the messengers of God's himself, is just empty boisterous noise (13:1), and persons doing so would be equivalent to the Old Testament "false prophets"; although in appearance they may seem to be "spiritual," in actuality they are not:

> Son of man, prophesy against the prophets of Israel, prophesy and say to those who prophesy out of their own minds: "Hear the word of the Lord!" Thus says the Lord God, Woe to the foolish prophets who follow *their own spirit*, and have seen nothing! ... My hand will be against the prophets who see delusive visions and who give lying divinations; *they shall not be in the council of my people*." (Ezek 13:2-3, 9)

Nonetheless, the same rule equally applies to the recipients of other gifts, including prophecy (1 Cor 13:2). Notice how Paul generalizes his verdict by bringing into the picture "understanding all mysteries and all knowledge" and "having all faith." Knowledge and faith have been introduced as gifts of the Spirit (12:8-9). Given that the two earlier mentions of "mysteries" in this letter are connected with the apostolic preaching (2:7; 4:1), it stands to reason to conclude that its occurrence here is directed toward the apostles who are at the head of the list of the recipients of the Spirit's gifts (12:28). Such should not be considered totally unexpected since later, in 2 Corinthians 11:10-15, Paul will unequivocally defend his love for the Corinthians by contrasting his apostolic behavior with that of his colleagues:

> As the truth of Christ is in me, this boast of mine shall not be silenced in the regions of Achaia. And why? Because *I do not love you?* God knows I do! And what I do I will continue to do, in order to undermine the claim of those who would like to claim that in their boasted mission they work on the same terms as we do. For such men are *false apostles*, deceitful workmen, disguising themselves as apostles of Christ. And no wonder, for even Satan disguises himself as an angel of light. So it is not strange if his servants also disguise themselves as servants of righteousness. Their end will correspond to their deeds.

It is only sincere love that functions as the standard of judgment concerning even the gifts of God's spirit. It is the sole rule that binds everyone and every behavior in God's church since it is nothing less than God's "law" (see Rom 8:2; 13:8-10; Gal 5:13-15; 6:2).

Vv. 4-7 ⁴ Ἡ ἀγάπη μακροθυμεῖ, χρηστεύεται ἡ ἀγάπη, οὐ ζηλοῖ, [ἡ ἀγάπη] οὐ περπερεύεται, οὐ φυσιοῦται, ⁵ οὐκ ἀσχημονεῖ, οὐ ζητεῖ τὰ ἑαυτῆς, οὐ παροξύνεται, οὐ λογίζεται τὸ κακόν, ⁶ οὐ χαίρει ἐπὶ τῇ ἀδικίᾳ, συγχαίρει δὲ τῇ ἀληθείᾳ· ⁷πάντα στέγει, πάντα πιστεύει, πάντα ἐλπίζει, πάντα ὑπομένει.

⁴Love is patient and kind; love is not jealous or boastful; ⁵it is not arrogant or rude. Love does not insist on its own way; it is not irritable or resentful; ⁶it does not rejoice at wrong, but rejoices in the right. ⁷Love bears all things, believes all things, hopes all things, endures all things.

One should not imagine that Paul found this "ode" in the form of a ready-made litany circulating in the churches or in society at large and incorporated it into his letter. In my discussion of the so-called "Christological hymns" (Phil 2:6-11 and Col 1:15-20) I concluded that they were ad hoc productions of the writer himself,[1] and so is the case here in 1 Corinthians 13:4-7. The description of true love fits perfectly within the argument of the chapter.

The entire passage is bracketed between "is patient" (*makrothymei*: is long suffering) and "endures (*hypomenei*; forbears) all things." The first is a quintessentially divine quality as is clear from Romans 2:4 and 9:22. It is a feature of God's Christ (1 Tim 1:16) and is required from the apostles (2 Cor 6:6; 2 Tim 3:10), the church leaders (2 Tim 4:2), and the believers (Gal 5:22;[2] Eph 4:2; Col 1:11; 3:12; 1 Thess 5:14; Heb 6:12). This patience is to be lived while one is enduring forbearance in all the difficulties pertaining to the life of the believer. The reason for such endurance is the hope of what lies

---

[1] See *C-Phil* 106-133 and *C-Col* 36-54.
[2] In this case it is, together with love, an expression of the fruit of the Spirit.

ahead. This can be seen in that it immediately follows "love hopes everything" in the list.[3]

On the other hand, "patience" is coupled with "kindness" (*khrēstevetai*), which pairing is enhanced by the fact that the long list of love's qualifications that follow this verse are all in the negative (1 Cor 10:4b-6a). To the hearer's ear, then, patience and kindness go hand in hand; one is to be patient while being kind. In Galatians 5:22, and also in Romans 2:4; 2 Corinthians 6:6; and Colossians 3:12, one finds the same sequence of patience and kindness and both, together with love, are the fruit of the Spirit. However, what is striking in our text (1 Cor 13:4) is that they are singled out as a pair. In my discussion of the noun *khrēstologia* (fair talk, kind talk) in Romans (16:18), I commented on the play between the assonant *Khristos* (Christ) and *khrēstos* (kind; meek).[4] Similarly here, the two verbs that positively qualify love—*makrothymei* and *khrēstevetai*—are meant to establish in the hearers' ears that the love they are expected to emulate is that of God and his Christ or, more precisely, God's love expressed through his Christ's behavior (Rom 5:1-11; 8:35-39).

The first negative directive concerning love that is singled out is jealousy, which speaks directly to the main reason for the writing of the letter: discord within God's one church. The expression of jealousy (*zēloi*; is jealous, 13:4) produces strife (*eris*; 3:3), which in turn splits (*erides*; quarreling, 1:11) the one church. Indeed, jealousy prohibits the zeal (*zēloute*; earnestly desire, 1 Cor 12:31) for the higher gifts.

---

[3] I have discussed in detail how *hypomonē* (forbearance; endurance) and *elpis* (hope) function together as the two sides of the same coin; see *1 Thess* 39-41.

[4] See *C-Rom* 283-4. The same wordplay can be detected in Mt 11:30 where Jesus refers to his yoke as *khrēstos* (easy, kind).

The following directives are coupled in pairs. The second and third negative directives (*ou perperevetai* [is not boastful], *ou physioutai* [is not arrogant]) go hand in hand in that the arrogant are often boastful. The attitude of *physioutai* (being "puffed up") was the object of Paul's criticism earlier in the letter (4:8 and in 8:1). The following *ouk askhēmonei* (is not rude) harks back to what Paul wrote a few verses earlier: "On the contrary, the parts of the body which seem to be weaker are indispensable, and those parts of the body which we think less honorable we invest with the greater honor, and our unpresentable (*askhēmona*) parts are treated with greater modesty (*evskhēmosynēn*; respect, honor), which our more presentable (*evskhēmona*) parts do not require." (12:22-24a) The counterpart of disregard toward the others is "seeking one's interest," which is prohibited. The next pair of negative directives, *ou paroxynetai, ou logizetai to kakon* (is not irritable or resentful), means "does not provoke to wrath and does not reckon evil (for others)." These two attitudes are the exclusive right of God as judge of all. Yet, if God himself opted for forbearance and kindness (Rom 2:4), then the Corinthians are to follow his example and never indulge in expressing their own judgment of others: "Beloved, never avenge yourselves, but leave it to the wrath of God; for it is written, 'Vengeance is mine, I will repay, says the Lord' ... Who are you to pass judgment on the servant of another? It is before his own master that he stands or falls. And he will be upheld, for the Master is able to make him stand." (Rom 12:19; 14:4). The last pair of directives is "(love) does not rejoice at wrong (*epi tē adikia*; over unrighteousness), but rejoices in the right (*tē alētheia*; truth as sworn to in court)" (1 Cor 13:6). Unrighteousness and right are legal terms that corroborate a judicial setting where God alone is the judge and his judgment is one of loving mercy through Jesus Christ (Rom 5:1-11; 8:31-39).

The passage ends with a foursome that functions as steps leading to the Kingdom and is a fitting conclusion to what was announced as "the more excellent way" (1 Cor 12:31b). The first step is "bearing (*stegei*; enduring) everything (*panta*)." If patience was invitation to emulate God and kindness another to imitate Christ (13:4a), then the invitation to "bear" all things is to follow in Paul's footsteps. Indeed earlier in the letter, when describing his behavior as an apostle with divine authority, Paul wrote: "If others share this rightful claim upon you, do not we still more? Nevertheless, we have not made use of this right, but *we endure anything* (*panta stegomen*; bear everything; endure all; bear all) rather than put an obstacle in the way of the gospel of Christ." (9:12) He explained the aim of such behavior a few verses later with the words "I do it all (*panta*) for the sake of the gospel, that I may share in (be a partaker of) its blessings" (v.23). In turn, such partaking takes place through the acceptance of the prize (*brabeion*) at the end of the race (v.24), and that prize is the coming Kingdom: "Brethren, I do not consider that I have made it my own; but one thing I do, forgetting what lies behind and straining forward to what lies ahead, I press on toward the goal for the prize (*brabeion*) of the upward call of God in Christ Jesus … But our commonwealth is in heaven, and from it we await a Savior, the Lord Jesus Christ." (Phil 3:13-14, 20) Along with love that endures everything, the other steps on that "way" are trust (faith) and hope, as Paul explicitly teaches:

> We always thank God, the Father of our Lord Jesus Christ, when we pray for you, because we have heard of your faith in Christ Jesus and of the love which you have for all the saints, because of the hope laid up for you in heaven. (Col 1:3-5)

> We give thanks to God always for you all, constantly mentioning you in our prayers, remembering before our God and Father your

work of faith and labor of love and steadfastness of hope in our Lord Jesus Christ. (1 Thess 1:2-3)

Having mentioned hope, Paul wraps up the passage with forbearance (*hypomenei*), the other facet of hope, which forms an *inclusio* with patience (*makrothymei*; 1 Cor 13:4). This is to underscore that the believers are always "on the way," and the spiritual gifts are not a sign that the Kingdom is already here and one can hail, "mission accomplished." Like the spiritual gifts given in the wilderness (1 Cor 10:3-4), the gifts bestowed on the church members are to sustain God's congregation on that way; mishandling those gifts can lead to a calamitous consequence: "Nevertheless with most of them God was not pleased; for they were overthrown in the wilderness." (v.5)

Vv. 8-13 ⁸ Ἡ ἀγάπη οὐδέποτε πίπτει· εἴτε δὲ προφητεῖαι, καταργηθήσονται· εἴτε γλῶσσαι, παύσονται· εἴτε γνῶσις, καταργηθήσεται. ⁹ ἐκ μέρους γὰρ γινώσκομεν καὶ ἐκ μέρους προφητεύομεν· ¹⁰ ὅταν δὲ ἔλθῃ τὸ τέλειον, τὸ ἐκ μέρους καταργηθήσεται. ¹¹ ὅτε ἤμην νήπιος, ἐλάλουν ὡς νήπιος, ἐφρόνουν ὡς νήπιος, ἐλογιζόμην ὡς νήπιος· ὅτε γέγονα ἀνήρ, κατήργηκα τὰ τοῦ νηπίου. ¹² βλέπομεν γὰρ ἄρτι δι' ἐσόπτρου ἐν αἰνίγματι, τότε δὲ πρόσωπον πρὸς πρόσωπον· ἄρτι γινώσκω ἐκ μέρους, τότε δὲ ἐπιγνώσομαι καθὼς καὶ ἐπεγνώσθην. ¹³ Νυνὶ δὲ μένει πίστις, ἐλπίς, ἀγάπη, τὰ τρία ταῦτα· μείζων δὲ τούτων ἡ ἀγάπη.

> ⁸*Love never ends; as for prophecies, they will pass away; as for tongues, they will cease; as for knowledge, it will pass away.* ⁹*For our knowledge is imperfect and our prophecy is imperfect;* ¹⁰*but when the perfect comes, the imperfect will pass away.* ¹¹*When I was a child, I spoke like a child, I thought like a child, I reasoned like a child; when I became a man, I gave up childish ways.* ¹²*For now we see in a mirror dimly, but then face to face. Now I know in part; then I shall understand fully, even as I*

have been fully understood. ¹³*So faith, hope, love abide, these three; but the greatest of these is love.*

In the Pauline gospel, love never fails (*piptei*; falls [during the race], is short of attaining the goal) because it is anchored in trust (faith) while it awaits, in sure hope, the coming Kingdom.[5] Love is the basic necessary attitude required of each and every believer. It is not a function given to one and not to another. In other words, whereas an individual believer can proceed "on the way" without this or that spiritual gift, he cannot attain the prized goal without the necessary condition of love for the others. Indeed, in order to emphasize this point, Paul writes that all gifts are bound to cease since they are merely functional. This not only applies to prophecy and speaking in tongues, but even to wisdom and knowledge which have the place of honor in the first list of gifts (1 Cor 12:8-10). Since wisdom and knowledge are linked to the gift of apostleship, what Paul is actually saying sounds thus: "If apostleship will find its end when the Lord comes, no less will prophecy and speaking in tongues!"

A major difficulty raised by the original Greek in 1 Corinthians 13:8-13 is the meaning of *ek merous* that is translated thrice as "imperfect" in vv.9-10 and once as "in part" in v.12, and earlier in 12:27 it was rendered as "individually." All the other instances of prepositional *merous* found in the Pauline corpus are part of the phrase *apo merous* (Rom 11:25; 15:15,[6] 24;[7] 2 Cor 1:14; 2:5) where it is always taken to mean "partly, to some extent." Consequently, the expressions *ek merous* and *apo merous* do not seem to bear the same connotation. Furthermore,

---

[5] RSV's "ends" does not render the connotation of the original *piptei* (falls) since it is influenced by v.13 where love is said to "abide."

[6] Translated as "on some points" in RSV.

[7] Translated as "for a little" in RSV.

why would *ek merous* have two different meanings within the same context (1 Cor 12-13)? On the other hand, it stands to reason to assume that the first instance (12:27) is the controlling factor concerning the meaning and function of *ek merous*. There the meaning "partly" does not fit since the result would be that v.27b (you are partly members of it) would contradict v.27a (you are the body of Christ). The intention is rather to underscore what was repeatedly expressed earlier: "For just as the body is one and has many members (*melē*), and all the members (*melē*) of the body, though many, are one body, so it is with Christ … For the body does not consist of one member (*melos*) but of many … As it is, there are many parts (*melē*), yet one body." (vv.12, 14, 20) The meaning of these verses is so evident that RSV did not shy from translating *melē* as "parts" instead of "members" in v.20. That is to say, *meros* (part) is equivalent to *melos* (member) throughout chapters 12-13 and does not connote an undefined part (portion) of a totality and, by extension, an imperfection when compared with the fullness (*teleion*; perfection, totality; 13:10). Put otherwise, in the church community, the believers are to accede to the full knowledge that only Paul has and which he communicates through *all* his writings that are to be repeatedly heard at church gatherings (Col 4:16).

With that in mind, a closer look at the similarity between the vocabulary of 1 Corinthians 13:1-3 and vv.8-13 will betray that the intention is to belittle speaking in tongues and, more so, prophecy since Paul is going to side with the latter over the former in chapter 14. If the apostle is functional, then certainly the second in line, the prophet, is also functional. The harshness exhibited against the end of prophecy and its counterpart, knowledge, when compared to the softness used to speak of the end of speaking in tongues, is telling:

> Love never ends (falls); as for prophecies, they will pass away (*katargēthēsontai*; will be destroyed; will be rendered invalid, obsolete); as for tongues, they will cease (*pavsontai*); as for knowledge, it will pass away (*katargēthēsetai*). For our knowledge is imperfect (*ek merous*) and our prophecy is imperfect (*ek merous*); but when the perfect comes, the imperfect (*ek merous*) will pass away (*katargēthēsetai*). (vv.8-10)

Not only is the verb used with tongues gentler than the one describing prophecy, but it is prophetic knowledge that is the main subject of imperfection when the perfect comes (vv. 9-10). This belittlement of prophecy is in view of the following chapter where Paul unequivocally expresses his preference for prophecy over speaking in tongues and wants to ensure that his assessment not be misunderstood: prophecy is only *functionally*, and *not absolutely*, to be preferred, as will become clear in chapter 14. By the same token, one is to understand the phrase *ek merous* against what Paul is about to write in that chapter:

> Let two or three prophets speak, and let the others weigh what is said (*diakrinetōsan*; discern [the value of what is said]; emit a discerning judgment). If a revelation is made to another sitting by, let the first be silent. For you can all prophesy *one by one* (*kath' hena*), so that all may learn and all be encouraged; and the spirits of prophets are subject to prophets. (vv.29-32).

Here it is clear that both the prophets are to speak *individually* and that the speech of each is bound to assessment, as Paul ordains elsewhere: "Do not quench the Spirit, do not despise prophesying, but test everything." (1 Thess 5:19-21a) Consequently, *ek merous* in 1 Corinthians 13:9-10 has the meaning of "individually" as in 12:27, but also reflects that the individual prophet is only a "part" of the totality, which is Christ himself whose full body is the church and thus represents *to teleion* (the fullness, the perfection; 13:10). Such perfection "comes" (13:10), that is, it will not be revealed except at Christ's "coming." Thus the fullness (perfection) of what each member is "partly" doing is ahead, and that is why each of the Corinthians should forbear "in hope" (v.7a) while exercising his personal gift *in love*, which is *the "way"* required of one and all (12:31).

The first of the two examples appealed to in 13:11-12 corroborates this conclusion: "When I was a child (*nēpios*; babe), I spoke like a child (*nēpios*; babe), I thought like a child (*nēpios*; babe), I reasoned (*elogizomēn*; reckoned) like a child (*nēpios*; babe); when I became a man, I gave up childish (*tou nēpiou*; of the babe) ways." (v.11) The fivefold mention of the term *nēpios* that occurred only once before (3:1) cannot but be intended to bring to mind what Paul wrote there: "But I, brethren, could not address (*lalēsai*; speak to) you as spiritual men, but as men of the flesh, as babes [*nēpiois*] in Christ." In turn, this statement harks back, through the use of the verb *lalō* (speak), to 2:6 (Yet among the mature [*teleiois*; perfect] we do impart [*laloumen*; speak] wisdom, although it is not a wisdom of this age or of the rulers of this age, who are doomed to pass away [*katargoumenōn*]) where we hear the two main terms, "perfect" and "pass away," of the passage 13:8-10. The perfection (full maturity) will always lie ahead of the Corinthians who thus have no valid reason to boast of their personal spiritual gifts. This, in turn, explains why the second and final example takes the phrase *ek merous* and blends it with a terminology used earlier to speak of love as being more beneficial for the church than knowledge: "For now we see in a mirror dimly, but then face to face. Now I know (*ginōskō*) in part (*ek merous*); then I shall understand fully (*epignōsomai*), even as I have been fully understood (*epegnōsthēn*)" (v.12). Compare with 8:1-3:

> Now concerning food offered to idols: we know that "all of us possess knowledge (*gnōsis*)." "Knowledge" (*gnōsis*) puffs up (*physioi*),[8] but love builds up (*oikodomei*).[9] If any one imagines that he knows (*egnōkenai*) something, he does not yet know (*egnō*) as he ought to know (*gnōnai*). But if one loves God, one is known (*egnōstai*) by him.

In 13:12 Paul is saying that what will lead the Corinthians into God's kingdom is for them to love fully (and not partly), that is to say, to unconditionally love the others just as God loved them fully and unconditionally. Only such a "way" of living will make them full partners in the Kingdom's table fellowship, a partnership they trusted (believed) in and for which they hope. In this sense, although trust (faith) and hope must abide in our daily lives together with love, it is love that is, functionally, the greatest (v.13). As Paul eloquently wrote in Galatians, "For through the Spirit, by *faith*, we wait for the *hope* of righteousness. For in Christ Jesus neither circumcision nor uncircumcision is of any avail, but *faith working through love*." (5:5-6)

---

[8] This verb was used earlier in chapter 13 (v.4; *physioutai*).
[9] This Greek root will be used profusely in chapter 14.

Chapter 14

Vv. 1-25 ¹Διώκετε τὴν ἀγάπην, ζηλοῦτε δὲ τὰ πνευματικά, μᾶλλον δὲ ἵνα προφητεύητε. ² ὁ γὰρ λαλῶν γλώσσῃ οὐκ ἀνθρώποις λαλεῖ ἀλλὰ θεῷ· οὐδεὶς γὰρ ἀκούει, πνεύματι δὲ λαλεῖ μυστήρια· ³ ὁ δὲ προφητεύων ἀνθρώποις λαλεῖ οἰκοδομὴν καὶ παράκλησιν καὶ παραμυθίαν. ⁴ ὁ λαλῶν γλώσσῃ ἑαυτὸν οἰκοδομεῖ· ὁ δὲ προφητεύων ἐκκλησίαν οἰκοδομεῖ. ⁵ θέλω δὲ πάντας ὑμᾶς λαλεῖν γλώσσαις, μᾶλλον δὲ ἵνα προφητεύητε· μείζων δὲ ὁ προφητεύων ἢ ὁ λαλῶν γλώσσαις ἐκτὸς εἰ μὴ διερμηνεύῃ, ἵνα ἡ ἐκκλησία οἰκοδομὴν λάβῃ. ⁶ Νῦν δέ, ἀδελφοί, ἐὰν ἔλθω πρὸς ὑμᾶς γλώσσαις λαλῶν, τί ὑμᾶς ὠφελήσω ἐὰν μὴ ὑμῖν λαλήσω ἢ ἐν ἀποκαλύψει ἢ ἐν γνώσει ἢ ἐν προφητείᾳ ἢ [ἐν] διδαχῇ; ⁷ ὅμως τὰ ἄψυχα φωνὴν διδόντα, εἴτε αὐλὸς εἴτε κιθάρα, ἐὰν διαστολὴν τοῖς φθόγγοις μὴ δῷ, πῶς γνωσθήσεται τὸ αὐλούμενον ἢ τὸ κιθαριζόμενον; ⁸ καὶ γὰρ ἐὰν ἄδηλον σάλπιγξ φωνὴν δῷ, τίς παρασκευάσεται εἰς πόλεμον; ⁹οὕτως καὶ ὑμεῖς διὰ τῆς γλώσσης ἐὰν μὴ εὔσημον λόγον δῶτε, πῶς γνωσθήσεται τὸ λαλούμενον; ἔσεσθε γὰρ εἰς ἀέρα λαλοῦντες. ¹⁰ τοσαῦτα εἰ τύχοι γένη φωνῶν εἰσιν ἐν κόσμῳ καὶ οὐδὲν ἄφωνον· ¹¹ ἐὰν οὖν μὴ εἰδῶ τὴν δύναμιν τῆς φωνῆς, ἔσομαι τῷ λαλοῦντι βάρβαρος καὶ ὁ λαλῶν ἐν ἐμοὶ βάρβαρος. ¹² οὕτως καὶ ὑμεῖς, ἐπεὶ ζηλωταί ἐστε πνευμάτων, πρὸς τὴν οἰκοδομὴν τῆς ἐκκλησίας ζητεῖτε ἵνα περισσεύητε. ¹³ Διὸ ὁ λαλῶν γλώσσῃ προσευχέσθω ἵνα διερμηνεύῃ. ¹⁴ ἐὰν [γὰρ] προσεύχωμαι γλώσσῃ, τὸ πνεῦμά μου προσεύχεται, ὁ δὲ νοῦς μου ἄκαρπός ἐστιν. ¹⁵ τί οὖν ἐστιν; προσεύξομαι τῷ πνεύματι, προσεύξομαι δὲ καὶ τῷ νοΐ· ψαλῶ τῷ πνεύματι, ψαλῶ δὲ καὶ τῷ νοΐ. ¹⁶ ἐπεὶ ἐὰν εὐλογῇς [ἐν] πνεύματι, ὁ ἀναπληρῶν τὸν τόπον τοῦ ἰδιώτου πῶς ἐρεῖ τὸ ἀμὴν ἐπὶ τῇ σῇ εὐχαριστίᾳ; ἐπειδὴ τί λέγεις οὐκ οἶδεν· ¹⁷ σὺ μὲν γὰρ καλῶς εὐχαριστεῖς ἀλλ' ὁ ἕτερος οὐκ οἰκοδομεῖται. ¹⁸ Εὐχαριστῶ τῷ θεῷ, πάντων ὑμῶν μᾶλλον γλώσσαις λαλῶ· ¹⁹ ἀλλὰ ἐν ἐκκλησίᾳ θέλω πέντε λόγους τῷ νοΐ μου λαλῆσαι, ἵνα καὶ ἄλλους κατηχήσω, ἢ μυρίους λόγους ἐν γλώσσῃ. ²⁰ Ἀδελφοί, μὴ παιδία γίνεσθε ταῖς φρεσὶν ἀλλὰ τῇ κακίᾳ νηπιάζετε, ταῖς δὲ φρεσὶν τέλειοι γίνεσθε. ²¹ ἐν τῷ νόμῳ γέγραπται ὅτι ἐν ἑτερογλώσσοις καὶ ἐν χείλεσιν ἑτέρων λαλήσω τῷ λαῷ τούτῳ καὶ οὐδ' οὕτως εἰσακούσονταί μου, λέγει κύριος. ²² ὥστε αἱ γλῶσσαι εἰς σημεῖόν εἰσιν οὐ τοῖς πιστεύουσιν ἀλλὰ τοῖς ἀπίστοις, ἡ δὲ προφητεία οὐ τοῖς ἀπίστοις ἀλλὰ τοῖς πιστεύουσιν. ²³ Ἐὰν οὖν συνέλθῃ ἡ ἐκκλησία ὅλη ἐπὶ τὸ αὐτὸ καὶ πάντες λαλῶσιν γλώσσαις, εἰσέλθωσιν δὲ ἰδιῶται ἢ ἄπιστοι, οὐκ ἐροῦσιν ὅτι μαίνεσθε; ²⁴ ἐὰν δὲ πάντες προφητεύωσιν, εἰσέλθῃ δέ τις ἄπιστος ἢ ἰδιώτης, ἐλέγχεται ὑπὸ πάντων, ἀνακρίνεται ὑπὸ πάντων, ²⁵ τὰ κρυπτὰ τῆς καρδίας αὐτοῦ φανερὰ γίνεται, καὶ οὕτως πεσὼν ἐπὶ πρόσωπον προσκυνήσει τῷ θεῷ ἀπαγγέλλων ὅτι ὄντως ὁ θεὸς ἐν ὑμῖν ἐστιν.

¹ *Make love your aim, and earnestly desire the spiritual gifts, especially that you may prophesy.* ²*For one who speaks in a tongue speaks not to men but to God; for no one understands him, but he utters mysteries in the Spirit.* ³*On the other hand, he who prophesies speaks to men for their upbuilding and encouragement and consolation.* ⁴*He who speaks in a tongue edifies himself, but he who prophesies edifies the church.* ⁵*Now I want you all to speak in tongues, but even more to prophesy. He who prophesies is greater than he who speaks in tongues, unless some one interprets, so that the church may be edified.* ⁶*Now, brethren, if I come to you speaking in tongues, how shall I benefit you unless I bring you some revelation or knowledge or prophecy or teaching?* ⁷*If even lifeless instruments, such as the flute or the harp, do not give distinct notes, how will any one know what is played?* ⁸*And if the bugle gives an indistinct sound, who will get ready for battle?* ⁹*So with yourselves; if you in a tongue utter speech that is not intelligible, how will any one know what is said? For you will be speaking into the air.* ¹⁰*There are doubtless many different languages in the world, and none is without meaning;* ¹¹*but if I do not know the meaning of the language, I shall be a foreigner to the speaker*

and the speaker a foreigner to me. ⁱ²So with yourselves; since you are eager for manifestations of the Spirit, strive to excel in building up the church. ¹³Therefore, he who speaks in a tongue should pray for the power to interpret. ¹⁴For if I pray in a tongue, my spirit prays but my mind is unfruitful. ¹⁵What am I to do? I will pray with the spirit and I will pray with the mind also; I will sing with the spirit and I will sing with the mind also. ¹⁶Otherwise, if you bless with the spirit, how can any one in the position of an outsider say the "Amen" to your thanksgiving when he does not know what you are saying? ¹⁷For you may give thanks well enough, but the other man is not edified. ¹⁸I thank God that I speak in tongues more than you all; ¹⁹nevertheless, in church I would rather speak five words with my mind, in order to instruct others, than ten thousand words in a tongue. ²⁰Brethren, do not be children in your thinking; be babes in evil, but in thinking be mature. ²¹In the law it is written, "By men of strange tongues and by the lips of foreigners will I speak to this people, and even then they will not listen to me, says the Lord." ²²Thus, tongues are a sign not for believers but for unbelievers, while prophecy is not for unbelievers but for believers. ²³If, therefore, the whole church assembles and all speak in tongues, and outsiders or unbelievers enter, will they not say that you are mad? ²⁴But if all prophesy, and an unbeliever or outsider enters, he is convicted by all, he is called to account by all, ²⁵the secrets of his heart are disclosed; and so, falling on his face, he will worship God and declare that God is really among you.

After writing in detail why and how to continually pursue (*diōkete*; make it one's aim) the "way" of love (1 Cor 14:1a; see 12:31b), Paul moves on to the spiritual gifts (14:1b; see 12:31a) and, in this matter, he does not hide his preference for prophecy over speaking in tongues (14:1c). The reason for this is clear: although the speaker in a tongue talks, the others cannot possibly "listen" (*akouei*; hear, and thus understand; v.2) and thus be edified into the one body of Christ. Therefore, the speaker in a tongue would not be acting toward "the common good" which is God's ultimate intention behind his imparting his gifts to "every one" (12:4-7). By speaking something that only God understands, it as though he is speaking only to God and, in so doing, he is hiding God's word from the people instead of sharing it with them. Such is, at best, ludicrous and, at worst, blasphemous since, after all, God is in no need of hearing his own word! The prophet, on the other hand, speaks to the people for their "upbuilding (*oikodomēn*; edification) and encouragement (*paraklēsin*; exhortation) and consolation" (14:3). The centrality of the idea of edification, which pervades the entire chapter, is evident in the following verse: "He who speaks in a tongue edifies himself, but he who prophesies edifies the church." (v.4) Since the church as a community, and not the individual member, is God's concern (1:1-2; 3:16-17; 10:32; 11:22; 12:28), the one who edifies it has the place of honor. Actually the original Greek of 14:4 reflects an ironic statement concerning the speakers in tongues. The verb *oikodomei* (edifies) literally means "builds a house" and thus assumes a multiplicity of stones (see e.g. 3:10-15) and thus many individuals in the case of the church. To build oneself, that is to say, to build with one stone is oxymoronic. However, in order not to give absolute value to the precedence of prophecy over speaking in tongues for the edification of the church, Paul immediately adds that, should there be an interpreter, then the speaker in a tongue would function similarly to the prophet (v.5) since, in that case, the message reaching the hearers would be understood.

Paul uses common examples to underscore the necessity of transmitting the message, and not merely uttering it. The ultimate aim of all the gifts is for the benefit of the common members. Such applies not only to prophecy and teaching, but also to revelation and knowledge. Unless these are imparted to others, the verdict of 1 Corinthians 8:1-3 would apply. In scripture knowledge is not tantamount to amassing information about a certain matter; rather knowledge is communicated by God through revelation on his part in order for the speaker to function as his medium (Is 6:1-13; Jer 1:4-10; Ezek 2:1-3:7; Jon 2:10-3:3; 4:1-11; Gal 1:15-16). Moreover, since people are to receive the message, it must be comprehensible to them (1 Cor 14:6-10); otherwise, both the speaker and the recipients would be de facto "barbarians"[1] to one another (v.11). This must have hit a sensitive chord in the ears of the Corinthians who were inhabitants of the capital city of the Roman province Achaia, a geographical area encompassing ancient Greece including Athens and Sparta. Ancient Greeks prided themselves of being Hellenes and not barbarians, and Paul is literally leveling this differentiation! The edification of the entire church membership is to be desired and sought after in excellence (v.12) by those endowed with the manifestations of the Spirit (*zēlōtai pnevmatōn*). Therefore, when a speaker in a tongue is to pray in the midst of the congregation as a prophet would (11:4-5), there should be an interpreter present to impart the "revelation," be it the speaker himself or someone else who is fluent in that same tongue (v.13).[2]

The following passage (vv.14-19) not only corroborates this understanding of the communal prayer but also goes hand in hand with what we find in Colossians, namely, that the main

---

[1] RSV uses the smoother sounding "foreigner" for *barbaros* in v.11.
[2] The original Greek allows either interpretation.

aspect of such communal prayer is thanksgiving.[3] This, in turn, confirms that the church gathering was essentially one at table fellowship during which the members, through their elders, thanked God not only for the earthly food but also and more importantly for the "spiritual" bread imparted through the reading of scripture and exhortatory comments on such reading. Notice the sequence "psalmody" (v.15),[4] "blessing" (v.16), and "thanksgiving" (vv.16-18). In comments on Colossians 3:16, I explained that the phrase "singing psalms" referred to reciting from the Book of Psalms as representative of the "scriptural story."[5] After reciting from "scripture," the wine and bread are blessed (1 Cor 10:16), which in turn is followed by "thanksgiving" (v.30). The exhortation through intelligible words in conjunction with the reading from scripture is imperative not only for instruction (14:19) but also to make sure that the recipients understand and acknowledge their submission to that teaching through their "Amen" (v.16). It is in this way that they are edified (v.17), that is to say, built up into the temple of God (3:10-17) and the body of Christ (10:16-17; 12:12, 27).

Having finished his examples, Paul reverts back to his main point which is that, practically speaking, prophecy is to be preferred over the gift of tongues. He begins by inviting the Corinthians to remain babes in matters of evil doing, but mature (*teleioi*; perfect) as Christ is[6] in their manner of thinking. To back his teaching, he uses "In the law it is written" to denote scripture in its totality before the actual reference to Isaiah

---

[3] See my comments in *C-Col* 64, 87, 93.
[4] The original Greek, translated as "sing" in RSV, is actually the verb *psallō* literally meaning "psalm (as verb), intone a psalm."
[5] See my comments in *C-Col* 85-7.
[6] See my comments earlier on 1 Cor 13:10.

28:11-12, which he rephrases to mirror a classic teaching in the Prophets[7] whereby God punishes his people with nations whose language is foreign and thus confusing rather than understandable. Paul does this to impress on the Corinthian hearers that what they are allowing in their gatherings will lead to divine punishment rather than edification. He then proceeds to explain why (1 Cor 14:22-25). According to scripture, "strange" languages are a sign of punishment of those who do not trust God. Hopefully, the prophetic word will educate and edify those who openly trust in its teaching (v.22). If only those who have the gift of tongues speak, then the outsiders (*idiōtai*; commoners) or unbelievers will think that the church is a meeting of mad people (v.23). Conversely, if only those who are granted the gift of prophecy speak, then the outsider or unbeliever would be convicted by their divine utterance (v.24). The hidden secrets of the unbeliever's heart will be revealed (v.25a), as they would be on judgment day (Rom 2:16), bringing him to acknowledge that indeed God, the judge of all, is actually presiding in the church (1 Cor 14:25b). This is precisely the function of the church gathering (11:17-34) as is evident from the use of the same phraseology in 11:20 and 14:23: "When you meet together" (*Synerkhomenōn epi to avto*; When you assemble for the same purpose)"; "If, therefore, the whole church assembles" (*synelthē epi to avto*; assembles [is assembled] for the same purpose).[8]

Vv. 26-40 ²⁶ Τί οὖν ἐστιν, ἀδελφοί; ὅταν συνέρχησθε, ἕκαστος ψαλμὸν ἔχει, διδαχὴν ἔχει, ἀποκάλυψιν ἔχει, γλῶσσαν ἔχει, ἑρμηνείαν ἔχει· πάντα πρὸς οἰκοδομὴν

---

[7] Notice at the end of the quotation Paul's intentional "prophetic" style addition "says the Lord," which is not in the original.

[8] *Synerkhmenōn* (active participle) and *synelthē* (indicative aorist) are two different forms of the same verb *synerkhomai* (assemble, come together).

γινέσθω. ²⁷ εἴτε γλώσσῃ τις λαλεῖ, κατὰ δύο ἢ τὸ πλεῖστον τρεῖς καὶ ἀνὰ μέρος, καὶ εἷς διερμηνευέτω· ²⁸ ἐὰν δὲ μὴ ᾖ διερμηνευτής, σιγάτω ἐν ἐκκλησίᾳ, ἑαυτῷ δὲ λαλείτω καὶ τῷ θεῷ. ²⁹ προφῆται δὲ δύο ἢ τρεῖς λαλείτωσαν καὶ οἱ ἄλλοι διακρινέτωσαν· ³⁰ ἐὰν δὲ ἄλλῳ ἀποκαλυφθῇ καθημένῳ, ὁ πρῶτος σιγάτω. ³¹ δύνασθε γὰρ καθ' ἕνα πάντες προφητεύειν, ἵνα πάντες μανθάνωσιν καὶ πάντες παρακαλῶνται. ³² καὶ πνεύματα προφητῶν προφήταις ὑποτάσσεται, ³³ οὐ γάρ ἐστιν ἀκαταστασίας ὁ θεὸς ἀλλὰ εἰρήνης. Ὡς ἐν πάσαις ταῖς ἐκκλησίαις τῶν ἁγίων ³⁴ αἱ γυναῖκες ἐν ταῖς ἐκκλησίαις σιγάτωσαν· οὐ γὰρ ἐπιτρέπεται αὐταῖς λαλεῖν, ἀλλὰ ὑποτασσέσθωσαν, καθὼς καὶ ὁ νόμος λέγει. ³⁵ εἰ δέ τι μαθεῖν θέλουσιν, ἐν οἴκῳ τοὺς ἰδίους ἄνδρας ἐπερωτάτωσαν· αἰσχρὸν γάρ ἐστιν γυναικὶ λαλεῖν ἐν ἐκκλησίᾳ. ³⁶ ἢ ἀφ' ὑμῶν ὁ λόγος τοῦ θεοῦ ἐξῆλθεν, ἢ εἰς ὑμᾶς μόνους κατήντησεν; ³⁷ Εἴ τις δοκεῖ προφήτης εἶναι ἢ πνευματικός, ἐπιγινωσκέτω ἃ γράφω ὑμῖν ὅτι κυρίου ἐστὶν ἐντολή· ³⁸ εἰ δέ τις ἀγνοεῖ, ἀγνοεῖται. ³⁹ Ὥστε, ἀδελφοί [μου], ζηλοῦτε τὸ προφητεύειν καὶ τὸ λαλεῖν μὴ κωλύετε γλώσσαις· ⁴⁰ πάντα δὲ εὐσχημόνως καὶ κατὰ τάξιν γινέσθω.

²⁶*What then, brethren? When you come together, each one has a hymn, a lesson, a revelation, a tongue, or an interpretation. Let all things be done for edification.* ²⁷*If any speak in a tongue, let there be only two or at most three, and each in turn; and let one interpret.* ²⁸*But if there is no one to interpret, let each of them keep silence in church and speak to himself and to God.* ²⁹*Let two or three prophets speak, and let the others weigh what is said.* ³⁰*If a revelation is made to another sitting by, let the first be silent.* ³¹*For you can all prophesy one by one, so that all may learn and all be encouraged;* ³²*and the spirits of prophets are subject to prophets.* ³³*For God is not a God of confusion but of peace. As in all the churches of the saints,* ³⁴*the women should keep silence in the churches. For they are not permitted to speak, but should be subordinate, as even the law says.* ³⁵*If there is anything they desire to know, let them ask their husbands at*

> *home. For it is shameful for a woman to speak in church.* [36]*What! Did the word of God originate with you, or are you the only ones it has reached?* [37]*If any one thinks that he is a prophet, or spiritual, he should acknowledge that what I am writing to you is a command of the Lord.* [38]*If any one does not recognize this, he is not recognized.* [39]*So, my brethren, earnestly desire to prophesy, and do not forbid speaking in tongues;* [40]*but all things should be done decently and in order.*

Paul ends this chapter by giving instructions on how to keep order (*kata taxin*; 14:40) at the congregational meetings for the edification of the church: "Let all things (*panta*) be done for edification (*oikodomēn*)." (v.26c) Since edification is the aim of each and every "psalm, lesson (*didakhē*; teaching), revelation, tongue, or interpretation" (v.26b), two conditions are required in the case of the gift of tongues: (1) a limited number of speakers who would speak "each in turn" (*ana merous*), and (2) an interpreter be present (v.27). The first condition ensures that the congregational gatherings are not used to show off or to promote a competition among those endowed with a gift; rather "'All things (*panta*) are lawful,' but not all things (*panta*) are helpful (*sympherei*; for the common good). 'All things (*panta*) are lawful,' but not all things (*panta*) build up (*oikodomei*). Let no one seek his own good, but the good of his neighbor (*heterou*; other)" (10:23-24) The neighbor (other) at the gatherings is the receiver of the message, not its dispenser. "To each (person with a gift) is given the manifestation of the Spirit for the common good (*to sympheron*)" (12:7). The condition of the common good underscores the necessity that the message be clear and understandable (14:16, 24-25). For that reason, if there is no one to interpret during the gathering (*en ekklēsia*), let the speaker in a tongue keep silent and reserve to himself and God what he is prompted to utter (v.28),[9] just as Paul himself does (vv.18-19).

The same rules that limit the number of speakers (v.29a) and require orderliness (vv.30-31a), which apply to speaking in tongues, also apply to prophecy, obviously without any restriction regarding the need for an interpreter. However, another kind of control does apply: whatever a prophet says is to be judged with discernment (*diakrinetōsan*) by the other prophets present (v.29b); indeed, "the spirits of prophets are subject to prophets" (v.32) and the Apostle's rule is: "Do not quench the Spirit, do not despise prophesying, but test everything." (1 Thess 5:19-21a) The aim of the rules of orderliness regarding prophecy is the same as that concerning speaking in tongues, "so that all may learn and all be encouraged (*parakalōntai*; be comforted, be exhorted)" (v.31b) through intelligible words (v.19). The ultimate reason is that, through the prophet's teaching, the God of peace (v.33b) is leading the church toward the final goal, the peace of his kingdom (1:3).[10] Thus any slight *akatastasia* (disorderliness; disturbance; unruliness; tumult) is to be averted in his church (14:33a).[11]

Verses 33b-36 are considered by many scholars as a later insertion since they appear to contradict what Paul wrote earlier in 11:5 regarding "any woman who prays or prophesies." Here Paul is instructing that "the women should keep silence in the churches. For they are not permitted to speak, but should be subordinate, as even the law says. If there is anything they desire

---

[9] The context militates for understanding that this action be done between the speaker and God and thus preferably at home, since he is to keep silence "in church."
[10] See my comments earlier on this verse.
[11] In Luke 21:9 *akatastasias* (tumults) occurs as a parallel to *polemous* (wars), the opposite of peace.

to know, let them ask their husbands at home. For it is shameful for a woman to speak in church." (14:34-35) The possibility that 11:33b-36 is a later insertion would stand only if "the women" in 14:34 and "any woman" of 11:5 were referring to the same subject matter. However, this does not seem to be the case. In chapter 11, woman is compared with man in general and not specifically with her husband.[12] In chapter 14 "the women" are specifically wives since the further reference is to "their *own* men (*tous idious andras*)[13] at home (*en oikō*)" (v.35). Still, the real difference between the "woman" of chapter 11 and "the women" of chapter 14 is that the former "prophesies" and thus teaches as prophets do (14:31), whereas the latter seek to learn (v.35). Thus, it is incorrect to presume that 14:33b-36 is dealing with the same subject matter as 11:2-16.

To determine what 14:33b-36 is talking about and what dilemma it is trying to solve or at least avoid, we can begin with the three verbs it uses: "keep silence" (*sigatōsan*)," "be subordinate" (*hypotassesthōsan*), and "learn" (*mathein*). These were the same verbs just used in conjunction with how the prophets are to behave in the church: "If a revelation is made to another sitting by, let the first be silent (*sigatō*). For you can all prophesy one by one, so that all may learn (*manthanōsin*) and all be encouraged; and the spirits of prophets are subject (*hypotassetai*) to prophets." (vv.30-32) What Paul is driving at is a case of "all the more so": "If the prophets, who are granted Paul's preferred spiritual gift, should keep silent to maintain the good order necessary for the membership at large to learn and remember that their teaching is subordained to the discernment

---

[12] RSV is misleading when in the same verse (11:3) it translates the same original *anēr/andros* once into "man" and once into "her husband." See my comments earlier on that verse.
[13] Which RSV renders correctly as "their husbands."

of other prophets, all the more so are regular members of the community bound by these rules." But why does Paul single out the wives to the exclusion of the husbands? Why does he not phrase his instruction in a more encompassing way? Before engaging the matter let me point out one more element in our passage (vv.33b-36) that brings to mind the second part of chapter 11 which discusses the differentiation between the church (gathering) and one's own house (11:21-22). This difference is the function of homes as "house churches" (Rom 16:5; 1 Cor 16:19; Col 4:15; Philem 2). In other words, church gatherings took place in "houses" similar to the homes of the guests, and the "church rules" Paul introduced in chapters 11 and 14 sometimes clashed with the common "household rules." When the community gathered together as a church, Paul had to ensure that his church rules, and not the household rules, were enforced.

In order to solve the alleged contradiction between chapters 11 and 14, one is to take into account the structure and rules governing a Roman household, which was essentially a hierarchy where everybody, including the wife, was "subordained" (*hypotassetai*) to the paterfamilias.[14] Paul hastens to say that this is a matter of (Roman as well as scriptural) law: "but should be subordinate, as even the law says." (v.34b) This is precisely the centerpiece in Paul's argument since it is surrounded by two parallel statements: "the women should keep silence *in the churches, for they are not permitted to speak*" (v.34a) and "If there is anything they desire to know, let them ask their husbands at home, *for it is shameful for a woman to speak in church*" (v.35).[15]

---

[14] See my comments on Col 3:18-4:1 in *C-Col* 87-92.
[15] The request in v.34b actually forms the center of a chiastic structure: [A] As in all the churches of the saints, [B] the women should keep silence in the churches. For they are not permitted to speak, [C] but should be subordinate, as even the law says.

As I explained in my discussion of 11:17-34, church gatherings took place as a *symposion* (festive table fellowship). In a Roman household, the *symposion* was essentially a social festivity around a common table where socio-political and philosophical ideas were debated. Those usually allowed to speak were the host and the free adult members of the guest households. However, the church gatherings (*ekklēsiai*) instituted by Paul after the manner of the synagogal meetings (*synagōgai*) revolved around scriptural readings followed by exhortational comments on those readings, which were delivered by the leading members of the gathering. The lack of discussion insured that the Lord's instruction inscribed in scripture be heard unequivocally as well as authoritatively. In the absence of an apostle and in order to maintain the tradition of the *symposion*, Paul allowed more than one voice on the condition that those two or three voices be sanctioned by God's spirit (14:27-32). Nonetheless, it was difficult to restrain all free Roman guests from speaking as they were used to doing. Moreover, such stricture would have offended them and might have led to their eventual refusal to attend such meetings. This would have been counterproductive to the dissemination of the gospel word through gatherings held at houses of believing Roman patricians such as Lydia (Acts 16:15), Jason (17:5-7), Prisca and Aquila (Rom 16:3-5; 1 Cor 16:19), and Philemon (Philem 1-2).

The Roman household head was usually the husband, the paterfamilias, and very rarely the widow until her eldest son became of age or the eldest daughter in an all-female progeny. So, out of deference, Paul's instructions in 1 Corinthians

---

[B'] If there is anything they desire to know, let them ask their husbands at home. For it is shameful for a woman to speak in church. [A'] What! Did the word of God originate with you, or are you the only ones it has reached?

14:33b-36 allowed a guest paterfamilias to speak—especially that some of the prophets were women—*however only to seek learning*. Nevertheless, in order not to open the door to a give and take at instructional church gatherings, he charged that the guest paterfamilias' wife—who was the second senior member of the family and usually engaged freely in discussions at *symposia*—would refrain from doing so when at a church gathering and wait to inquire from, or even discuss with, her husband privately in their own home. Consequently, the text in question is not dealing with "women" in general, but rather with the wives of the guest Roman patricians present at church gatherings.[16]

To support his stand Paul uses the same approach that he used in chapter 11. In both cases he refers to the unacceptable attitude of women as being *aiskhron* (disgraceful [11:6]; shameful [14:35]). In the first case, however, he appeals to nature (11:14-15), while in the second case he appeals to the (Roman as well as scriptural) law of subordination, which makes his case much more forceful. On the other hand, just as he did in 11:16 in the case of the women prophets, Paul appeals to the tradition of the churches he established and, since the issue is quite sensitive, reference to that tradition is made at the outset (14:33b-34a). Furthermore, to underscore the authority as well as value of this reference to the Pauline tradition, the Apostle ends with the rhetorical question: "What! Did the word of God originate with you, or are you the only ones it has reached?" (v.36) Still both statements (vv.33b-34a and v.36) seem to take into

---

[16] It does not stand to reason that all women would be targeted in a text just following reference to prophets that could be women. On the other hand, the assumption is that the host wife, being herself a believer (Philem 2; see my comments in *C-Col* 110-11), would have been aware of the rule and would have abstained from speaking.

consideration the Jewish synagogal tradition,[17] as is the case in 11:2-16. This is done intentionally in order to forego any undue criticism from the Jerusalem church authorities, which criticism could have jeopardized Paul's mission among the Gentiles.[18]

In speaking of the "churches of the saints" (1 Cor 14:33b) instead of "the churches of God" (11:16) Paul is clearly referring to the believers and, more specifically, the leaders of the Jerusalem church (16:1-3). In particular Paul is concerned with the acceptance of the offering of the Gentiles which Paul is to carry to those leaders in Jerusalem. Should those leaders endorse the reception of that offering, it would confirm their full endorsement of his mission (Rom 15:25-26, 31). Since that offering is the topic of 1 Corinthians 16, it stands to reason that the same concern, which was also expressed in Romans 15, was on Paul's mind in 1 Corinthians 14.

Paul then rephrases his oblique appeal to "the Law" in v.34 into the unequivocal "a command(ment) (*entolē*) of the Lord" in v.37. The original Greek is even more forceful: "If any one thinks (*dokei*; considers) that he is a prophet, or spiritual, he should acknowledge that what I am writing (*graphō*; from the same root as *graphē* [scripture]) to you is a command(ment) of the Lord." That Paul intended his instruction to be of no less than scriptural (divine) authority is corroborated in the following verdict which he iterates with the same "If any one (*ei tis*)" of v.37: "If any one (be he even a prophet [v.37]) does not recognize this, he is not (to be) recognized (by the community and thus he is to be put to silence by the other prophets [v.30])."

---

[17] This concern was primary on his mind as is evident in his intentional use of the phrase "the law says (*ho nomos legei*)" (v.34) which brings to mind the Mosaic law over and beyond the Roman law.
[18] See earlier my comments on 1 Cor 11:2-16.

(v.38) The conclusion of the entire chapter concerning prophecy (So, my brethren, earnestly desire to prophesy; v.39a) was stated at the outset (earnestly desire the spiritual gifts, especially that you may prophesy; v.1b). Speaking in tongues, however, is also a spiritual gift and should not be forbidden (hindered; v.39b) on the conditions enunciated earlier. At any rate, everything is to be done decently (*evskhēmonōs*)—which has the opposite meaning of *aiskhron* (shameful, disgraceful; v.35)—and in order (according to order; *kata taxin* [which is of the same root as *hypotassesthōsan* of v.34 and *hypotassetai* of v.32], v.40). The intention is to stress that without orderliness the edification of the church would be jeopardized. This is evident in the similar grammatical syntax of vv.26 and 40: "*Let all things be done* (*panta ginesthō*) for edification" (v.26); "but *all things should be done* (*panta ginesthō*) decently and in order." (v.40)

Chapter 15

Vv. 1-11 ¹Γνωρίζω δὲ ὑμῖν, ἀδελφοί, τὸ εὐαγγέλιον ὃ εὐηγγελισάμην ὑμῖν, ὃ καὶ παρελάβετε, ἐν ᾧ καὶ ἑστήκατε, ² δι' οὗ καὶ σῴζεσθε, τίνι λόγῳ εὐηγγελισάμην ὑμῖν εἰ κατέχετε, ἐκτὸς εἰ μὴ εἰκῇ ἐπιστεύσατε. ³ παρέδωκα γὰρ ὑμῖν ἐν πρώτοις, ὃ καὶ παρέλαβον, ὅτι Χριστὸς ἀπέθανεν ὑπὲρ τῶν ἁμαρτιῶν ἡμῶν κατὰ τὰς γραφὰς ⁴ καὶ ὅτι ἐτάφη καὶ ὅτι ἐγήγερται τῇ ἡμέρᾳ τῇ τρίτῃ κατὰ τὰς γραφὰς ⁵ καὶ ὅτι ὤφθη Κηφᾷ εἶτα τοῖς δώδεκα· ⁶ ἔπειτα ὤφθη ἐπάνω πεντακοσίοις ἀδελφοῖς ἐφάπαξ, ἐξ ὧν οἱ πλείονες μένουσιν ἕως ἄρτι, τινὲς δὲ ἐκοιμήθησαν· ⁷ἔπειτα ὤφθη Ἰακώβῳ εἶτα τοῖς ἀποστόλοις πᾶσιν· ⁸ ἔσχατον δὲ πάντων ὡσπερεὶ τῷ ἐκτρώματι ὤφθη κἀμοί. ⁹ Ἐγὼ γάρ εἰμι ὁ ἐλάχιστος τῶν ἀποστόλων ὃς οὐκ εἰμὶ ἱκανὸς καλεῖσθαι ἀπόστολος, διότι ἐδίωξα τὴν ἐκκλησίαν τοῦ θεοῦ· ¹⁰ χάριτι δὲ θεοῦ εἰμι ὅ εἰμι, καὶ ἡ χάρις αὐτοῦ ἡ εἰς ἐμὲ οὐ κενὴ ἐγενήθη, ἀλλὰ περισσότερον αὐτῶν πάντων ἐκοπίασα, οὐκ ἐγὼ δὲ ἀλλὰ ἡ χάρις τοῦ θεοῦ [ἡ] σὺν ἐμοί. ¹¹ εἴτε οὖν ἐγὼ εἴτε ἐκεῖνοι, οὕτως κηρύσσομεν καὶ οὕτως ἐπιστεύσατε.

¹Now I would remind you, brethren, in what terms I preached to you the gospel, which you received, in which you stand, ²by which you are saved, if you hold it fast—unless you believed in vain. ³For I delivered to you as of first importance what I also received, that Christ died for our sins in accordance with the scriptures, ⁴that he was buried, that he was raised on the third day in accordance with the scriptures, ⁵and that he appeared to Cephas, then to the twelve. ⁶Then he appeared to more than five hundred brethren at one time, most of whom are still alive, though some have fallen asleep. ⁷Then he appeared to James, then to all the apostles. ⁸Last of all, as to one untimely born, he appeared also to me. ⁹For I am the least of the apostles, unfit to be called an apostle, because I persecuted the church of God. ¹⁰But by the grace of God I am what I am, and his grace toward me was not in vain. On the contrary, I worked harder than any of them, though it was not I, but the grace of God which is with me. ¹¹Whether then it was I or they, so we preach and so you believed.

The RSV translation of *gnōrizō* (make known; make understand; reveal) into "I would remind" reflects a distinct interpretational bias, especially in view of the fact that the earlier *gnōrizō* in 12:3 was translated as "I want [you] to understand." The bias is even more evident when the other New Testament instances render the meaning as outright information[1] rather than apologetic reminder.[2] I am pointing out this flagrant inconsistency because it reflects the traditional and still widespread exegetical assumption that here Paul is just conveying the "common" gospel preached by all the apostles. However, if that were the case, why would he bother to "remind" the Corinthians of something so well known and do so in such detailed manner that it took over 55 verses (15:3-57)? To say that they must have forgotten or rather misunderstood or misinterpreted the Pauline message is an invalid argument since nowhere in the entire letter do we hear this. We are informed right from the beginning that the primary reason for writing the letter is the dissension within the community caused by siding with different apostles, namely, Paul, Apollos, and Cephas. Since Paul and Apollos are presented as companions working in unison in God's field in Corinth (3:4-9), the "outsider" then is Cephas. This is confirmed in chapter 9 in his apologia where Paul claims

---

[1] "We want [you] to know (*gnōrizomen*)" (2 Cor 8:1); "I would have [you] know (*gnōrizō*)" (Gal 1:11); "I cannot tell (*ou gnōrizō*)" (Phil 1:22); "be made known (*gnōrizesthai*)" (4:6).

[2] Notice RSV's conditional "I *would* remind you" instead of the plain "I am reminding [you]" or "I want (intend) to remind [you]."

to be the *sole* apostle to the Corinthians,[3] and differentiates between his and Barnabas' behavior, on the one hand, and that of "the other apostles and the brothers of the Lord and Cephas," on the other hand (vv.5-6).

In 2 Corinthians Paul revisits the same subject. In 3:1-3 he claims to be the *sole* apostle to the Corinthians. Later, in chapter 11, he iterates that point by addressing the Corinthians in these terms: "I betrothed you to Christ to present you as a pure bride to her one husband." (v.2) However, it is what he writes a few verses later in that same chapter that sheds a clear light on how he perceives those "others" with whom he compares himself in 1 Corinthians 9:5-6. The parallelism in thought and intent between 1 Corinthians 9 and 2 Corinthians 11 is evident in that, in both cases, he is defending his decision to be self-sufficient and not burden his addressees financially or otherwise:

> This is my defense to those who would examine me. Do we not have the right to our food and drink? Do we not have the right to be accompanied by a wife, as the other apostles and the brothers of the Lord and Cephas? Or is it only Barnabas and I who have no right to refrain from working for a living? (1 Cor 9:3-6)

> Did I commit a sin in abasing myself so that you might be exalted, because I preached God's gospel without cost to you? I robbed other churches by accepting support from them in order to serve you. And when I was with you and was in want, I did not burden any one, for my needs were supplied by the brethren who came from Macedonia. So I refrained and will refrain from burdening you in any way. As the truth of Christ is in me, this boast of mine shall not be silenced in the regions of Achaia. And why? Because I do not love you? God knows I do! And what I do I will continue

---

[3] That does not contradict what he writes in chapter 3 where he alone is the one who "planted" and "laid the foundation." See earlier my comments on that chapter.

to do, in order to undermine the claim of those who would like to claim that in their boasted mission they work on the same terms as we do. (2 Cor 11:7-12)

Still, his description of the "others" reveals that he is at odds with them not only behaviorally but also, and more importantly, regarding the content of the preaching:

> But I am afraid that as the serpent deceived Eve by his cunning, your thoughts will be led astray from a sincere and pure devotion to Christ. For if some one comes and preaches another Jesus than the one we preached, or if you receive a different spirit from the one you received, or if you accept a different gospel from the one you accepted, you submit to it readily enough. I think that I am not in the least inferior to these superlative apostles ... For such men are false apostles, deceitful workmen, disguising themselves as apostles of Christ. And no wonder, for even Satan disguises himself as an angel of light. So it is not strange if his servants also disguise themselves as servants of righteousness. Their end will correspond to their deeds ... For you gladly bear with fools, being wise yourselves! For you bear it if a man makes slaves of you, or preys upon you, or takes advantage of you, or puts on airs, or strikes you in the face. (2 Cor 11:3-5, 13-15, 19-20)[4]

In its extreme harshness, this last passage reminds us of Galatians 2:11-14 where Paul castigates the "others" for having betrayed the *one* gospel they all agreed on (vv.7-10), which is the gospel that he had been preaching (1:11-24) and which he stood for uncompromisingly at the Jerusalem summit (2:1-6). Put otherwise, Paul's gospel, which originated in God and his Christ, is the *one* valid gospel they all agreed on. It is precisely that

---

[4] Jesus himself in the Gospels castigates Peter in a similar fashion *after* the latter's correctly worded confession: "But turning and seeing his disciples, he rebuked Peter, and said, 'Get behind me, Satan! For you are not on the side of God, but of men.'" (Mk 8:33; see also Mt 16:23)

gospel which Paul consigned to writing in Galatians (1:8-9; 3:1; 6:11) and which the "others" should have been preaching *all along* and should still be preaching *now*. Galatians 2:7-10 excludes or at least dismisses the others *as a reference*, and the hearers are to give full attention to what follows as being the authoritative teaching of their sole father. 1 Corinthians 15:1-11 functions in precisely the same way. The only valid apostle in Corinth is Paul and he alone,[5] and the Corinthians are invited to open their ears and hearts to what he is about to say. They do not have license to check with those "others" as to the veracity of his message.[6] Indeed, at the outset, he is threatening them with an unequivocal caveat: "Now *I am making you aware (gnōrizō)*, brethren, in what terms *I preached* to you the gospel, which *you received*, in which *you stand*, by which you are saved, *if* you hold it fast—*unless* you believed in vain" (vv.1-2).

The most commonly held view is that the message Paul "delivered" (v.3) to the Corinthians, who "received" it from him (v.1), must also have been "received" by Paul through the same kind of medium. This would reflect the purported Pharisaic tradition of handing down that which one has received. The fallacy of such stand is evident on two counts: (1) we never hear of the Corinthians, including their leaders, being given free rein to further hand down what they received; (2) while they received the message from *the man* Paul, he himself received it according to the following terms: "For I would have you know (*gnōrizō*; I am making you aware), brethren, that the gospel which was preached by me is not man's gospel. For I did not receive it from man, nor was I taught it, but it came through a revelation of

---

[5] See Rom 15:20 and 2 Cor 10:15-18.
[6] See the detailed discussion of that passage in my article "Paul, the One Apostle of the One Gospel" in *The Journal of the Orthodox Center for the Advancement of Biblical Studies (JOCABS)* 2 (2009).

Jesus Christ." (Gal 1:11-12) Thus, Paul's gospel has a divine origin, which in turn makes it incontrovertibly authoritative. Furthermore, this is the gospel the Corinthians received "at first" (*en prōtois*)[7] from Paul (1 Cor 15:3a), which makes it the only gospel valid for them, especially since they already accepted it and stand in it (v.1); any change of mind on their part boils down to following another gospel and thus following another Jesus and another Spirit (2 Cor 11:4). In so doing, they would be declaring "cursed is (the) Jesus" whom Paul preached to them (1 Cor 12:3), and as a result they would fall under a divine "curse" (Gal 1:8-9). Like the Galatians, they would be betraying the gospel Paul preached to them "at first" (*to proteron*; 4:13) and would be "deserting him who called you in the grace of Christ and turning to a different gospel—not that there is another gospel, but there are some who trouble you and want to pervert the gospel of Christ" (1:6-7). The closeness in thought and intent between the two letters is borne out by the similarity in phraseology:

> Now I would remind you, brethren, in what terms *I preached to you the gospel* (*to evangelion ho evēngelisamēn hymin*), which you received (*parelabete*), in which you stand, by which you are saved, if you hold it fast—unless you believed *in vain* (*eikē*). For I delivered to you *at first* (*en prōtois*) what I also received. (1 Cor 15:1-3)

> I am afraid I have labored over you *in vain* (*eikē*) … you know it was because of a bodily ailment that *I preached the gospel to you* (*evēngelisamēn hymin*) *at first* (*to proteron*); and though my condition was a trial to you, you did not scorn or despise me, but

---

[7] RSV dodges the issue by incorrectly translating *en prōtois* into the bland "as of first importance" under the influence of the classical pervading theological assumption that the "raising of Jesus stands at the heart of the Christian faith," which has unfortunately become a rallying cry among all Christian denominations.

received me (*edexasthe me*) as an angel of God, *as Christ Jesus.* (Gal 4:11, 13-14)[8]

Paul's gospel, which he received "from the Lord" (1 Cor 11:23)[9] or through divine revelation (Gal 1:11-12) and delivered to the Corinthians consists of four elements (1 Cor 15:3-5), each introduced with the conjunction "that" (*hoti*) and the last three linked through the conjunction "and" (*kai*) to the preceding statement in the original Greek: (1) that Christ died for our sins in accordance with the scriptures, (2) and that he was buried, (3) and that he was raised on the third day in accordance with the scriptures, (4) and that he appeared to Cephas. In my commentaries on Romans, Philippians, and Colossians I have repeatedly shown that Isaiah 53 was pivotal in Paul's thought when dealing with Christ's death on the cross as an expiatory sacrifice willed by God himself, especially that the servant spoken of in Isaiah is God's one messenger to the nations as well as to the scattered sheep of Israel (Is 42:6-7; 49:6).

It is that background that accounts for the first statement "that Christ died for our sins in accordance with the scriptures." The function of the terse second statement "that he was buried" is to underscore the reality of the death of God's Christ—who was expected to be victorious and not succumb to death—in order to prepare for God's intervention against the verdict of the mighty of this world (1 Cor 2:6-9), the leaders of both Israel and the nations.[10] The third statement, "that he was raised on the third

---

[8] The close parallelism makes it virtually impossible to understand *en prōtois* in 1 Cor 15:3 as meaning "as of first importance."

[9] Notice the exactly similar formula in 1 Cor 11:23 (For I received [from the Lord] what I also delivered to you, that…) and 15:3 (For I delivered to you [at first] what I also received, that…).

[10] See Acts 4:26-28 (The kings of the earth set themselves in array, and the rulers were gathered together, against the Lord and against his Anointed [*Christ*]—for truly in this

day in accordance with the scriptures," announces that God overturned the invalid verdict of those leaders by openly declaring the righteousness of the one they put to death as unrighteous (Is 53:11). The function of God's "raising" his Christ, who was unjustly condemned, is to make him stand upright in a court of law and "subject everything"—including those who judged him—"under him" (1 Cor 15:27b-28a). As in the case of the death, the raising is "in accordance with the scriptures," that is to say, according to God's plan:

> Yet it was *the will of the Lord* to bruise him; he has put him to grief; when he makes himself an offering for sin, he shall see his offspring, he shall prolong his days; *the will of the Lord* shall prosper in his hand; he shall see the fruit of the travail of his soul and be satisfied; by his knowledge shall the righteous one, my servant, make many to be accounted righteous; and he shall bear their iniquities. Therefore *I will divide him a portion with the great, and he shall divide the spoil with the strong*; because he poured out his soul to death, and was numbered with the transgressors; yet he bore the sin of many, and made intercession for the transgressors. (Is 53:10-12)

The phrase "on the third day" expresses the "indeedness" of Christ being raised. Scripturally, the number three connotes full and unequivocal confirmation of that which has been tested not only once, but twice, and has passed the tests.[11] There are many examples of this in scripture, but the most telling and impressive example for our case is found in Hosea:

---

city there were gathered together against thy holy *servant* Jesus, whom thou didst anoint, both Herod and Pontius Pilate, with the Gentiles and the peoples of Israel, to do *whatever thy hand and thy plan had predestined to take place*).

[11] See further on three and other numbers used in scripture the "Excursus on Number Symbolism" in *NTI₃* 22-5.

Come, let us return to the Lord; for he has torn, that he may heal us; he has stricken, and he will bind us up. After two days he will revive us; on the third day he will raise us up, that we may live before him. Let us know, let us press on to know the Lord; *his going forth is sure* (*nakon*; is established) *as the dawn*; he will come to us as the showers, as the spring rains that water the earth. (6:1-3)

Jesus "indeed" was buried for two full days. Yet, as the judge of the court of appeal, God intervened and, in his justice, overturned the unjust verdict by raising his "righteous one." Finally, the fourth statement "that he appeared to Cephas" conveys the necessary medium through which the news of God's raising up his Christ was communicated to the world, for unless the "gospel" (*evangelion*) is "heralded," the gospel news is moot: "so we preach (*kēryssomen*; herald) and so you believed. Now if Christ is preached (*kēryssetai*; heralded) as raised from the dead…" (1 Cor 15:11b-12a)

The question that remains is why Paul singled out Peter as the necessary medium of communication. Let me begin by pointing out that what applies to Peter applies also to Paul: "But when he who had set me apart before I was born, and had called me through his grace, was pleased to reveal his Son to me, *in order that* (*hina*) I might preach (*evangelizōmai*) him among the Gentiles, I did not confer with flesh and blood…" (Gal 1:15-16) Furthermore, in that same letter Paul singles out Peter and himself as *the* apostles bound to carry the same gospel, the one to the Jews of the diaspora and the other to the nations (2:7-8). In Galatians we hear the sequence Peter, then Paul, and then the mention of the grace granted to Paul. We find that same sequence here in 1 Corinthians:

... but on the contrary, when they saw that I had been entrusted with the gospel to the uncircumcised, just as Peter had been entrusted with the gospel to the circumcised, for he who worked through Peter for the mission to the circumcised worked through me also (*kai emoi*) for the Gentiles, and when they perceived the grace that was given to me... (Gal 2:7-9a)

... he appeared to Cephas ... Last of all, as to one untimely born, he appeared also to me (*kamoi*)[12] ... But by the grace of God I am what I am, and his grace toward me was not in vain. (1 Cor 15:5, 8, 10)[13]

It is reasonable then to conclude that Paul's intent in 1 Corinthians is to stress Peter's subsequent failure (Gal 2:11-14). In Galatians 2:1-14, however, along with Peter there is reference to Barnabas, James, John, and even "certain men from James" dubbed as the "circumcision party" (v.12) who *one and all* betrayed the cause of the one gospel, leaving Paul as its only champion, Similarly, 1 Corinthians 15:5-7 is aiming at the same: Paul alone is preaching what the others are supposed to be preaching but are not.[14]

The phraseology as well as the structure of these verses is symbolic. After the first "appeared" we hear of "the twelve" together with Peter. Since twelve is the number of the tribes of

---

[12] A contraction of *kai emoi*.

[13] The closeness between the two letters is further reflected in that "For I am the least of the apostles, unfit to be called an apostle, because I persecuted the church of God" (1 Cor 15:9) is also a trademark of Galatians: "For you have heard of my former life in Judaism, how I persecuted the church of God violently and tried to destroy it ... But when he who had set me apart before I was born, and had called me through his grace..." (1:13, 15)

[14] See the more detailed discussion in my article "Paul, the One Apostle of the One Gospel" in *The Journal of the Orthodox Center for the Advancement of Biblical Studies* (*JOCABS*) 2 (2009).

the scriptural Israel, this addition is to underscore that, as in Galatians 2:7-8, Peter was assigned as the apostle to the Jewish diaspora.[15] The five hundred after the second "appeared" (1 Cor 15:6) functions as a bridge between Peter and his group (v.5) and James and the others (v.7): the "five" points to the five books of the Law, the "hundred"—a multiple of 10—is reflective of the totality, in this case of the totality of the people of that Law.[16] The last cluster after the third "appeared" is the most intriguing since it links James with "all the apostles." If one keeps in mind the closeness between Galatians and 1 Corinthians, then it is intended to be inclusive of Barnabas. This close companion of Paul had a change of mind between the meeting at Jerusalem (Gal 2:1-10) and the incident at Antioch when he succumbed to the pressure from James, joining his party and leaving Paul as the sole valid apostle of the gospel (vv.11-14). Here also 1 Corinthians seems to be reflecting this change of mind on Barnabas' part. Earlier in chapter 9, Barnabas was in Paul's camp versus James, the brother of the Lord, and Cephas; hence "Do we not have the right to be accompanied by a wife, as the other apostles and the brothers of the Lord and Cephas? Or is it only Barnabas and I who have no right to refrain from working for a living?" (vv.5-6).[17] However here in chapter 15, the phraseology concerning James' colleagues changes from "the other apostles" to "all the apostles" (v.9), that is to say, inclusive of Barnabas.

---

[15] See also Mt 19:27-28 (Then Peter said in reply, "Lo, we have left everything and followed you. What then shall we have?" Jesus said to them, "Truly, I say to you, in the new world, when the Son of man shall sit on his glorious throne, you who have followed me will also sit on twelve thrones, judging the twelve tribes of Israel…") and Jas 1:1 (James, a servant of God and of the Lord Jesus Christ, to the twelve tribes in the Dispersion: Greeting).

[16] See further on these numbers the "Excursus on Number Symbolism" in *NTI₃* 22-5.

[17] See my comments on those verses.

Consequently, Paul remains the only apostle faithful to the cause of the gospel (vv.10-11) in spite of all signs to the contrary: being the last (v.8), the least (v.9a) and, to top it off, unworthy of that honor because he persecuted the church of God (v.9b). Being the "least of the apostles" would have sufficed to underscore Paul's unworthiness, so the "last" seems to point to something else. Indeed, the metaphor of "untimely born," and thus "early," does not correspond to "last." The clue to the understanding of the function of v.8 is revealed later in the chapter where both "early" and "last" are used of Christ in a positive sense: the "first fruits" (vv.20 and 23) and the "last Adam" (v.45).[18] So what Paul is saying in v.8 is that the "untimely born" weakling who should not have been considered in the running,[19] nevertheless, was chosen *last* in order to be the fulfillment of "all the apostles" that preceded him.[20] No one familiar with scripture could possibly miss the background of this imagery:

> Behold, my servant shall prosper, he shall be exalted and lifted up, and shall be very high. As many were astonished at him—his appearance was so marred, beyond human semblance, and his form beyond that of the sons of men—so shall he startle many nations; kings shall shut their mouths because of him; for that which has not been told them they shall see, and that which they have not heard they shall understand. Who has believed what we have heard? And to whom has the arm of the Lord been revealed? For he grew up before him like a young plant, and like a root out

---

[18] The corresponding one metaphor that brings together both elements is the well-known "the alpha and the omega" (Rev 1:8; 21:6; 22:13).

[19] Similarly to the case of Jeremiah who complains to God that he is unfit because of his young age (Jer 1:6) and thus lacking in maturity, and yet God chooses him in spite of his inadequacy (vv.7-10).

[20] Notice the play on "all" between v.7b and 8a: "… then to *all* (*pasin*) the apostles. Last of (these) *all* (*pantōn*)…"

of dry ground; he had no form or comeliness that we should look at him, and no beauty that we should desire him. He was despised and rejected by men; a man of sorrows, and acquainted with grief; and as one from whom men hide their faces he was despised, and we esteemed him not. (Is 52:13-53:3)[21]

Paul was the "least" among the apostles and not even worthy (*hikanos*; fit) to be one since, at one point, he persecuted the church of God (1 Cor 15:9). He has no reason to assume that being chosen by God was due to his intrinsic value. Rather it was an act of gracefulness on God's part, and the success of his endeavor is not so much linked to his own effort, but to God's gratuitous will (v.10). Given all this, v.11 sounds baffling at first sight since it seems to state that both Paul and the others are preaching the same gospel. However, the present tense *kēryssomen* (we preach; we are preaching) is to be taken as describing the content of the gospel rather than the action of the apostles. My understanding is confirmed by the verse immediately following, which is commenting on v.11 and uses the passive voice: "Now if Christ *is preached* (*kēryssetai*) as raised from the dead." (v.12a) Paul is simply saying in v.11 that this is how the gospel ought to be preached and, not necessarily, that it was actually so preached by all the apostles. This is similar to what Paul did in Galatians. When he included Peter as his co-apostle bound to preach the *same* gospel (vv.7-8), he was not necessarily saying that Peter actually did so. Indeed, a few verses later (vv.11-14) he does write that Peter betrayed the

---

[21] My readers should not be astonished that the same imagery applies to Paul as well as Christ. We encountered the same phenomenon in Colossians, where both are presented as implementing in their flesh the sufferings willed for them by God, as well as Philippians, where both are compared to "obedient slaves." In both instances I showed that the background was also Is 53. See my comments in *C-Col* 54-9 and *C-Phil* 109-10.

commitment he was bound to. And this is precisely what he does here in 1 Corinthians. At the end of 15:11 Paul refers to the Corinthians' response to the preaching of the gospel (so we preach [present tense]) in the past tense (and so you believed), which corresponds to what he wrote in vv.1-3 where the past tense is used to describe that behavior as well as his apostolic activity in Corinth. Add to this that he alone is their apostle (9:2). So the other apostles are included with the view of their being put under judgment should they not be preaching what Paul is defining as the gospel: "We are even found to be misrepresenting God, because we testified of God that he raised Christ, whom he did not raise if it is true that the dead are not raised." (15:15) One should not be amazed that Paul is including himself under that same judgment since he does the same in Galatians (1:8-9). Consequently, Paul's inclusion of the others is a literary device aimed at dismissing them as a reference and keeping himself as the sole apostle to the Corinthians and the one who exclusively laid the foundation (1 Cor 3:10).[22]

A classic example of such an approach is when a mother says to her children, "You can bet your life that what I am telling you is so. Even if you asked your aunts and uncles, they will confirm it." This statement is in no way giving license to the children to call their aunts and uncles, but is essentially a prohibition to do so. Indeed, if her siblings dare to contradict her, the mother can always belie them by telling the children, "Your aunt said so because she is need of your attention, while I am not; I know for a fact that this is not what she originally said to me." This actually sounds quite similar to what Paul wrote earlier:

---

[22] See for more detail my article "Paul, the One Apostle of the One Gospel" in *The Journal of the Orthodox Center for the Advancement of Biblical Studies (JOCABS)* 2 (2009).

I do not write this to make you ashamed, but to admonish you as my beloved children. For though you have countless guides in Christ, you do not have many fathers. For I became your father in Christ Jesus through the gospel ... Some are arrogant, as though I were not coming to you. But I will come to you soon, if the Lord wills, and I will find out not the talk of these arrogant people but their power. For the kingdom of God does not consist in talk but in power. What do you wish? Shall I come to you with a rod, or with love in a spirit of gentleness? (4:14-15, 18-21)

Vv. 12-19 ¹² Εἰ δὲ Χριστὸς κηρύσσεται ὅτι ἐκ νεκρῶν ἐγήγερται, πῶς λέγουσιν ἐν ὑμῖν τινες ὅτι ἀνάστασις νεκρῶν οὐκ ἔστιν; ¹³ εἰ δὲ ἀνάστασις νεκρῶν οὐκ ἔστιν, οὐδὲ Χριστὸς ἐγήγερται· ¹⁴ εἰ δὲ Χριστὸς οὐκ ἐγήγερται, κενὸν ἄρα [καὶ] τὸ κήρυγμα ἡμῶν, κενὴ καὶ ἡ πίστις ὑμῶν· ¹⁵ εὑρισκόμεθα δὲ καὶ ψευδομάρτυρες τοῦ θεοῦ, ὅτι ἐμαρτυρήσαμεν κατὰ τοῦ θεοῦ ὅτι ἤγειρεν τὸν Χριστόν, ὃν οὐκ ἤγειρεν εἴπερ ἄρα νεκροὶ οὐκ ἐγείρονται. ¹⁶ εἰ γὰρ νεκροὶ οὐκ ἐγείρονται, οὐδὲ Χριστὸς ἐγήγερται· ¹⁷ εἰ δὲ Χριστὸς οὐκ ἐγήγερται, ματαία ἡ πίστις ὑμῶν, ἔτι ἐστὲ ἐν ταῖς ἁμαρτίαις ὑμῶν, ¹⁸ ἄρα καὶ οἱ κοιμηθέντες ἐν Χριστῷ ἀπώλοντο. ¹⁹ εἰ ἐν τῇ ζωῇ ταύτῃ ἐν Χριστῷ ἠλπικότες ἐσμὲν μόνον, ἐλεεινότεροι πάντων ἀνθρώπων ἐσμέν.

¹²Now if Christ is preached as raised from the dead, how can some of you say that there is no resurrection of the dead? ¹³But if there is no resurrection of the dead, then Christ has not been raised; ¹⁴if Christ has not been raised, then our preaching is in vain and your faith is in vain. ¹⁵We are even found to be misrepresenting God, because we testified of God that he raised Christ, whom he did not raise if it is true that the dead are not raised. ¹⁶For if the dead are not raised, then Christ has not been raised. ¹⁷If Christ has not been raised, your faith is futile and you are still in your sins. ¹⁸Then those also who have fallen asleep in Christ have perished. ¹⁹If for this life only we have hoped in Christ, we are of all men most to be pitied.

A common, though subconscious, understanding of 1 Corinthians 15:12 is to hear yet mentally dismiss "is preached" (*kēryssetai*) and simply remember "If Christ was raised from the dead,"[23] thus making "is preached" a secondary statement that could have been omitted. For most of us, Christ being raised from the dead is a "visible fact" that we could have been privy to had we been at the right place at the right time. However, such an assumption contradicts the immediate context where we repeatedly hear of Christ "having appeared [to someone]" and not having been seen by someone. It is not because Paul "has seen" the Lord Jesus that he is an apostle. Rather he was granted to see the Lord because he was chosen to be an apostle (Gal 1:11-16). In Acts, we are told, no less than three times (9:3-6; 22:6-8; 26:12-15), that Paul did see the risen Lord, or rather the risen Lord appeared to him, at the gates of Damascus, that is to say, "at the wrong place and the wrong time" compared to the other apostles. Listening more closely to the first two accounts we are struck with an apparent discrepancy: "The men who were traveling with him stood speechless, hearing the voice but seeing no one" (9:7); "Now those who were with me saw the light but did not hear the voice of the one who was speaking to me." (22:9) A discrepancy *within the one book* cannot be but a literary device used by the author, in this case, to say that those who were in Saul's immediate company were not privy to the appearing Lord's *entire* message; the core of the Lord's *words* were *addressed exclusively to Saul* and not to those in his company since they were not chosen by God. As we hear a few verses later: "But the Lord said to him [Ananias], 'Go, for he [Saul] is a

---

[23] I have tried a stratagem many times in the classroom and in my talks, to read the verse by omitting "is preached." None of the listeners corrected me or even reacted as though I was misreading the verse, including those who are well acquainted with scripture.

chosen instrument of mine to carry my name before the Gentiles and kings and the sons of Israel; for I will show him how much he must suffer for the sake of my name.'" (9:15-16) Thus the message concerning the raising of Christ from the dead is a "packaged" message that includes the correct meaning and function of that raising. A case in point is that even Peter's correctly worded confession is not tantamount to the veracity of his understanding of it:

> And he asked them, "But who do you say that I am?" Peter answered him, "You are the Christ." And he charged them to tell no one about him. And he began to teach them that the Son of man must suffer many things, and be rejected by the elders and the chief priests and the scribes, and be killed, and after three days rise again. And he said this plainly. And Peter took him, and began to rebuke him. But turning and seeing his disciples, he rebuked Peter, and said, "Get behind me, Satan! For you are not on the side of God, but of men." (Mk 8:29-33)

In 1 Corinthians 15:12-19, Paul is explaining the correct meaning and function of *his preaching* which the Corinthians *received* (vv.1-2) in order to secure that their reception of it would not prove to be in vain (vv.2, 14, 17). As in 4:14-21, he is handling the matter of the gospel as a father would and not opening it for debate.

Another common mistake rampant in classical theological discourse concerning the passage 15:12-19 is that it is Christ being raised from the dead that is the basis for the coming resurrection of the dead. This blatantly contradicts vv.13-14a, v.15b and 16-17a where *thrice* the direction of the argument is inverse: "But if there is no resurrection of the dead, then Christ has not been raised; if Christ has not been raised, then ... because we testified of God that he raised Christ, whom he did not raise if it is true that the dead are not raised. For if the dead are not raised, then Christ has not been raised. If Christ has not been raised, (then)…"[24] In v.12, we do not have a statement of fact, but merely a rhetorical question expressing the Apostle's amazement at some of the Corinthians' hypothetical refusal of his preaching that they already accepted: "Now if Christ is preached as raised from the dead, *how can some of you* say that there is no resurrection of the dead?" If the *coming* resurrection of the dead is the basis of the possibility of God's raising his Christ from the dead, it is because we already hear of it in the Old Testament scripture: "And many of those[25] who sleep in the dust of the earth shall awake, some to everlasting life, and some to shame and everlasting contempt. And those who are wise shall shine like the brightness of the firmament; and those who turn many to righteousness, like the stars for ever and ever." (Dan 12:2-3)[26] This is precisely the reason Paul is utterly amazed that some of the Corinthians are factually refusing a teaching that is "in accordance with the scriptures" or, as he usually says, "As it is written." The consequence of such a stand is catastrophic as is clear from its repetition (vv.14b and 17b): "…then our preaching (*kērygma*; heralding) is in vain and *your faith is in vain*"; "… *your faith is futile* and you are still in your sins." Moreover, if they are still in their sins, then the Corinthians will be raised—since, "as it is written," resurrection there shall be!—

---

[24] Notice the forcefulness of the phraseology that reflects the "factuality" of the resurrection of the dead. After having referred to "the resurrection of the dead" (v.13a; see also v.12b) Paul uses twice the present tense "the dead are raised (*egeirontai*)" instead of the future tense "the dead will be raised ([*ex*]*egerthēsontai*)" as in Daniel.

[25] In the sense of "as many as they be" as is clear from the original Hebrew.

[26] Later in 1 Cor it will become clear that that passage was on Paul's mind since he will use its phraseology in "describing" the "how" of the resurrection of the dead (vv.35-41).

"to shame and everlasting contempt" instead of "to everlasting life."

The centrality of Paul's preaching in his argument can be seen in the factual statement he inserts between the two conditional statements in vv.13-14 and 16-17: "We are even found to be misrepresenting (*psevdomartyres*; false witnesses [bearers of false witness] to) God, because we testified (*emartyrēsamen*; witnessed) of God that he raised Christ, whom he did not raise if it is true that the dead are not raised." (v.15) This is not an invitation to pursue a mental exercise about the raising of the Christ or the resurrection of the dead, as has often become the case in classical theology. Rather it is meant to make the believers aware that even "those also who have fallen asleep *in Christ* have perished (*apōlonto*)" (v.18). Put otherwise, "being in or communing with Christ" is not enough. One must "walk the way" as Paul previously underscored in 10:1-11, at the conclusion of which we hear: "We must not put the Lord to the test, as some of them did and were destroyed (*apōllynto*; perished) by serpents; nor grumble, as some of them did and were destroyed (*apōlonto*; perished) by the Destroyer." (vv.9-10) Paul preached the gospel word to those in Corinth hoping they would trust in it and be saved: "For Christ did not send me to baptize but to preach the gospel, and not with eloquent wisdom, lest the cross of Christ be emptied of its power. For the word of the cross is folly to those who are perishing (*apollymenois*), but to us who are being saved (*sōzomenois*) it is the power of God." (1:17-18) Indeed, "If for this life only we have hoped in Christ, we are of all men most to be pitied (*eleeinoteroi*; most in need of [God's mercy])" (15:19).

Vv. 20-28 ²⁰ Νυνὶ δὲ Χριστὸς ἐγήγερται ἐκ νεκρῶν ἀπαρχὴ τῶν κεκοιμημένων. ²¹ ἐπειδὴ γὰρ δι' ἀνθρώπου θάνατος, καὶ δι' ἀνθρώπου ἀνάστασις νεκρῶν. ²² ὥσπερ γὰρ ἐν τῷ Ἀδὰμ πάντες ἀποθνῄσκουσιν, οὕτως καὶ ἐν τῷ Χριστῷ πάντες ζῳοποιηθήσονται. ²³ Ἕκαστος δὲ ἐν τῷ ἰδίῳ τάγματι· ἀπαρχὴ Χριστός, ἔπειτα οἱ τοῦ Χριστοῦ ἐν τῇ παρουσίᾳ αὐτοῦ, ²⁴ εἶτα τὸ τέλος, ὅταν παραδιδῷ τὴν βασιλείαν τῷ θεῷ καὶ πατρί, ὅταν καταργήσῃ πᾶσαν ἀρχὴν καὶ πᾶσαν ἐξουσίαν καὶ δύναμιν. ²⁵ δεῖ γὰρ αὐτὸν βασιλεύειν ἄχρι οὗ θῇ πάντας τοὺς ἐχθροὺς ὑπὸ τοὺς πόδας αὐτοῦ. ²⁶ ἔσχατος ἐχθρὸς καταργεῖται ὁ θάνατος· ²⁷ πάντα γὰρ ὑπέταξεν ὑπὸ τοὺς πόδας αὐτοῦ. ὅταν δὲ εἴπῃ ὅτι πάντα ὑποτέτακται, δῆλον ὅτι ἐκτὸς τοῦ ὑποτάξαντος αὐτῷ τὰ πάντα. ²⁸ ὅταν δὲ ὑποταγῇ αὐτῷ τὰ πάντα, τότε [καὶ] αὐτὸς ὁ υἱὸς ὑποταγήσεται τῷ ὑποτάξαντι αὐτῷ τὰ πάντα, ἵνα ᾖ ὁ θεὸς [τὰ] πάντα ἐν πᾶσιν.

²⁰*But in fact Christ has been raised from the dead, the first fruits of those who have fallen asleep.* ²¹*For as by a man came death, by a man has come also the resurrection of the dead.* ²²*For as in Adam all die, so also in Christ shall all be made alive.* ²³*But each in his own order: Christ the first fruits, then at his coming those who belong to Christ.* ²⁴*Then comes the end, when he delivers the kingdom to God the Father after destroying every rule and every authority and power.* ²⁵*For he must reign until he has put all his enemies under his feet.* ²⁶*The last enemy to be destroyed is death.* ²⁷*"For God has put all things in subjection under his feet." But when it says, "All things are put in subjection under him," it is plain that he is excepted who put all things under him.* ²⁸*When all things are subjected to him, then the Son himself will also be subjected to him who put all things under him, that God may be everything to every one.*

Here again, by translating only in this instance *nyni* as "in fact" and not simply "now," as it usually does,[27] RSV is forcing the text to say what has become the classical theological assumption

---

[27] The only exception being "as it is" (1 Cor 12:18).

of the "factuality" of Christ's raising while overlooking the fact that 15:20 picks up the statement of v.12a, namely, that Christ *is preached* as raised from the dead, in order for Paul to comment on it. In so doing, he begins by referring to the content of the preaching as having been "now" received by the Corinthians and then proceeds to explain its functionality. The raised Christ is the first fruits (*aparkhē*) of those who have fallen asleep and will remain so until the day assigned by God for their common resurrection. The choice of first fruits (*aparkhē*) over first-born (*prōtotokos*), which is found elsewhere in conjunction with the believers in general (Rom 8:29) as well as with the dead (Col 1:18; Rev 1:5), is in view of the agricultural metaphor that Paul will use later to describe the manner of the resurrection; indeed, in the LXX *aparkhē* is the usual translation of different Hebrew nouns that refer to the first fruits. This liberty Paul took is warranted due to the intimate parallelism in scripture between the human/animal (mammal) "first" and the agricultural "first": the same Hebrew root *bkr* is found in both the mammal *bekor* (first-born; firstling) and the agricultural *bikkurim* (first fruits).[28] In this particular context (1 Cor 15:20-28), however, the intent behind the use of "first fruits" is to draw the hearers' attention to the time that *necessarily* will have to elapse between the raising of Christ as "first fruits" and the resurrection of all the other deceased, which will take place when "the time is ripe."

Verse 21 is looking ahead toward the agricultural metaphor in vv.35-41, while vv. 22-23 are written in view of what Paul will say in vv.42-49 where Christ is spoken of as "the last Adam" (v.45b). These verses (21-23) are a condensed rendition of the

---

[28] Which is also reflected in the Greek where the former is translated as *prōtotokos* (from the verb *tiktō* meaning "bear, be pregnant with, give birth") and the latter as *prōtogenēmata* (from the verb *ginomai* meaning "be, become, be produced, be born").

more elaborate passage in Romans 5:12-21.[29] In scripture Adam functions as "first (fruits)" to all other humans who are on the path of death through the divine verdict of punishment. Christ, on the other hand, functions as "first (fruits)" to all human beings on the path that hopefully will lead to the divine verdict of life through righteousness (Dan 12:3), should they abide by God's will. However—and this is the main point—"each in his own order: Christ the first fruits, *then at his coming* those who belong to Christ (are Christ's). *Then* (comes) the end" (1 Cor 15:23-24a). It is only at that second "then" of "*the* end" that Christ, before the eyes of all "who belong to him," will deliver the *basileian* (factual rule associated with kingship) back to his God and Father (v.24b), after he will have "destroyed every rule and every authority and power" (v.24c) which earlier condemned him to the shameful death of the cross (2:8).[30] In view of that end, Christ must exercise the rule he was granted at his raising from the dead until God has put (*thē*) all possible enemies under his feet,[31] including the last enemy, death itself (15:26), from whose grip all those who belong to Christ will be delivered. This stress on the fact that death is the *last* enemy to be destroyed is intended as a reminder to the Corinthians that death still awaits them and, if so, they are not as "spiritual" as they think (see

---

[29] See my comments on that passage in *C-Rom* 109-15.

[30] The link to 1 Cor 2:8, where "rulers" (*arkhontōn*) are referred to, is evident in that in 1 Cor 15:24 we hear "every rule (*arkhēn*) and every authority and power." Not only is "rule" mentioned first, but it is also underscored given that "authority" and "power" are lumped together after a single "every."

[31] Debating as to whether the subject of "has put" is Christ or God is irrelevant since the gift of subjecting the enemies is granted by God to his Christ, as will be stated in v.27. However, given that the statement "until he has put all his enemies under his feet" (v.25b) is a verbatim quotation from LXX 109:1b (Hebrew 110:1b), it is preferable to assume that the subject of "has put" is God. This is substantiated by the fact that the first part of v. 25a (he [Christ] must reign) reflects the first part of the psalm's first verse: "The Lord says to my lord: 'Sit at my right hand.'" (v.1a)

earlier 3:1-3), but rather are mere "living souls" bound to return to dust (v.45a).

In order to back his teaching Paul, as usual, refers to the authoritative scripture: "For 'he [God] has put all things in subjection (*hypetaxen*; sub-ordained, subjected) under his feet.'" (v.27a, quoting Ps 8:6). At first sight, it is strange that Paul would quote Psalm 8 after having quoted Psalm 110 [LXX 109] in 1 Corinthians 15:25b.[32] Yet, the reason is evident. While Psalm 110 deals with the king *as king*, Psalm 8 speaks of the king as "man" and "son of man," which in Hebrew are *'adam* and *ben 'adam*, and in Greek *anthrōpos* and *hyios anthrōpou*, respectively. Thus, Paul's intention is to link the conclusion of this passage to its point of departure: "For as by [a] man (*anthrōpou*) came death, by [a] man (*anthrōpou*) has come also the resurrection of the dead. For as in *Adam* all die, so also in Christ shall all be made alive." (1 Cor 15:21-22) However, the "all" that is subjected to Christ does not include his God and Father who subjected everything to Christ (v.27). At the end Christ himself will be subjected to the one God of "all" (v.28). After all, Jesus, as an anointed king, is a "man" (v.21b).

Vv. 29-34 ²⁹ Ἐπεὶ τί ποιήσουσιν οἱ βαπτιζόμενοι ὑπὲρ τῶν νεκρῶν; εἰ ὅλως νεκροὶ οὐκ ἐγείρονται, τί καὶ βαπτίζονται ὑπὲρ αὐτῶν; ³⁰ Τί καὶ ἡμεῖς κινδυνεύομεν πᾶσαν ὥραν; ³¹ καθ' ἡμέραν ἀποθνήσκω, νὴ τὴν ὑμετέραν καύχησιν, [ἀδελφοί,] ἣν ἔχω ἐν Χριστῷ Ἰησοῦ τῷ κυρίῳ ἡμῶν. ³² εἰ κατὰ ἄνθρωπον ἐθηριομάχησα ἐν Ἐφέσῳ, τί μοι τὸ ὄφελος; εἰ νεκροὶ οὐκ ἐγείρονται, φάγωμεν καὶ πίωμεν, αὔριον γὰρ ἀποθνήσκομεν. ³³ μὴ πλανᾶσθε· φθείρουσιν ἤθη χρηστὰ ὁμιλίαι κακαί. ³⁴ ἐκνήψατε δικαίως καὶ μὴ ἁμαρτάνετε, ἀγνωσίαν γὰρ θεοῦ τινες ἔχουσιν, πρὸς ἐντροπὴν ὑμῖν λαλῶ.

---

[32] RSV blurs the clear differentiation between the two passages from Psalms since it translates both verbs *thē* (1 Cor 15:25) and *hypetaxen* (v.27) as "has put."

> ²⁹ *Otherwise, what do people mean by being baptized on behalf of the dead? If the dead are not raised at all, why are people baptized on their behalf?* ³⁰*Why am I in peril every hour?* ³¹*I protest, brethren, by my pride in you which I have in Christ Jesus our Lord, I die every day!* ³²*What do I gain if, humanly speaking, I fought with beasts at Ephesus? If the dead are not raised, "Let us eat and drink, for tomorrow we die."* ³³*Do not be deceived: "Bad company ruins good morals."* ³⁴*Come to your right mind, and sin no more. For some have no knowledge of God. I say this to your shame.*

Paul gives two very serious examples of the utter irrationality "if the dead are not raised" (v.29 and vv. 30-32) followed by a conclusion of warning to the Corinthians (vv.33-34). The first is an argument ad hominem: some of the Corinthians are actually undertaking baptism "on behalf (in the name of) the dead." The reason behind such behavior appears to emulate the Thessalonians' worry concerning those who were baptized, that is to say, "those who died in Christ" before his return: would those dead be part of the Lord's retinue at his coming? (1 Thess 4:15-18) The Corinthians' dilemma, however, is somewhat different. Given that, according to Paul, the baptized have a better chance to be raised unto life eternal as was Christ (Rom 6:1-9), then it would stand to reason to give that chance to believing "catechumens" who happen to die before being baptized and thus some were getting baptized "for their sake, in their stead" (*hyper tōn nekrōn*; 1 Cor 15:29). Hence Paul's rhetorical question, "Why would one do that 'if the dead are not raised'"? The other example is personal. "If the dead are not raised," why would Paul undergo a life of continuous danger (v.30), experience near death (v.31a; see also 2 Cor 1:8), fight beasts in the arena (v.32a), even die for the sake of the gospel, and still find pride in what he is doing (1 Cor 15:31b)? He should rather live thus: "Let us eat and drink, for tomorrow we die" (v.32b; see also Is 22:13; 56:12; Lk 12:19). Yet Paul cautions against a deception that leads to punishable deeds (1 Cor 15:33) since divine judgment is coming.

RSV's "Come to your right mind" (v.34) is totally inaccurate. It does not correctly render the original *eknēpsate dikaiōs* that literally means "stand up (arise) sober, righteously (in righteousness)," a clear reflection of (righteous) judgment terminology, which is confirmed in the parallel "sin no more." This is corroborated in that the reason given, "For some have no (lack of) knowledge (*agnōsian*) of God," is also legal terminology since, for all practical purposes, knowledge of God is knowledge of his will inscribed in the Law.[33] Further evidence is that the verb *nēphō* (be sober)—whence *eknēpsate*—found twice in 1 Thessalonians 5:1-11 (vv.6 and 8) speaks of the Lord's coming to judge, which immediately follows 4:15-18 that deals with a concern similar to that found in 1 Corinthians 15:29. Having warned the Corinthians not to take lightly the coming resurrection as a prelude to divine judgment, Paul ends with "I say this to your shame (*pros entropēn hymin*)" (v.34) that has an effect similar to that of "I do not write this to make you ashamed (*ouk entrepōn hymas*) but to admonish you" (4:14) with which he earlier prefaced his reproving remark, "What do you wish? Shall I come to you with a rod, or with love in a spirit of gentleness?" (4:21). Paul's aim is to warn the Corinthians of the coming judgment, as can be seen in his use of the same caveat, "Do not

---

[33] See earlier 1 Cor 14:7-38 and my comments thereon. See also the classic text "And so, from the day we heard of it, we have not ceased to pray for you, asking that you may be filled with the knowledge of his will in all spiritual wisdom and understanding, to lead a life worthy of the Lord, fully pleasing to him, bearing fruit in every good work and increasing in the knowledge of God" (Col 1:9-10) and my comments thereon in *C-Col* 37-42.

be deceived" (1 Cor 15:33a), that he wielded earlier in conjunction with the final judgment (6:9).

Vv. 35-49 ³⁵ Ἀλλὰ ἐρεῖ τις· πῶς ἐγείρονται οἱ νεκροί; ποίῳ δὲ σώματι ἔρχονται; ³⁶ ἄφρων, σὺ ὃ σπείρεις, οὐ ζῳοποιεῖται ἐὰν μὴ ἀποθάνῃ· ³⁷καὶ ὃ σπείρεις, οὐ τὸ σῶμα τὸ γενησόμενον σπείρεις ἀλλὰ γυμνὸν κόκκον εἰ τύχοι σίτου ἤ τινος τῶν λοιπῶν· ³⁸ὁ δὲ θεὸς δίδωσιν αὐτῷ σῶμα καθὼς ἠθέλησεν, καὶ ἑκάστῳ τῶν σπερμάτων ἴδιον σῶμα. ³⁹Οὐ πᾶσα σὰρξ ἡ αὐτὴ σάρξ ἀλλὰ ἄλλη μὲν ἀνθρώπων, ἄλλη δὲ σὰρξ κτηνῶν, ἄλλη δὲ σὰρξ πτηνῶν, ἄλλη δὲ ἰχθύων. ⁴⁰καὶ σώματα ἐπουράνια, καὶ σώματα ἐπίγεια· ἀλλὰ ἑτέρα μὲν ἡ τῶν ἐπουρανίων δόξα, ἑτέρα δὲ ἡ τῶν ἐπιγείων. ⁴¹ἄλλη δόξα ἡλίου, καὶ ἄλλη δόξα σελήνης, καὶ ἄλλη δόξα ἀστέρων· ἀστὴρ γὰρ ἀστέρος διαφέρει ἐν δόξῃ. ⁴²οὕτως καὶ ἡ ἀνάστασις τῶν νεκρῶν. σπείρεται ἐν φθορᾷ, ἐγείρεται ἐν ἀφθαρσίᾳ· ⁴³σπείρεται ἐν ἀτιμίᾳ, ἐγείρεται ἐν δόξῃ· σπείρεται ἐν ἀσθενείᾳ, ἐγείρεται ἐν δυνάμει· ⁴⁴σπείρεται σῶμα ψυχικόν, ἐγείρεται σῶμα πνευματικόν. Εἰ ἔστιν σῶμα ψυχικόν, ἔστιν καὶ πνευματικόν. ⁴⁵οὕτως καὶ γέγραπται· ἐγένετο ὁ πρῶτος ἄνθρωπος Ἀδὰμ εἰς ψυχὴν ζῶσαν, ὁ ἔσχατος Ἀδὰμ εἰς πνεῦμα ζῳοποιοῦν. ⁴⁶ἀλλ' οὐ πρῶτον τὸ πνευματικὸν ἀλλὰ τὸ ψυχικόν, ἔπειτα τὸ πνευματικόν. ⁴⁷ὁ πρῶτος ἄνθρωπος ἐκ γῆς χοϊκός, ὁ δεύτερος ἄνθρωπος ἐξ οὐρανοῦ. ⁴⁸οἷος ὁ χοϊκός, τοιοῦτοι καὶ οἱ χοϊκοί, καὶ οἷος ὁ ἐπουράνιος, τοιοῦτοι καὶ οἱ ἐπουράνιοι· ⁴⁹καὶ καθὼς ἐφορέσαμεν τὴν εἰκόνα τοῦ χοϊκοῦ, φορέσομεν καὶ τὴν εἰκόνα τοῦ ἐπουρανίου. ⁵⁰Τοῦτο δέ φημι, ἀδελφοί, ὅτι σὰρξ καὶ αἷμα βασιλείαν θεοῦ κληρονομῆσαι οὐ δύναται οὐδὲ ἡ φθορὰ τὴν ἀφθαρσίαν κληρονομεῖ.

³⁵*But some one will ask, "How are the dead raised? With what kind of body do they come?"* ³⁶*You foolish man! What you sow does not come to life unless it dies.* ³⁷*And what you sow is not the body which is to be, but a bare kernel, perhaps of wheat or of some other grain.* ³⁸*But God gives it a body as he has chosen, and to each kind of seed its own body.* ³⁹*For not all flesh is alike,*

but there is one kind for men, another for animals, another for birds, and another for fish. ⁴⁰There are celestial bodies and there are terrestrial bodies; but the glory of the celestial is one, and the glory of the terrestrial is another. ⁴¹There is one glory of the sun, and another glory of the moon, and another glory of the stars; for star differs from star in glory. ⁴²So is it with the resurrection of the dead. What is sown is perishable, what is raised is imperishable. ⁴³It is sown in dishonor, it is raised in glory. It is sown in weakness, it is raised in power. ⁴⁴It is sown a physical body, it is raised a spiritual body. If there is a physical body, there is also a spiritual body. ⁴⁵Thus it is written, "The first man Adam became a living being"; the last Adam became a life-giving spirit. ⁴⁶But it is not the spiritual which is first but the physical, and then the spiritual. ⁴⁷The first man was from the earth, a man of dust; the second man is from heaven. ⁴⁸As was the man of dust, so are those who are of the dust; and as is the man of heaven, so are those who are of heaven. ⁴⁹Just as we have borne the image of the man of dust, we shall also bear the image of the man of heaven. ⁵⁰I tell you this, brethren: flesh and blood cannot inherit the kingdom of God, nor does the perishable inherit the imperishable.

In tackling the manner of the resurrection, Paul utilizes the imagery of sowing which he used in Galatians in conjunction with the final judgment: "Do not be deceived; God is not mocked, for whatever a man sows, that he will also reap. For he who sows to his own flesh will from the flesh reap corruption; but he who sows to the Spirit will from the Spirit reap eternal life." (6:7-8) Given the similarity in phraseology as well as the introductory caveat "Do not be deceived," no one can possibly miss that 1 Corinthians 15:35-50 is an expansion of the two verses in Galatians. However in 1 Corinthians Paul's main concern is to stress the *necessity* of death before one could reach "spiritual" life: "What you sow does not come to life *unless* (*ean mē*) it dies." (v.36) Then, he details his agricultural example in order to show his hearers that something can and does come out of something unimpressive (vv.37-38). Then, given that in both cases one deals with a "seed" (*sperma*), he moves from the agricultural realm to the human realm since his concern in this chapter is man (v.39). He universalizes his point by referring to the heavenly realm versus the earthly one (vv.40-41), which allows him to introduce the term *doxa* that connotes "splendor," which applies to both the heavenly bodies and the scriptural divine "glory." This, in turn, facilitates the move to the resurrection with which he deals in terms of divine reality versus human realm (vv.42-50): "So is it with the resurrection of the dead." (v.42a) This statement is in answer to the original question of v.35 (How are the dead raised? With what kind of body do they come?).

Paul builds his argument (vv.42-50) using the same three steps of vv.36-41: agriculture, human or earthly realm, divine or celestial realm. In revisiting his agricultural example, he begins with the term *phthora* (corruption, dissolution of the seed kernel; perishable [RSV]) that he links to "power" (vv.42b-43) which is at the heart of the Corinthian correspondence since it not only pervades it but actually brackets it: it is found early in the letter (1 Cor 1:17-18) and near the end of his correspondence (2 Cor 13:3-4). This is not surprising since, in scripture, "power" is the other facet of the spirit (*pnevma; ruaḥ*; mighty wind). This intimate connection between "power" and "spirit" is evident from the sequence "It is sown in weakness, it is raised in power" (15:43b) followed by "It is sown a physical body, it is raised a spiritual body. If there is a physical body, there is also a spiritual body. Thus it is written, 'The first man Adam became a living being'; the last Adam became a life-giving spirit" (vv.44-45). Paul explains the path from *phthora* (corruption) to "power" by using three contrasting pairs that link vv.36-41 and vv.42-50: the former passage dealing with natural examples and phenomena is written *in view of* the latter passage that deals with the subject matter itself. The first pair contrasts the agricultural *phthora* (corruption; v.42a) with *aphtharsia* (the status of being imperishable; v.42b), a term that connotes the "divine" realm in Greco-Roman mythological terminology, which Paul uses extensively in vv.50-54. The second pair builds on "glory" that was introduced in vv.40-41 and is coupled with its antonym *atimia* (dishonor, disrepute; v.43a). The last pair is the classic weakness versus power (v.43b). These last two opposing pairs appeared earlier in a passage where Paul used irony against the Corinthians (We are fools for Christ's sake, but you are wise in Christ. We are weak, but you are strong. You are held in honor [*endoxoi*; glorious], but we in disrepute [*atimoi*]; 4:10) in a passage (vv.6-13) immediately following the reference to the coming judgment which *all without exception* shall undergo (vv.1-5) and immediately preceding a passage (vv.14-21) introduced with "I do not write this to make you ashamed" (v.14a). Shame is repeated again in 15:34b (I say this to your shame) just before the lengthy passage we are discussing (vv.35-58). Consequently, the two pairs in 15:43 are meant to recall what Paul wrote in 4:10 and to remind the "spiritual" Corinthians, who are behaving as though there is no resurrection of the dead, of the coming judgment *of all*. At that judgment, appearances will be turned around since the true glory and power are still ahead and not already here or already attained.

Having thus aroused his hearers' attentiveness Paul moves directly to the main subject of the "body" posed in his original questions, "How are the dead raised? With what kind of body (*sōma*) do they come?" (15:35): "It is sown a physical (*psykhikon*) body, it is raised a spiritual body. If there is a physical (*psykhikon*) body, there is also a spiritual body." (v.44). By translating *psykhikon* into "physical" RSV completely blurs the original's intent even more so than it did when it translated the same *psykhikos*[34] into "unspiritual" in 2:14.[35] As I explained when dealing with 2:13-15, the real opposition is that between "flesh" and "spirit." The other facet of "flesh" in scripture is *nepheš* (breath) whose usual Greek translation is *psykhē*. The common English rendering of *psykhē* as "soul" is misleading since it leads to confusion between the original Hebrew connotation of animal and human breathing, on the one hand, and the Platonic understanding of "soul" as the self-standing eternal "element" that dwells in a given body but remains independent of it, on the other hand. These two views are worlds apart since the breathing starts at birth and ceases at death. Accordingly, the scriptural "breath(ing)" has nothing to do with the Platonic soul which is totally un-fleshly. Curtailing the soul into being only immortal, but not eternal, as was done in Christian thought, does not eliminate the tension since it still views the "soul" as an "element" independent of the body, as reflected in the traditional phrase "the human being is made of a soul and a body"; furthermore, at their "separation" at death the soul survives while the body decomposes and is no more.[36] In Hebrew, the "breath(ing)" is merely a physical, or rather—scripturally

---

[34] Grammatically, *psykhikon* is the neutral gender form while *psykhikos* is the masculine gender form.

[35] At least, "unspiritual" reflects the opposition between *psykhikos* and *pnevmatikos* (spiritual), whereas the translation of 15:44 completely eschews that *opposition* and seems to refer simply to two *different* "kinds" or "manners" of existence.

[36] Similarly, linking the one soul to one body in Christian thought, in opposition to the Platonic concept of re-incarnation of the eternal soul in different bodies, does not entirely eliminate the notion of two different "composites."

speaking—"fleshly" attribute of an animal or a human body while it is "alive." The hold of the Platonic philosophical view of the "soul" over Christian thought can readily be seen in the factual equation in the minds of the great majority of Christians between "soul" and "spirit." Speaking of three different parts of the human being, body, soul, and spirit, does not solve the dilemma either, since, in the common understanding, the latter two are not bodily whereas, in scripture, the "soul" as breathing is integrally "bodily" and thus is not divine, while the "divine" is exclusively "spirit" in scripture. This is precisely why, in 15:44, Paul underscores through repetition the opposition between "spirit" and "soul" by confining the function of the soul to the body *until death*, and relegating the function of the spirit to the human *post-resurrectional* status: "It is *sown* a physical (*psykhikon*; soul-ly) body, it is *raised* a spiritual body." Thus, the same body functions differently at two subsequent stages: "soul-ly" before death and "spiritually" at the resurrection, just as the seed and the plant, which comes out of that seed, have two different functions as well as appearances.

As usual, in order to back his statement concerning the human "soul," especially when it goes counter his addressees' or opponents' belief, Paul appeals to scripture itself: "Thus it is indeed (*kai*; also)[37] written, 'The first man Adam became (was made into) a living being (*psykhēn zōsan*).'" (vv.45a) The full verse from which the quotation is taken reads: "then the Lord God formed man (*ha'adam*) of dust from the ground (*ha'adamah*), and breathed (*wayyiphphah*) into his nostrils the breath (*nišmat*; breeze) of life (*ḥayyim*); and man (*ha'adam*) became a living (*ḥayyah*) being (*nepheš*; breathing) (LXX *psykhēn*

---

[37] Which is omitted in RSV.

zōsan)." (Gen 2:7) Thus, the "breeze" *of life* that God "breathed" into the *nostrils* of the being formed out of the ground rendered that being a *living breathing* (being). Although the first "man" was not "born" out of the womb, in order to make him human the way the rest of us are, the biblical author had no choice but to describe his beginning as a human being in the same way we all start life: by breathing. We cease living our life when we stop breathing. That is all there is to it: as Paul simply puts it, our body—the actual *form* (Gen 2:7) of our existence—is a breathing body (*sōma psykhikon*).[38] However, since the raised Christ is our first fruits and we, at the resurrection, shall hopefully be deemed among "those who belong to him" (1 Cor 15:23), then Christ—and not the first Adam[39]—is the standard we shall assume in our raised being. Since Christ is raised as life-giving—and not simply "living"—spirit (*pnevma zōopoioun*) (v.45b), our body will be "spiritual" (*pnevmatikon*), that is to say, under the aegis of that life-giving spirit, instead of just "soul-ly" (*psykhikon*) (v.44).

Having established his teaching, Paul hurries to say: "But it is not the spiritual which is *first* but the physical (soul-ly), and *then* the spiritual." (v.46) As in the case of v.36, this statement is intended to underscore to the Corinthians that they cannot be "spiritual" as they claim, that is to say, before becoming "spiritual" they would have to die and *then* be raised *in order to be judged* as all, even their Apostle, are bound (4:1-5). The fact that this is precisely what he was driving at all along is evident in that he immediately repeats the same thought no less than four more times in four different ways:

---

[38] For the meaning of the Greek *sōma* see *C-Col* 75.
[39] Notice how Paul adds the adjective "first" to the original quotation from Gen 2:7 in order to introduce Christ as the "last" Adam (1 Cor 15:45).

The *first* man was from the earth, a man of dust; the *second* man is from heaven. As was the man of dust, so are *those who are of the dust*; and as is the man of heaven, so are *those who are of heaven*. Just as *we have borne* (past tense) the image of the man of dust, *we shall also bear* (future tense) the image of the man of heaven. I tell you this, brethren: flesh and blood *cannot* inherit the kingdom of God, nor does *the perishable inherit the imperishable*. (15:47-50)[40]

The stress on the "heavenly" origin of both the "second man," Christ (v.47b), and those who belong to him (v.48b) brings to mind other Pauline statements that underscore the futurity of our "spiritual" resurrection:

But our commonwealth is *in heaven*, and from it *we await* a Savior, the Lord Jesus Christ, who *will change* our lowly body to be like his glorious body, by the power which enables him even to subject all things to himself. (Phil 3:20-21)

For the Lord himself *will descend from heaven* with a cry of command, with the archangel's call, and with the sound of the trumpet of God. And the dead in Christ *will rise first*; *then* we who are alive, who are left, *shall be caught up* together with them in the *clouds* to meet the Lord in the *air*; and so we shall always be with the Lord. (1 Thess 4:16-17)

This is evidence of the righteous judgment of God, that you may be made worthy of the kingdom of God, for which you are suffering—since indeed God deems it just to repay with affliction those who afflict you, and to grant rest with us to you who are afflicted, *when the Lord Jesus is revealed from heaven* with his mighty angels in flaming fire, inflicting vengeance upon those who

---

[40] Notice how Paul here adduces in v.50 the same imagery of inheritance of the kingdom that he used earlier (6:9-10) in conjunction with the coming divine judgment of the world (vv.1-8).

do not know God and upon those who do not obey the gospel of our Lord Jesus. (2 Thess 1:5-8)

Vv. 51-58 ⁵¹ ἰδοὺ μυστήριον ὑμῖν λέγω· πάντες οὐ κοιμηθησόμεθα, πάντες δὲ ἀλλαγησόμεθα, ⁵²ἐν ἀτόμῳ, ἐν ῥιπῇ ὀφθαλμοῦ, ἐν τῇ ἐσχάτῃ σάλπιγγι· σαλπίσει γὰρ καὶ οἱ νεκροὶ ἐγερθήσονται ἄφθαρτοι καὶ ἡμεῖς ἀλλαγησόμεθα. ⁵³Δεῖ γὰρ τὸ φθαρτὸν τοῦτο ἐνδύσασθαι ἀφθαρσίαν καὶ τὸ θνητὸν τοῦτο ἐνδύσασθαι ἀθανασίαν. ⁵⁴ὅταν δὲ τὸ φθαρτὸν τοῦτο ἐνδύσηται ἀφθαρσίαν καὶ τὸ θνητὸν τοῦτο ἐνδύσηται ἀθανασίαν, τότε γενήσεται ὁ λόγος ὁ γεγραμμένος· κατεπόθη ὁ θάνατος εἰς νῖκος. ⁵⁵ποῦ σου, θάνατε, τὸ νῖκος; ποῦ σου, θάνατε, τὸ κέντρον; ⁵⁶τὸ δὲ κέντρον τοῦ θανάτου ἡ ἁμαρτία, ἡ δὲ δύναμις τῆς ἁμαρτίας ὁ νόμος· ⁵⁷τῷ δὲ θεῷ χάρις τῷ διδόντι ἡμῖν τὸ νῖκος διὰ τοῦ κυρίου ἡμῶν Ἰησοῦ Χριστοῦ. ⁵⁸ Ὥστε, ἀδελφοί μου ἀγαπητοί, ἑδραῖοι γίνεσθε, ἀμετακίνητοι, περισσεύοντες ἐν τῷ ἔργῳ τοῦ κυρίου πάντοτε, εἰδότες ὅτι ὁ κόπος ὑμῶν οὐκ ἔστιν κενὸς ἐν κυρίῳ.

> ⁵¹Lo! I tell you a mystery. We shall not all sleep, but we shall all be changed, ⁵²in a moment, in the twinkling of an eye, at the last trumpet. For the trumpet will sound, and the dead will be raised imperishable, and we shall be changed. ⁵³For this perishable nature must put on the imperishable, and this mortal nature must put on immortality. ⁵⁴When the perishable puts on the imperishable, and the mortal puts on immortality, then shall come to pass the saying that is written: "Death is swallowed up in victory." ⁵⁵"O death, where is thy victory? O death, where is thy sting?" ⁵⁶The sting of death is sin, and the power of sin is the law. ⁵⁷But thanks be to God, who gives us the victory through our Lord Jesus Christ. ⁵⁸Therefore, my beloved brethren, be steadfast, immovable, always abounding in the work of the Lord, knowing that in the Lord your labor is not in vain.

As I explained in Romans and Colossians, "mystery" does not refer to something inexplicable that can only be understood after one has developed a certain mystical aptitude. In scripture "mystery" is something yet unknown to the addressees and that is about to be communicated to them.[41] Thus, its connotation is that of very special news, and its use is meant to draw the hearers' undivided attention to what is being relayed to them. As Paul also writes in 1 Thessalonians 4:15-18, in spite of his stress on the necessity of death (1 Cor 15:36) he concedes that some will still be alive at the Lord's coming (v.51a). This does not mean that his earlier statement in v.36 is invalid since none knows the exact time of the Lord's coming (1 Thess 5:1-3), and thus cannot gamble regarding this matter. But, more importantly, since the general resurrection will take place *in view of* the judgment and since one is to become "spiritual" in order to secure imperishability, then all, alive as well as dead, shall be "changed" (1 Cor 15:51b); indeed, even those who would be alive at the Lord's coming will have merely a "soul-ly" body. Having referred to the suddenness of the end (v.52a), Paul writes unequivocally that only those who are dead *will be raised* imperishable, while those who are still alive[42] *shall be changed* into that state. The "must" of v.53 corresponds to the earlier and only other "must" in this chapter: "For he must reign until he has put all his enemies under his feet. The last enemy to be destroyed is death." (vv.25-26) Indeed, the last enemy mentioned in v.26 is the subject matter of v.54, which begins by taking up the content of v.53: "For this perishable (nature) must put on the imperishable, and this mortal (nature) must put on immortality. When the perishable puts on the imperishable, and the mortal puts on immortality, then shall come to pass the

---

[41] See *C-Col* 56-59.
[42] As we hear in a parallel passage 1 Thess 4:14-17: "And the dead in Christ will rise first; then *we who are alive*…" (vv.16-17)

saying that is written: 'Death is swallowed up in victory.'" (vv.53-54)[43]

Once more Paul appeals to the incontrovertible authority of scripture in order to substantiate the "mystery" he is communicating here.[44] What is of utmost importance in this particular case is the unique introduction to the quotation "*then shall come to pass* the saying that is written" (v.54c). Such ensures that the first part of the quotation from Isaiah 25:8 be taken as a future, and not past, action.[45] Paul wants to make sure his hearers bear in mind that the victory over death, the last enemy, will take place at the Lord's coming, and until then death will reign over us since we are mortal and bound to die (1 Cor 15:53-54). Paul's main concern is death, and he rephrases the quotation from Hosea (13:14) in a way that makes death the subject of all three statements (1 Cor 15:54b-55). Whereas Hosea has Hades (Sheol) in the second line, Paul changes it into death,[46] the result being that death is heard as the main cadence. Also, given that death was introduced as "enemy" in 1 Corinthians 15:26, Paul stresses the victory over it by changing *dikē* (just penalty; just revenge) in LXX Hosea into *nikos* (victory) the result being that "victory over death" is heard twice.

---

[43] For the meaning of the metaphor of "putting on," see my comments in *Gal* 170-2 and in *C-Col* 66.
[44] Just as he did in Romans 11:25-27.
[45] The Greek aorist tense does not necessarily refer to an action in the past; rather it expresses assuredness that the action either did or would take place.
[46] The change is permissible in that twice in that verse Sheol (Hades) and death are used as parallels, parallelism being a basic feature of scriptural Hebrew poetry: "Shall I ransom them from the power of Sheol? Shall I redeem them from Death? O Death, where are your plagues (*dikē* [just penalty] in LXX)? O Sheol, where is your destruction (*kentron* [sting] in LXX)?"

However, and again lest the hearers think that the ultimate and consummate victory is behind them, Paul keeps the original "sting" in LXX Hosea, instead of changing it into "victory," in view of commenting on it in 1 Corinthians 15:56. As in the case with Adam, after whose likeness the Corinthians still are (v.49), death was introduced as the consequence of sin (vv.21-22; see also Rom 5:12). So long as death remains ahead of them, it is sin on their part that is the sting of death (1 Cor 15:56a). What Paul compresses in two verses (vv.56-57) is a compendium of what he detailed in Romans 6-8.[47] The introduction of sin and Law together with victory is used to build up to his conclusion in 1 Corinthians 15:58. The victory of Christ, as consequence of his trust in God, is already established; however the believers' victory, as consequence of the same kind of trust in God, is still ahead of them. That is why they, as well as the Apostle, are still *continually* death bound: "As it is written, 'For thy sake we are being killed *all the day long*; we are regarded as sheep to be slaughtered'" (Rom 8:36); "I die *every day*!" (1 Cor 15:31) That is why they should not behave as though they were already reigning with Christ in God's kingdom (4:8) but rather should *continually* and until the Lord's coming heed Paul's injunction: "*Therefore*, my beloved brethren, be steadfast, immovable, always abounding in the work of the Lord, knowing that in the Lord your labor is not in vain." (15:58)

---

[47] Rom 6:17-18, 20-21, 23; 7:7-12, 22-25a; 8:37-39.

Chapter 16

Vv. 1-4 ¹Περὶ δὲ τῆς λογείας τῆς εἰς τοὺς ἁγίους ὥσπερ διέταξα ταῖς ἐκκλησίαις τῆς Γαλατίας, οὕτως καὶ ὑμεῖς ποιήσατε. ² κατὰ μίαν σαββάτου ἕκαστος ὑμῶν παρ' ἑαυτῷ τιθέτω θησαυρίζων ὅ τι ἐὰν εὐοδῶται, ἵνα μὴ ὅταν ἔλθω τότε λογεῖαι γίνωνται. ³ ὅταν δὲ παραγένωμαι, οὓς ἐὰν δοκιμάσητε, δι' ἐπιστολῶν τούτους πέμψω ἀπενεγκεῖν τὴν χάριν ὑμῶν εἰς Ἰερουσαλήμ· ⁴ ἐὰν δὲ ἄξιον ᾖ τοῦ κἀμὲ πορεύεσθαι, σὺν ἐμοὶ πορεύσονται.

> ¹*Now concerning the contribution for the saints: as I directed the churches of Galatia, so you also are to do.* ²*On the first day of every week, each of you is to put something aside and store it up, as he may prosper, so that contributions need not be made when I come.* ³*And when I arrive, I will send those whom you accredit by letter to carry your gift to Jerusalem.* ⁴*If it seems advisable that I should go also, they will accompany me.*

As he committed himself at the Jerusalem meeting to "remember the poor" (Gal 2:10), Paul is asking the Corinthians to do their share, as he requests from all his churches (1 Cor 16:1; Rom 15:26; 2 Cor 8:1-2), and is suggesting they do so on the first day of the week so that they would not have to cram matters in when he comes to visit them (1 Cor 16:2). They would benefit more from his teaching instead of losing time on something they could do during his absence. The mention of the "first of the week" (*mian sabbatou*) suggests that regular church meal gatherings (1 Cor 11:17-34) took place on those days, as we hear in Acts 20:7: "On the first day of the week (*tē mia tōn sabbatōn*), when we were gathered together to break bread, Paul talked with them, intending to depart on the morrow; and he prolonged his speech until midnight." The original intent behind the choice of that day seems to have been parallel to Paul's concern with the collection for the "saints" in Jerusalem: not to break the bridge between Jews and Gentiles by always reminding the Gentiles that the good news that reached them is embedded in the scriptures of Israel. Since the synagogues refused to include the non-circumcised, Paul insisted that his church gatherings (*ekklēsiai*), which welcomed both Jews and Gentiles around the "word,"[1] convene to hear those same scriptures (the) immediately (following day) after it resounded in the synagogues. This is borne out in that striking Lukan description of what happened in Corinth itself:

> After this he left Athens and went to Corinth. And he found a Jew named Aquila, a native of Pontus, lately come from Italy with his wife Priscilla, because Claudius had commanded all the Jews to leave Rome. And he went to see them; and because he was of the same trade he stayed with them, and they worked, for by trade they were tentmakers. And he argued in the synagogue every sabbath, and persuaded Jews and Greeks. When Silas and Timothy arrived from Macedonia, Paul was occupied with preaching, testifying to the Jews that the Christ was Jesus. And when they opposed and reviled him, he shook out his garments and said to them, "Your blood be upon your heads! I am innocent. From now on I will go to the Gentiles." And he left there and went to the house of a man named Titius Justus, a worshiper of God; *his house was next door to* (*synomorousa*; bordering on)[2] *the synagogue.* Crispus, the ruler of the synagogue, believed in the Lord, together with all his household; and many of the

---

[1] Notice the end of Acts 20:7: "and he prolonged his speech (*dialegeto*; from the same root as *logos* [word]) until midnight."

[2] A unique instance in the New Testament. *synomorō* is a compound verb formed out of the preposition *syn* ([together] with) and the verb *homorō*, which is in turn a compound of *homo* (equal to; on the same level as) and the noun *horos* (marker stone [between two properties]).

Corinthians hearing Paul believed and were baptized. (Acts 18:1-8)

To make sure that the Corinthian collections reach Jerusalem with or without him, Paul obliquely invites his hearers to continue that tradition in his absence, that is to say, after his death (1 Cor 16:3-4). His reference to the collection as "grace" (*kharin*; gift [RSV]) is a constant reminder to the Corinthians that what they are doing is a debt on their part to acknowledge the "grace" that reached them out of Israel's scriptures: "For Macedonia and Achaia have been pleased to make some contribution for the poor among the saints at Jerusalem; they were pleased to do it, and indeed they are in debt (*opheiletai*) to them, for if the Gentiles have come to share in their spiritual blessings, they ought (*opheilousin*; are indebted) also to be of service to them in material blessings." (Rom 15:26-27)

Vv. 5-12 ⁵ Ἐλεύσομαι δὲ πρὸς ὑμᾶς ὅταν Μακεδονίαν διέλθω· Μακεδονίαν γὰρ διέρχομαι, ⁶ πρὸς ὑμᾶς δὲ τυχὸν παραμενῶ ἢ καὶ παραχειμάσω, ἵνα ὑμεῖς με προπέμψητε οὗ ἐὰν πορεύωμαι. ⁷ οὐ θέλω γὰρ ὑμᾶς ἄρτι ἐν παρόδῳ ἰδεῖν, ἐλπίζω γὰρ χρόνον τινὰ ἐπιμεῖναι πρὸς ὑμᾶς ἐὰν ὁ κύριος ἐπιτρέψῃ. ⁸ ἐπιμενῶ δὲ ἐν Ἐφέσῳ ἕως τῆς πεντηκοστῆς· ⁹ θύρα γάρ μοι ἀνέῳγεν μεγάλη καὶ ἐνεργής, καὶ ἀντικείμενοι πολλοί. ¹⁰ Ἐὰν δὲ ἔλθῃ Τιμόθεος, βλέπετε, ἵνα ἀφόβως γένηται πρὸς ὑμᾶς· τὸ γὰρ ἔργον κυρίου ἐργάζεται ὡς κἀγώ· ¹¹ μή τις οὖν αὐτὸν ἐξουθενήσῃ. προπέμψατε δὲ αὐτὸν ἐν εἰρήνῃ, ἵνα ἔλθῃ πρός με· ἐκδέχομαι γὰρ αὐτὸν μετὰ τῶν ἀδελφῶν. ¹² Περὶ δὲ Ἀπολλῶ τοῦ ἀδελφοῦ, πολλὰ παρεκάλεσα αὐτόν, ἵνα ἔλθῃ πρὸς ὑμᾶς μετὰ τῶν ἀδελφῶν· καὶ πάντως οὐκ ἦν θέλημα ἵνα νῦν ἔλθῃ· ἐλεύσεται δὲ ὅταν εὐκαιρήσῃ.

⁵*I will visit you after passing through Macedonia, for I intend to pass through Macedonia,* ⁶ *and perhaps I will stay with you or*

even spend the winter, so that you may speed me on my journey, wherever I go. ⁷For I do not want to see you now just in passing; I hope to spend some time with you, if the Lord permits. ⁸But I will stay in Ephesus until Pentecost, ⁹for a wide door for effective work has opened to me, and there are many adversaries. ¹⁰When Timothy comes, see that you put him at ease among you, for he is doing the work of the Lord, as I am. ¹¹So let no one despise him. Speed him on his way in peace, that he may return to me; for I am expecting him with the brethren. ¹²As for our brother Apollos, I strongly urged him to visit you with the other brethren, but it was not at all his will to come now. He will come when he has opportunity.

Paul uses a classic literary device in 1 Corinthians 16:5-8 to inform his addressees not to expect him soon and, most probably, never. He uses the same stratagem in Romans 15:22-33.³ That is why, in both cases, he is writing a detailed and encompassing letter.⁴ This is corroborated in the reference to Pentecost in conjunction with Ephesus. Indeed, the mention of Pentecost together with Ephesus is found elsewhere only in Acts 20:16 and there also in conjunction with his plan to visit Jerusalem.⁵ Such cannot be mere coincidence, when Pentecost is referred to only once more in the New Testament (Acts 2:1) where it is connected with the pouring out of the Spirit. Furthermore, the reason given for staying in Ephesus is that, in spite of the open door for his preaching, there are still many

---

³ See my comments on this passage in *C-Rom* 265-8.
⁴ The real reason may well be that Paul was already deceased—which is precisely why he is not coming—and the letters were written in his name. I have pointed out in all my commentaries on his letters how he dwells repeatedly on his "absence" while wishing to be "present."
⁵ In Acts 20 Paul hopes to reach Jerusalem before Pentecost whereas in 1 Corinthians he is planning to remain in Ephesus until then.

adversaries in that city. Thus, the situation is difficult, which is precisely what is related in Acts 20:17-38 that ends with the following comment: "And when he had spoken thus, he knelt down and prayed with them all. And they all wept and embraced Paul and kissed him, sorrowing most of all because of the word he had spoken, that they should see his face no more." (vv.36-38) In my comments on that entire passage I took the position that, most probably, Paul found his end in Ephesus.[6] If so, then the mention of Pentecost both here in 1 Corinthians and in Acts 20 makes sense only if we take it as an oblique reference to the coming in power of the Spirit that opened the mission to the Gentiles as well as the Jews, which is precisely its function in Acts 2. There we have the beginning of the apostolic activity and, in Acts 20, just before the mention of Pentecost (v.16) we hear, amid a great deal of opposition, of the Spirit being the bridge between the mission of Paul and that of the Ephesian elders after his demise:

> And now, behold, I am going to Jerusalem, bound in the Spirit, not knowing what shall befall me there; except that the Holy Spirit testifies to me in every city that imprisonment and afflictions await me[7] ... Take heed to yourselves and to all the flock, in which the Holy Spirit has made you overseers, to care for the church of God which he obtained with the blood of his own Son. I know that after my departure fierce wolves will come in among you, not sparing the flock; and from among your own selves will arise men speaking perverse things, to draw away the disciples after them. (vv.22-23, 28-30)

Here, in 1 Corinthians 16, we are presented with the end of Paul's mission when the Spirit, in spite of all adversity (v.9) is

---

[6] See *NTI₂* 259, 261 and also *NTI₁* 16.
[7] This statement parallels that in 1 Cor 15:31-32a.

"coming again with power" to raise the dead (1 Cor 15:42-46). Since the coming Spirit is as sudden as it is unexpected (v.52), it is understandable that the Corinthians might not be able to see Paul again (16:6-7).

However, the question remains as to why at all the reference to Pentecost in 1 Corinthians 16:8 when Paul could have said the same thing without its mention?[8] Is there something in that feast that prompted him to use it in conjunction with his apostolic activity in Ephesus? The Greek *tē pentēkostē* is a feminine adjective meaning "the fiftieth" and after which one is to supply *hēmera* (day), which is a feminine noun in Greek, as is clear from Tobit 2:1: "In the reign of Esarhaddon, therefore, I returned home, and my wife Anna was restored to me with my son Tobias. At the feast of Pentecost, which is the holy feast of seven Weeks, there was a good dinner and I took my place for the meal." That feast was the second major feast of the Old Testament cultic year: "Three times a year all your males shall appear before the Lord your God at the place which he will choose: at the feast of unleavened bread, at the feast of weeks, and at the feast of booths." (Deut 16:16) It was celebrated seven weeks after Passover in commemoration of the first fruits:

> You may not offer the passover sacrifice within any of your towns which the Lord your God gives you; but at the place which the Lord your God will choose, to make his name dwell in it, there you shall offer the passover sacrifice, in the evening at the going down of the sun, at the time you came out of Egypt. And you shall boil it and eat it at the place which the Lord your God will choose; and in the morning you shall turn and go to your tents. For six days you shall eat unleavened bread; and on the seventh

---

[8] My readers are reminded that appealing to Acts to explain 1 Corinthians is putting the cart before the horse since the latter was written before the former.

day there shall be a solemn assembly to the Lord your God; you shall do no work on it. You shall count seven weeks; begin to count the seven weeks from the time you first put the sickle to the standing grain. Then you shall keep the feast of weeks to the Lord your God with the tribute of a freewill offering from your hand, which you shall give as the Lord your God blesses you; and you shall rejoice before the Lord your God, you and your son and your daughter, your manservant (*'ebed*) and your maidservant, the Levite who is within your towns, the sojourner (*ger*), the fatherless, and the widow who are among you, at the place which the Lord your God will choose, to make his name dwell there. You shall remember that you were a slave (*'ebed*) in Egypt; and you shall be careful to observe these statutes. (vv.5-12)

As prescribed, this festivity of fruits is to include the "manservant" (*'ebed*; v.11) in remembrance of the fact that the addressee and thus main celebrant was himself a "slave" (*'ebed*; v.12) in Egypt whence he was liberated, which means that that feast was intrinsically related to that of Passover. However, we are told that the "sojourner" (*ger*; stranger, v.11) is also to be included. The mention of the *ger* is telling in view of what we hear elsewhere: "When a stranger (*ger*) sojourns with you in your land, you shall not do him wrong. The stranger (*ger*) who sojourns with you shall be to you as the native among you, and you shall love him as yourself; for you were strangers (*gerim*) in the land of Egypt: I am the Lord your God." (Lev 19:33-34)

Thus, Paul's choice to refer to Pentecost in conjunction with his prescribed collection in his Gentile churches, whose members were "once alienated from the commonwealth of Israel, and *strangers* to the covenants of promise" (Eph 2:12), makes perfect sense. His intention was to take their offering to Jerusalem at the appointed time of the "feast of weeks" when God will accept the common offering of both Jew and Gentile for what he did to both, free them from the bondage of Egypt at Passover; indeed the "fathers" who were delivered have become, through Paul, the fathers of the Gentile Corinthians (1 Cor 10:1). However, Paul's plans are frayed with difficulties (16:9a); and yet, his hope is firm in that the seed he planted (3:6) will find, beyond his own demise, its fruition at the hands of his junior colleagues who will celebrate the Pentecost at Jerusalem with the offering of the Gentiles.

As is the case in Philippians (2:19-24), here Timothy is also Paul's top adjutant. Should Paul not be able to come to Corinth, then Timothy would come and the Corinthians are to welcome him, accept his teaching and not despise him (1 Cor 16:11a). The reason is that Timothy "is doing the work of the Lord" as is Paul (1 Cor 16:10b) and thus would lead the Corinthians in doing what Paul has required of them (15:58). Yet even Timothy is bound to leave them, so the Corinthians are urged not to hold on to him and be ready to "speed him on his way" (*propempsate*; send him off) in (the) peace (of the Lord) so that he should "come to Paul who is expecting him" (16:11) to join him, opening the way for Stephanas, Fortunatus, and Achaicus (v.17) just as, in Philippi, Timothy had to step aside for Epaphroditus (Phil 2:25-30).[9]

However, the passage from the second generation (Timothy) to the third (Stephanas, Fortunatus, and Achaicus) might not be smooth. Just as Paul is encountering "adversaries" even in Ephesus where God has opened a "wide door for effective work" (1 Cor 16:9), so also in Corinth there are hurdles from within. Even Apollos, who watered the seed Paul planted there (3:6), is now tergiversating in carrying on the mission (16:12). What is

---

[9] See my comments in *C-Phil* 142-7 and also below on 1 Cor 16:15-18.

said of Apollos here seems to parallel how Luke speaks of him in Acts and, once more, in conjunction with Ephesus and Corinth (Acts 18:24-19:1). Although "an eloquent man, well versed in the scriptures" (18:24) Apollos needed to be corrected in his teaching by Priscilla and Aquila (v.26). When he reached Corinth (19:1a) nothing more is said of him; he disappears from Luke's horizon. Notable is the fact that this parallels what happened with Silas (v.5): he also "vanishes" at Corinth. Thus, like Silas and Barnabas,[10] Apollos ends up betraying Paul's gospel and becoming one of his "adversaries" in Ephesus (1 Cor 16:9); it is as though he did not want to go to Corinth (v.12) in order to remain in Ephesus and put hurdles in the way of Paul's preaching there (v.8). According to Luke's description, Apollos was "a native of Alexandria" (*Alexandreus tō genei*; Acts 18:24). Alexandria was famous as the city of Greek philosophy, which produced both the Jewish Philo and the Christian Origen who introduced the extraneous Platonic thought into the explication of scripture. This is precisely what Paul was fighting against in 1 Corinthians 1-2 and branded as "foolish human wisdom" (1:18-25). It thus stands to reason that Cephas and Apollos, the two named besides Paul in 1:12 and 3:22, in whose names divisions plagued the one church of God in Corinth, are those aimed at in Paul's statement "Jews demand signs and Greeks seek wisdom, but we preach Christ crucified, a stumbling block to Jews and folly to Gentiles" (1:22-23). And if Cephas betrayed the gospel (Gal 2:11-14), so did Apollos.

Vv. 13-24 ¹³ Γρηγορεῖτε, στήκετε ἐν τῇ πίστει, ἀνδρίζεσθε, κραταιοῦσθε. ¹⁴ πάντα ὑμῶν ἐν ἀγάπῃ γινέσθω. ¹⁵ Παρακαλῶ δὲ ὑμᾶς, ἀδελφοί· οἴδατε τὴν οἰκίαν Στεφανᾶ, ὅτι ἐστὶν ἀπαρχὴ τῆς Ἀχαΐας καὶ εἰς διακονίαν τοῖς ἁγίοις ἔταξαν

---

[10] See earlier my discussion of Barnabas in my comments on 1 Cor 15:1-11.

ἑαυτούς· ¹⁶ ἵνα καὶ ὑμεῖς ὑποτάσσησθε τοῖς τοιούτοις καὶ παντὶ τῷ συνεργοῦντι καὶ κοπιῶντι. ¹⁷ χαίρω δὲ ἐπὶ τῇ παρουσίᾳ Στεφανᾶ καὶ Φορτουνάτου καὶ Ἀχαϊκοῦ, ὅτι τὸ ὑμέτερον ὑστέρημα οὗτοι ἀνεπλήρωσαν· ¹⁸ ἀνέπαυσαν γὰρ τὸ ἐμὸν πνεῦμα καὶ τὸ ὑμῶν. ἐπιγινώσκετε οὖν τοὺς τοιούτους. ¹⁹ Ἀσπάζονται ὑμᾶς αἱ ἐκκλησίαι τῆς Ἀσίας. ἀσπάζεται ὑμᾶς ἐν κυρίῳ πολλὰ Ἀκύλας καὶ Πρίσκα σὺν τῇ κατ' οἶκον αὐτῶν ἐκκλησίᾳ. ²⁰ ἀσπάζονται ὑμᾶς οἱ ἀδελφοὶ πάντες. Ἀσπάσασθε ἀλλήλους ἐν φιλήματι ἁγίῳ. ²¹ Ὁ ἀσπασμὸς τῇ ἐμῇ χειρὶ Παύλου. ²² εἴ τις οὐ φιλεῖ τὸν κύριον, ἤτω ἀνάθεμα. μαράνα θά. ²³ ἡ χάρις τοῦ κυρίου Ἰησοῦ μεθ' ὑμῶν. ²⁴ ἡ ἀγάπη μου μετὰ πάντων ὑμῶν ἐν Χριστῷ Ἰησοῦ.

¹³Be watchful, stand firm in your faith, be courageous, be strong. ¹⁴Let all that you do be done in love. ¹⁵Now, brethren, you know that the household of Stephanas were the first converts in Achaia, and they have devoted themselves to the service of the saints; ¹⁶I urge you to be subject to such men and to every fellow worker and laborer. ¹⁷I rejoice at the coming of Stephanas and Fortunatus and Achaicus, because they have made up for your absence; ¹⁸for they refreshed my spirit as well as yours. Give recognition to such men. ¹⁹The churches of Asia send greetings. Aquila and Prisca, together with the church in their house, send you hearty greetings in the Lord. ²⁰All the brethren send greetings. Greet one another with a holy kiss. ²¹I, Paul, write this greeting with my own hand. ²²If any one has no love for the Lord, let him be accursed. Our Lord, come! ²³The grace of the Lord Jesus be with you. ²⁴My love be with you all in Christ Jesus. Amen.

Given the difficulties lying ahead of them—his own absence, Timothy's end, and Apollos' betrayal—Paul asks the Corinthians to stick with the basics: while being watchful for the Lord's coming, they are to continue to stand firm in their trust in the

Pauline gospel (1 Cor 16:13a) as they have been doing (15:1) and remain courageous and strong in the face of all adversities. They should use the Pauline standard of love for the others as the test of their trust in what Paul preached them. Paul's request in 16:13-14 parallels his recommendation to the Galatians: "For through the Spirit, by faith, we wait for the hope of righteousness. For in Christ Jesus neither circumcision nor uncircumcision is of any avail, but faith (trust) working through love." (Gal 5:5-6)

Just as he does in Philippians and Colossians, Paul prepares his hearers to be obedient to their local leaders, the third generation after that of Paul and of Timothy.[11] The chosen person for this purpose in Corinth is Stephanas, whose name means "crown" and thus is the prototype of the true witness to the cause of the gospel.[12] Actually, his household members were the "first converts" (*aparkhē*; first fruits) of Achaia who "devoted" (*etaxan*; put in an orderly manner) themselves to the *diakonian* (service at table fellowship) of the saints (1 Cor 16:15). The entire terminology reflects the fact that Stephanas' house was actually the main house church in Corinth. According to Paul, if Stephanas and his immediate family, the first fruits and the leaders, have dedicated themselves to the "service" of all, their example should induce all the Corinthians to follow suit[13] and "be subject to" (*hypotassēsthe* [from the same root as *etaxan*]; submit yourselves) "such men (*tois toioutois*) and to every fellow worker (*synergounti*) and laborer (*kopiōnti*; toiler)" (v.16). By

---

[11] See *C-Phil* 142-7 and *C-Col* 95-105.
[12] See earlier my comments on 1 Cor 1:16.
[13] RSV hides the original *hina kai hymeis hypotassēsthe* (*in order that* you also might be subject; v.16a) into "I urge you to be subject" as though Paul in v.16 was making another request unrelated to the former one in v.15. RSV dismisses even the original *kai* (also, too) before *hymeis* (you).

referring to Stephanas' family members as "such men" Paul was opening up the list to include Fortunatus and Achaicus in v.17. Furthermore, the two qualifications for the third generation leaders are "fellow worker" and "laborer (toiler)." Paul used the verb *kopiō* (labor, toil) earlier in conjunction with his apostolic activity (4:12; see also Col 1:29; 1 Tim 4:10). He now applies it to church leaders (see 1 Thess 5:12; 1 Tim 5:17) since they are supposed to carry on Paul's apostolic teaching. The same applies to "fellow worker" (*synergos* [noun]; *synergōn* [active participle]): Paul is God's fellow worker (3:9a), but so also is Epaphroditus Paul's "brother and fellow worker and fellow soldier" (Phil 2:25).[14] Therefore, the absence of Paul or Timothy should not be a problem. The "presence" (*parousia*; coming so as to be present with) of Stephanas, Fortunatus, and Achaicus should suffice to fulfill the Corinthians' needs and wants (1 Cor 16:17). The classic verse that plays on presence and absence is found in Philippians: "Therefore, my beloved, as you have always obeyed, so now, not only as in my presence (*parousia*) but much more in my absence (*apousia*), work out your own salvation with fear and trembling." (2:12)

RSV misses completely the intent of 1 Corinthians 16:17-18 in its translation: "I rejoice at the coming of Stephanas and Fortunatus and Achaicus, because they have made up for your absence; for they refreshed my spirit as well as yours. Give recognition to such men." Such a translation presupposes that the three leaders went to visit Paul in Ephesus, and their visit made up for Paul's missing the Corinthians. Such is definitely not Paul's intent: *anaplērō* (fulfill) and *hysterēma* (something missing; need; want) are translated elsewhere in RSV as "fulfill the needs and wants of others" (2 Cor 9:12; 11:9; Phil 2:30) or

---

[14] See also Phil 4:3; Col 4:11; Philem 24.

"what is missing for something to be complete" (Col 1:24). Furthermore, the other three instances of *anapavō* in Paul (2 Cor 7:13; Philem 7, 20), translated as "refresh" here in 1 Cor 16:18, are used in conjunction with fulfilling God's will and do not in the least denote giving satisfaction to someone who is emotionally missing someone else! At any rate, if this were the case, then Paul should have written simply "for they refreshed my spirit" and not "for they refreshed my spirit *as well as yours*," since the presumed psychological "refreshment" of the Corinthians would have taken place at the return of the emissaries and thus would have been in the future, not the past, which is implied in the past tense "refreshed." Rather, just as is the case with Philemon himself, both the refreshment felt by his subalterns (Philem 7) and the one he is required to give Paul (v.20) have to do with the duty of doing God's will. This is precisely what we have in 1 Corinthians. The behavior of the Corinthian leaders in doing what they are supposed to do, taking care of their flock, is what brings, at the same time, refreshment to both Paul and the recipients of their care. Moreover, that is why the Corinthians are required to "give recognition to such men" (1 Cor 16:18b) in being "submissive (subject)" to their instructions (v.16). A more accurate translation of vv.17-18 would be: "I rejoice at the coming of Stephanas and Fortunatus and Achaicus, because they have fulfilled what is still missing on your part in the matter of comprehending and implementing the gospel teaching; in so doing, they refreshed my spirit as well as yours. Give recognition to such men."

I have shown repeatedly in my commentaries on Romans, Philippians, Colossians, and Philemon that names are more functional than personal. The same is true in our passage here. Fortunatus is the Latin for the Greek Epaphroditus and thus intimates any Corinthian who would be chosen by divine providence to be a church leader.[15] The Greek *Akhaikos*[16] translates literally as someone from the province Achaia, whose capital was Corinth at the time. Hence, it is another free choice by God. The total message Paul is trying to communicate is that, in his absence and that of Timothy, the Corinthians will be led through God's "good fortune" (Fortunatus) by worthy leaders from among themselves (Achaicus), who will be deemed to bear witness (Stephanas) to the Pauline teaching. God will not abandon his field that was planted in Corinth by Paul (3:6, 9) as long as Paul's letter is read aloud to the Corinthian congregation so that not only the common members but also their leaders heed the Pauline gospel: "Paul and Timothy, servants of Christ Jesus, to all the saints in Christ Jesus who are at Philippi, with the bishops and deacons." (Phil 1:1)[17]

At the end of Romans Paul structures his lengthy greetings to remind his addressees that, although Rome is the capital of the empire and from it comes forth the imperial and senatorial edicts *urbi et orbi* (to the city [of Rome] and the world), it is from Ephesus, the Pauline headquarters, that the gospel of God's peace (Eph 6:13-17) goes forth.[18] This gospel is inscribed in the Pauline letters addressed to both all the capitals of the major Roman provinces of the East, including Ephesus itself, the capital of the Province Asia, and Rome, the capital of the empire and the center of the western provinces. Here, also, to the Corinthian church around Stephanas' house come greetings from "the churches of Asia" and from "Aquila and Prisca,

---

[15] See my comments on Epaphroditus in *C-Phil* 142-7 and his counterpart Epaphras in *C-Col* 32-6 and 100-2.

[16] Which becomes *Akhaikou* in the gentive case (complement of noun) just as *Fortounatos* changes into *Fortounatou*.

[17] See my comments on this verse in *C-Phil* 58-64.

[18] See my comments on Rom 16:1-5 in *C-Rom* 270-6.

together with the church in their house" (1 Cor 16:19). By pointing out that the greeting comes from "*all* the brethren" (v.20a) Paul is underscoring the oneness of "the churches of Asia" around the gospel. Paul intimated this in his earlier letter to the Galatians: "*Paul* an apostle—not from men nor through man, but through Jesus Christ and God the Father, who raised him from the dead—*and all the brethren who are with me, to the churches of Galatia…*" (1:1-2)

The holy kiss (1 Cor 16:20b) is the sign of brotherhood.[19] Refusing to kiss a brother in a tribal society, as was the Roman empire, was an expression of disagreement; when one declined to kiss the chief, it was perceived as outright dissent tantamount to betrayal, in which case the traitor was excised, declared *anathema* (cut out, accursed). Such would be a serious matter in the Pauline churches since the Lord is coming to judge. The Aramaic *Marana Tha*, which is found in the Greek original, means "(Our) Lord, come!" Still, the real test to the truthfulness of the brotherly kiss (v.20) is whether each is ready and willing to give the same kiss (*philei*) to the first-born (Rom 8:29), that is, to Christ, who is not *another brother*, but rather the Lord around whom the brotherhood takes life as well as shape.

"I, Paul, write this greeting with my own hand" is a literary device used to cluster the Pauline letters in order to show their unity, which is rooted in the one sender in spite of the multiplicity of addressed communities.[20] The first cluster combines Romans and 1 Corinthians and the second combines 2 Corinthians and Galatians. The split between 1 and 2 Corinthians is intentional: whatever applies to Rome in the West

---

[19] See my comments on Rom 16:16a in *C-Rom* 282.
[20] See Rev 2-3.

is to be heard across the Adriatic Sea in Corinth in Eastern Europe, and whatever applies to Corinth is to be heard across the Aegean Sea in Galatia in Asia Minor. The third cluster of Ephesians, Philippians, and Colossians puts the letter to the Macedonian Philippi *in between* the letters to two cities of the province Asia. Thus the message is clear: the teaching of each letter is authoritatively valid in *all* the churches. In turn, this is confirmed *literally* in Colossians where just before "I, Paul, write this greeting with my own hand" (4:18) we hear: "And when this letter has been read among you, have it read also in the church of the Laodiceans; and see that you read also the letter from Laodicea." (v.16)

RSV again misses the point by translating *ou philei* into "has no love" (1 Cor 16:22) thus obscuring the intended link between *philēmati* (kiss; v.20) and *philei* (v.22) that are from the same root *phil*—. It is highly improbable that *ou philei* here means "has no love" because "loving (*philein*) the Lord" would be a *hapax legomenon* (unique instance) in the New Testament; usually it is the verb *agapō* (from the same root as *agapē*) that is used to express the love one has for the Lord.[21] On the other hand, the proximity of *philēmati* (kiss) makes the case virtually impossible. "Kissing" the Lord (v.22a) is tantamount to being ready to receive him at his coming as corroborated in the appositional "Our Lord, come!" (v.22b).

At this point, Paul has nothing more to add except to bid the Corinthians the Lord's grace (16:23) with the hope that it would lead them to his promised peace (1:3) in God's kingdom, and to convey his paternal love (16:24) expressed in the instructions he

---

[21] See e.g. Rom 8:28 (We know that in everything God works for good with those who love [*agapōsin*] him, who are called according to his purpose).

just consigned for them in his lengthy letter. It would behoove them to accept those instructions, even when perceived as a "rod" rather than the expression of a "spirit of gentleness" (4:21) and live by them in order not to fall under the "rod" of the coming judge.

Further Reading

Commentaries and Studies

John Chrysostom, Homilies on 1 Corinthians in P. Schaff, ed., *The Nicene and Post-Nicene Fathers.* Grand Rapids, 1st Series, xii 1979: 1-269.

Aletti, J.-N. *Saint Paul: Epître aux Colossiens. Introduction, traduction et commentaire.* Etudes Bibliques, nouvelle série 20. Paris : Gabalda, 1993.

Barclay, J. M. G. *Colossians and Philemon.* T&T Clark Study Guides. London-New York: T&T Clark International, 2004.

Collins, R.F. *First Corinthians.* Sacra Pagina, 7. Collegeville, MN: Liturgical Press, 1999.

Coutsoumpos, P. *Community, Conflict and the Eucahrist in Roman Corinth. The Social Setting of Paul's Letter.* Lanham, MD-Oxford: University Press of America, 2006.

Fisk, B. N. *First Corinthians.* Interpretation Bible Studies. Louisville, KY: Geneva, 2000.

Fotopoulos, J. *Food Offered to Idols in Roman Corinth. A Social-Rhetorical Reconsideration of 1 Corinthians 8:1-11:1.* Wissenschaftliche Untersuchungen zum Neuen Testament 2. Reihe. Tübingen: Mohr Siebeck, 2003. Groundbreaking.

Hays, R. B. *First Corinthians.* Interpretation: A Bible Commentary for Teaching and Preaching. Louisville, KY: Knox, 1997.

Horsley, R. A. *1 Corinthians.* Abingdon New Testament Commentaries. Nashville, TN: Abingdon, 1998.

Johnson, A. F. *First Corinthians.* IVP New Testament Commentary, 7. Downers Grove, IL–Leicester, UK: InterVarsity, 2006.

Keener, C. S. *1-2 Corinthians.* New Cambridge Bible Commentary. Cambridge, UK–New York: Cambridge University Press, 2005.

Lockwood, G. J. *First Corinthians.* Concordia Commentary. St Louis, MO: Concordia, 2000.

Martin, D. B. *Slavery as Salvation: The Metaphor of Slavery in Pauline Christianity.* 1990.

Martin, D. B. *The Corinthian Body.* New Haven, CT–London: Yale University Press, 1995.

Murphy-O'Connor, J. *1 Corinthians.* Doubleday Bible Commentary. NY–London: Doubleday, 1998.

Soards, M. L. *1 Corinthians.* New International Bible Commentary. New Testament, 7. Peabody, MA: Hendrickson, 1999.

Thiselton, A. C. *The First Epistle to the Corinthians. A Commentary on the Greek Testament.* New International Greek Testament. Grand Rapids–Cambridge UK: Eerdmans, 2000.

Wright, N. T. *Paul for Everyone. 1 Corinthians.* Louisville, KY: Westminster John Knox, 2004.

Articles

BeDuhn, J. D. "'Because of the Angels': Unveiling Paul's Anthropology in 1 Corinthians 11." *Journal of Biblical Literature* 118 (1999) 295-320.

De Vos, C. S. "Stepmothers, Concubines and the Case of Πορνεία in 1 Corinthians 5." *Novum Testamentum* 44 (1998) 104-114.

Deming, W. "The Unity of 1 Corinthians 5-6." *Journal of Biblical Literature* 115 (1996) 289-312.

Ekem, J. D. K. "Does 1 Cor 11:2-16 legislate for 'head covering'?" *Neotestamentica* 35 (2001) 169-176.

Ekem, J. D. K. "'Spiritual Gifts' or 'Spiritual Persons'? 1 Corinthians 12:1a Revisited." *Neotestamentica* 38 (2004) 54-74. Opts for persons

Farla, P. "The Rhetorical Composition of 1 Cor 8,1-11,1." *Ephemerides Theologicae Lovanienses* 80 (2004) 144-166.

Fotopoulos, J. "Arguments Concerning Food Offered to Idols: Corinthian Quotations and Pauline Refutations in a Rhetorical *Partitio* (1 Corinthians 8:1-9)." *Catholic Biblical Quarterly* 67 (2005) 611-631.

Hollander, H. W. and van der Hout, G. E. "The Apostle Paul Calling Himself an Abortion: 1 Cor. 15:8 within the contest of 1 Cor. 15:8-10." *Novum Testamentum* 38 (1996) 224-236.

Hoskins, P. M. "The Use of Biblical and Extrabiblical Parallels in the Interpretation of First Corinthians 6:2-3." *Catholic Biblical Quarterly* 63 (2001) 287-297.

Kerr, D. P. "Paul and Apollos—Colleagues or Rivals?" *Journal for the Study of the New Testament* 77 (2000) 75-97.

Maccoby, H. "Paul and the Eucharist." *New Testament Studies* 37 (1991) 247-267.

Moiser, J. "1 Corinthians 15." *Irish Biblical Studies* 14 (1992) 10-30.

O'Day, G. R. "Jeremiah 9:22-23 and 1 Corinthians 1:26-31: A Study in Intertextuality." *Journal of Biblical Literature* 109 (1990) 259-267.

Passakos, D. C. "Eucharist in First Corinthians: A Sociological Study." *Revue Biblique* 104 (1997) 192-210.

Patrick, J. E. "Living Rewards for Dead Apostles; 'Baptized for the Dead' in 1 Corinthians 15.29." *New Testament Studies* 52 (2006) 71-85.

Roberts, P. "Seers or Overseers?" *Expository Times* 108 (1997) 301-305.

Schottroff, L. "Holiness and Justice: Exegetical Comments on 1 Corinthians 11.17-34." *Journal for the Study of the New Testament* 79 (2000) 51-60.

Sigountos, J. G. "The Genre of 1 Corinthians 13." *New Testament Studies* 40 (1994) 246-260.

Smit, J. F. M. "Tongues and Prophecy: Deciphering 1 Cor 14,22." *Biblica* 75 (1994) 175-190.

Taylor, N. H. "Baptism for the Dead (1 Cor 15:29)?" *Neotestamentica* 36 (2002) 111-120.

Tyler, R. L. "The History of Interpretation of τὸ μὴ ὑπὲρ ἃ γέγραπται in 1 Corinthians 4:6." *Restoration Quarterly* 43 (2001) 243-252.

Van Unnik, W. C. "The Meaning of 1 Corinthians 12:31." *Novum Testamentum* 35 (1993) 142-159.

Witherington, B. "Why Not Idol Meat? Is It What You Eat or Where You Eat It?" *Bible Review* 10 (1994) 38-43, 54-55.

www.ingramcontent.com/pod-product-compliance
Lightning Source LLC
Chambersburg PA
CBHW022104150426
43195CB00008B/263